Sun Country Banker

BOOKS *by* JOSEPH LEACH

The Typical Texan: Biography of an American Myth (Dallas: Southern Methodist University Press, 1952)

Bright Particular Star: The Life and Times of Charlotte Cushman (New Haven: Yale University Press, 1970)

What Then Is This American, This New Woman? (El Paso: Texas Western Press, 1974)

Sun Country Banker: The Life and the Bank of Samuel Doak Young (El Paso: Mangan Books, 1989)

Sun Country Banker

The Life and the Bank
of Samuel Doak Young

by JOSEPH LEACH

Mangan books

FIRST EDITION

Library of Congress Catalog No. 88-90911
ISBN 0-930208-26-9

PRINTED IN THE UNITED STATES OF AMERICA

Design: Frank Mangan

MANGAN BOOKS
6245 Snowheights Court
El Paso, Texas 79912

To the Secretaries

Especially Marie Halleran,
Bertha Bull Knight,
Laura Rutter,
Christine Gill,
Ramona Mullins,
Faye Hartman,
and
"Ground Control"

They also served – and valiantly

CONTENTS

FOREWORD

Books and stories rarely get written about the meek, the cautious, or the merely lucky. To interest the writer (be he fictionist, poet, playwright, historian, or biographer), the person whose life will eventually fill the writer's pages brings to his living a drive, a vigor of spirit that sooner or later takes charge of the artist's pencil and writes its own story. The lustrous spirit who "wrote" the life of Samuel Doak Young was Sam D. himself, and he wrote it out of the random materials available to him.

In producing these pages, I have tracked the boy who began his story in the Piney Woods of East Texas, the youth who ventured into the larger field of Texas itself, and the man who took on the nation and a sizable spread of the world and burned his brand on it. "Sam Young was here. Sam Young passed by. Let others take note as they will."

In the ensuing chapters, many voices speak of many things, but the fact that they speak with such force about Young attests to the drama that Sam himself brought to his scene and to the difference his "passing by here" made in the lives of those who knew him.

In preparing this book, I have enjoyed the assistance of countless generous people. To list them all by name would far exceed the space available to me, but I am most eager to express my thanks here to those many individuals whose names appear in the text itself and especially to the following people: Phebe Young Armstrong, Barbara Austin, Joe Ayres, Ellen Bell, Agnes Bryan, Hilliard Bryan, Karl Conrad, Gary Conwell, Dorothy Cook, Jack Curlin, T. S. Currie, Jack Darling, Gregory H. Dillon, Sarah Jane Dodds, Jeanette Dority, Barbara Eaves, Lila Evans, Dr. Walter Feinberg, Jim Ferguson, Judy Fields, Ashby Foote, June Fore, Rachel Garcia, Malcolm Harris, Faye Hartman, Paul Harvey, Sr., Bill Heaton, Martha Goodman Herman, Robert T. Hoover, Jr., Susan Jeffery, Tom Hussmann, Teresa Irvin,

Mr. and Mrs. Cooper Jacoway, Charles Johnson, Martin Kern, Walt Klinikowski, Anne Leach, Jonathan Leach, Joseph Leach, Jr., Leslie Levy, Fred McVay, Maria Montes, Joseph Moreno, Paul Mueller, Dolores Najera, Jesus Ojeda, Henry Ortiz, Margaret Young Parker, Joseph A. Pratt, Jerry Roberts, Olga Roderick, Leo Schuster, Jr., Skip Schmulbach, Abner Sheffield, Frances Roderick Smith, Margaret Stocker, Connie and Reba Strickland, Chuck Tapp, Irma Portillo, James Turnage, Willie Villasenor, W. S. Warnock, Jr., Helen Wheatley, Florene Williamson, and Linda Wilson.

To my publishers, Judy and Frank Mangan, I owe special thanks for their excellent editorial advice and skill in book production.

For her unflagging good cheer and assistance with the project from start to finish, I am profoundly grateful to my wife, Dorothy Ann.

Joseph Leach

El Paso
November 1, 1988

Sun Country Banker

SAM D. YOUNG

1

A LITTLE ACORN

ONE SUMMER MORNING IN 1903 Sam Young asked his hard-working mother, "Now that I'm already seven years old, can't I work too? Maybe sell things on the trains when they stop? If you could parch me some peanuts" — smiling up at her, he tugged at her skirts — "I bet we could make us some money."

Fanny, his twenty-nine-year-old mother, dried her hands on her apron. "Why, son — " She studied his question a moment. "Why, son, I reckon we could," she nodded. "I could pop you some corn, I could make popcorn balls. Maybe you and I" — she patted his cheek — "well, it's worth a good try."[1]

Smiling a kind of secret between them, neither mother nor son thought of anything much beyond Sam's happy notion. But in Fanny Young's kitchen that morning a die was cast into a much greater scene than the little frame house they called home or the little hometown they called Woodville.

Woodville, Texas is a mighty far piece from Athens and Hong Kong. And its Steward Hotel was a far cry from New York's Waldorf-Astoria. In his ninetieth year, Samuel Doak Young, the far-ranging traveler whose story spanned those distances, turned and looked back, back to his roots in East Texas.

Those roots were firmly entangled among the liveoaks, the loblolly pines, black hickory, cypress and alligator swamps in the vast forest known now as the Big Thicket. Since times prehistoric those woods had witnessed a passing parade of red men, then European explorers and adventurers. For nearly a century before Sam's own arrival, they had known too the horses and wagons of American settlers moving in from back east to clear fields — on Mexican land — for their plows and sites for new homes and communities.

Among the intrepid colonists who rolled in from Tennessee in 1831 came the Rev. Samuel Doak McMahon and his wife Phebe. They settled with their seven children in Sabine County. The McMahons were sturdy Presbyterian stock, but soon after breaking ground for a field and constructing the necessary log house and outbuildings, McMahon turned to other matters equally urgent. In 1832 during the Texas Revolution, Major McMahon as a battalion commander led his troop of American volunteers against Mexican troops at the Battle of Nacogdoches.

Soon after that battle McMahon changed his church affiliation and in 1833, as a Methodist lay preacher, he and his neighbors built a log church just large enough to seat the forty-eight founding families. Constructed from trees felled on the spot, the small building with its tower and bell was the first Methodist church erected on what became Republic of Texas soil three years later when General Sam Houston's Texas forces defeated General Santa Anna's Mexican forces at San Jacinto.[2]

Worshippers who gathered in that chapel heard McMahon's Bible-thumping orations Sunday after Sunday. Through the years they also heard the stirring sermons of many a circuit-riding preacher, one of whom, the Rev. Acton Young, took for his bride the sixteen-year-old Margaret Tabitha McMahon.

During the next twelve years, Acton established a mission church at Woodville in Tyler County. He became presiding elder over all the Methodist congregations in an area extending from Woodville sixty miles south to the Gulf coast. He and Margaret became the parents of a daughter Phebe, a son Sam, a daughter Ettina, and a son Charles Acton born on November 18, 1862.

On the other side of the county Thomas Sims, who had escaped imminent death on a Civil War battlefield only to spend gruelling months in a Yankee prison in Ohio, had settled his family on a farm in the Neches River bottom. It was there that his twenty-year-old daughter

Sarah Frances, after a few brief years of schooling in a one-room log cabin, married Charles Acton Young in February 1894.[3]

Woodville at that time was typical of the small crossroad communities scattered among Tyler County's rolling hills and clear streams. Stretching in all directions, the Big Thicket's virgin forests afforded ample lumber and firewood but posed frustrations for any young farmer impatient to rid his acres of stumps and get his corn, his sorghum cane, and cotton into the ground in time for an early fall crop.

Woodville itself – except for the Tyler County Courthouse, a few stores, one bank, three wooden churches, two schools, two modest roadside hotels, a lumber mill, and the Texas and New Orleans Railroad trains puffing into town twice a day – was mostly a cluster of rambling, white painted houses, with their barns and outbuildings sheltered under spreading oak trees. The unpaved roads leading south and southwest to Beaumont and Houston and north to Lufkin and Nacogdoches were like sharp razor cuts slashed through the pines. If most of the Woodville men packed sidearms, that fact said no more about them or their town than that common practice said about any other Texas community where every man was quick on the draw to defend his women, his children, or oftentimes his good name.

There was little to suggest that Woodville was a place to grow rich. Its 1,800 people were so close to their pioneer past that it was a rare child indeed who grew up there ignorant of the hopes that had brought his God-fearing forebears into these woods. These early religious folks were determined to instill in their little acorns an abiding zeal and ambition to become mighty oaks – "to make something of yourselves in the eyes of the Lord."

That parental admonition had been preached again and again by the good Rev. Acton Young to his son Charlie, but as in the case of many another preacher's boy, those sermons had fallen on deaf ears. Nevertheless, the admonitions ceased only with Acton's death. A year later, Charlie quit school at age twelve.[4] In his late teens when he left home to drive a wagon in a traveling circus, it was clear to his mother and his motherly big sister Phebe (whom the family called "Daughtie") that whatever religious zeal their six-foot-two Charlie possessed, he was not preacher material. By age thirty-two, he was the double-fisted, hard-drinking owner of six saloons in sawmill towns out in the county.

The union between Charlie the black sheep, however, and rock-solid Baptist Sarah Frances Sims (whom he called "Fanny") started with plenty of religious zeal in the wife. During the wedding ceremony, tall Charlie's outstretched arm sheltered little Fanny who shyly smiled up at him. But once they were married, if Fanny the blue-eyed brunette – all four-feet-eleven inches of her – did not immediately set out to remold her strapping blond husband, she clearly aimed to sand off his rough edges. Within a year Charlie had broken a small piece of land on Little Cypress Creek, had sold his saloons, and was running a general store at the crossroads in town.[5] Fanny was nursing their first offspring, a daughter whom Daughtie had already named "Charlie" before the stork delivered a girl in 1894. To distinguish between the family's two Charlies, Daughtie nicknamed the baby "Teah."

Their home was a small wooden frame structure typical of Woodville abodes, its wide porch and front walk bordered with Fanny's roses and red verbenas.[6]

By the time their second child, Samuel Doak Young (whom they named for his uncle) arrived on November 15, 1896, the family had settled down to normal domesticity and storekeeping. But Charlie had retained from his bachelor days one handy skill. Whenever too many young toughs loitered around his store, he doubled his fists and cleared them out of his way.

For brown-haired little Sam and auburn-haired Teah, family life centered in a compromise between their father's loud orders and their mother's gentle lessons from Scripture. Two years later, when Daughtie and her husband Bronson Cooper and their four children moved to Beaumont, the better to play Bronson's new role as a U. S. congressman, they turned their two-story house over to Fanny and Charlie. By then, Sam and Teah were already learning the Bible verses that helped their mother bring peace into the household that now included baby brother Cooper, born in 1898.

"In all thy ways," Fanny taught her children from Proverbs, "acknowledge Him, and He shall direct thy paths."

By 1901, when Sam was big enough to help with the supper dishes, Fanny stood him on a soap box at her side and explained the new verse she had just had him recite. One night when he was puzzled about Proverbs 16:3, "Commit thy works unto the Lord and thy thoughts shall be established," she admonished him softly. "Trust the Lord with all thine heart, son, and as the Lord says, 'Lean not to thine own understanding.'"

Sam's parents, Charlie and Fanny Young in Woodville, Texas, 1925.

Smiling, she went on to explain, "It's all right to ask questions about what you read in the Bible. But don't worry about what you can't understand yet. The important thing is to keep your faith. Keep your faith strong."[7]

Though young Sam considered washing dishes a painful chore, those times with his mother had sealed a special bond between them by the time another little brother, Thomas, arrived on the scene. "Now, we've had our good visit," Fanny often told him on long summer evenings. "So head on out to the back porch and rig up your bucket. We've had a good rain, and the cistern's brim full, so take yourself a nice cool shower bath under that bucket you punched full of holes." In winter, the Saturday baths took place in a wash tub behind the wood stove.

From earliest childhood Sam had sensed his mother's staunch fiber, but he never saw a clearer example of it than on the day she took him and Teah fishing on Big Cypress Creek. Leaning against a tree stump, she was baiting Sam's hook when he saw her suddenly freeze, stare at her feet, and point toward a cotton-mouth moccasin. It was coiled next to the stump, its bared fangs rising to strike. In a moment another snake circled around the hem of Fanny's long skirt. Unflinching, Fanny waited stock still till the snakes wriggled away.

A similar moment occurred one afternoon when Sam and the family were walking along their quiet street toward home. From just up ahead, a gunshot rang out. Charlie shoved his screaming family behind him, shouting, "Damn you, Tom Bullett!" When the smoke cleared, a black-bearded face and black eyes were glaring at Charlie from behind a big oak. In a flash, Charlie was firing straight back, but Bullett had already fled.

Charlie never explained Bullett's anger, but six-year-old Sam never forgot the blast of that shot or Fanny's tearful outcry, "Oh my Lord, Charlie, pray God there won't be a next time!" Later, when Charlie's brother (whom the family called "Buddy Sam") lay in wait for Bullett, the blackbeard never showed up, nor was he ever again seen around town.

At least once every summer Fanny's faith in God's mercy came to her help when a warning scurried through town that a hurricane was blowing up from the Gulf. Calmly, she called her brood to the porch, gathered them close, and watched the southern skies darken to black, the clouds boil up angry and green. With the rain gusting in torrents, she helped them all pray for the strength to stand firm.

There were other times no less frightening when the "storm" was Papa Charlie himself, roaring home from too much imbibing at a corner saloon. Once, when he came in raving at the children, little Fanny threw out her arms. "Now, you hush! Don't you dare touch these children! They haven't done anything and you know it!"

Stunned, Charlie glared at her, then collapsed in a chair.[8]

There were also bitter moments when Charlie concluded some business deal that to Fanny made no possible sense: the time he sold off a large piece of his farm at a profit of only twenty-five cents an acre,[9] times when he simply gave up trying to balance his chaotic books at the store. There were equally hard moments when Fanny had to accept clothes from Uncle Bronson and Daughtie in Beaumont and financial help from Buddy Sam, who now lived with the family. It was Buddy Sam, not Charlie, who bought the children new shoes.

In the fall of 1902 Sam was through with his summer games when he started to school. In a room full of squirming children seated two to a desk, he began the long routine of mastering the three R's under such stern taskmasters as Mrs. Lucy Shivers. Smaller than most of the others, Sam sat still and a little reserved until the teacher's question brought him alert and he shot up his hand.

Riding a little gray mule named Scotty to school each morning, he carried his biscuits and bacon in a tin bucket. That lunch was only a taste of the three ample meals that Fanny served every day. Though she lacked many of life's other essentials, her children never went hungry. Hands washed and faces a'shine, they hustled into their chairs at the table, the plates resting face down away from the flies. They waited till the "Amen," then dived into the bounty from Fanny's own garden: butter beans, turnip greens, new potatoes and sweet corn. After chicken and dumplings and cold buttermilk, she often served apple cobbler or Sam's special favorite, hot biscuits and fig preserves.

With the arrival in 1903 of a fifth little mouth to feed, William Chapman, Sam began earning most of his own keep by working the T&NO passenger trains after school and on Saturdays, selling Fanny's popcorn and peanuts. When he could shoulder heavier loads, he peddled the *Saturday Blade and Gazette* newspaper all over town. Each time he brought home his pennies and nickels, his mother patted his cheek. "Sambo, you're my hard-working young man. I'm proud of you."[10]

But all work and no play, however vital the added income for the family, was not the full story. Summer saw its share of highjinks when

Sam and his friends Mayo McBride, Alonzo Wright, Johnny Reid, Clyde Smith, Cullee and Edward Mann and their little brother Thomas stripped to the skin for spread-eagle dives into the best swimming hole in Big Turkey Creek. Gladly, Fanny counted those gleeful splashings as baths.

In the late fall, riding bareback through the woods, the boys hunted possums, grabbing the biggest from the low trees by their tails. Squirrel hunting was almost as easy. When they spotted a target high in an oak, they watched till it leaped for the next tree, then gunned it down in midair. Their sacks of squirrels, Teah (who had become the family cook at age eleven) served fried, along with red beans, corn bread and cream gravy.

One especially good game they played involved their own telephone, a couple of cans and a hay wire stretched along a fence row. With a hole punched in the base of each can, each boy slid his can back and forth on the wire, and the screeching carried along to the far end. Even better things happened when a boy screamed "Boo!" into his can, blasting the faraway ears.

With the birth of child number six, Mike Welker, in 1906, Charlie put ten-year-old Sam to work at the store. For a nickel a week he unloaded the delivery wagons and restocked the shelves, cut piece goods with the great scissors that hung from a string near the counter. Quickly, he became adept at delivering the day's cash to the bank, but his special job after supper was sweeping the store. His Saturday nickel he could spend as he liked, most times on a peppermint stick or a molasses candy bar sprinkled with coconut.[11] Or better still, he could spend it on a Horatio Alger book in Beaumont on the happy occasions when the T&NO conductor let him catch a free ride. Once, Uncle Bronson and Daughtie took him to a big circus; once they let him wander alone on the beach to stare at a dead whale.

Back at the store, Sam learned by sad experience to put a tight cover on the coffee barrel before locking up for the night. One morning he found a mother cat snugly at home on the coffee beans, calmly licking her newborn kittens. Grimly, Charlie threw out at least half the new coffee. After that, when Cooper was big enough to help out, Sam put him to work, restocking shelves and sweeping.

Working with Cooper out at the farm during summer vacations, Sam soon knew that sweating behind a plow was no role for him. But with Cooper eager to do all the plowing and chop the firewood if Sam took over his chores at the store, the brothers gladly contracted a deal.

A Beaumont wedding in 1907, the year Sam was eleven, brought a momentary break from the Woodville routine when his cousin Margaret Cooper married Henderson Jacoway. After driving the newlyweds in a buggy to the T&NO station, Sam was loading their baggage onto the Pullman for the trip to their home in Little Rock when the groom reached in his pocket. "Sambo," he smiled, "I've got something I think you might like. Here now, you take it." Henderson handed him a bright, heavy coin. "The date on that silver dollar makes it, well, just right for you."

Sam examined the dollar. "1896! The year I was born!"[12]

Boarding the train, the Jacoways waved. "Come see us sometime!" as Sam fingered, deep in his pocket, the most cash he had ever owned at one time.

In 1908, just as twelve-year-old Sam was entering high school, the frustration of having too little money weighed especially heavily. He could not afford the "right" shirts and pants like the other boys wore. On top of that, he desperately wanted a bicycle, but when he approached his father about the necessary fifteen dollars, Charlie shook his head firmly. Now that Sam's Aunt Ettie had moved in to help with new baby Margaret, he explained, "The money just isn't there."

Charlie's response could hardly be argued, but Sam and Teah shared an outlook by now that neither one mentioned to their parents. With Mama always looking so haggard, with money always so tight, with the house always more and more crowded, did there have to be, as regular as sunrise, another new mouth to feed? Many times, fourteen-year-old Teah grumbled to Sam about the perpetual baby she always must carry around on her hip while she cooked supper.

Teah was right about always toting an infant, but another detail troubled Sam more. Wasn't it a little bit, well, not quite nice for his shy little Mama to be – he hesitated even to think it – always coming on awkward and slow and having another baby? What was the matter with Papa?

The matter with Charlie was no business of Sam's, but Sam did wish at times that Papa could express some affection for him. Beyond an occasional hearty slap on the back, Papa never paid compliments. It was Buddy Sam who shepherded the children to town when they needed new tablets or school books at Mr. Reid's store and praised them for working hard at their lessons.[13]

It seemed a godsend to Sam the summer of 1908 when Mrs. Steward who ran Woodville's better hotel told Charlie she needed somebody to man her front desk and "bell boy" her twenty-four rooms. When Charlie passed Sam the word that she could pay fifteen dollars a month, plus board and a room all to himself while he stayed on in school, Sam leaped at the job.

Fanny did not make Sam a speech when he gathered up his few clothes and made his way along the path to the street. Her goodbye was brief; he was only moving a few blocks away. But from that moment her special big son was out on his own.

The work at the hotel front desk – meeting salesmen just in off the train, settling boarders' complaints, making out customers' bills – quickly broadened Sam's world. Before many months, between dashes out to the street to grab up a suitcase, Sam began spinning ideas about increasing his monthly income. Too well, he remembered one of Fanny's Monday morning burdens at home. Until now, the Woodville housewives' hard work at their wash tubs had been the only way Woodville ever got its clothes clean. But now, with a hotel guest asking almost daily where a fellow could get his shirts laundered and his collars starched right, Sam could only shake his head.

Exasperated, one guest slapped the desk. "You mean in this whole blasted hick town there's not a single honest-to-god laundry? Where's the good old American enterprise around here?"

Sam's enterprise soon put him aboard the T&NO to Beaumont. Back from the big city, he had contracted a deal with the U-Need-A-Laundry, and he had had a quick chat with Henderson Jacoway, who was visiting in town.

"Sam, about that silver dollar I gave you last year," Henderson wanted to know, "how'd you spend it?"

"Spend it?" Sam patted his pocket. "I didn't spend it. I'm keeping it here. In case I ever get in a tight."[14]

Twice a week Sam and his new business partner Reginald Geisendorf collected soiled clothes in wicker baskets at the hotel. But soon – when one of Charlie's friends lent him a horse and his Aunt Ettie lent him a buggy – Sam took on the town. By the afternoon train twice a week, he dispatched his baskets to Beaumont. Two days later, he met the train, collected the fresh bundles, and quickly distributed them where they should go. To that enterprise he soon added a little cleaning and pressing business and hired a Cajun friend Marvin to do the actual work.

Familiar now with the clothing salesmen at the hotel, Sam himself began taking measurements for the suits he could order direct from a clothing factory in Chicago. In a few weeks, when his own special tailor-made outfit arrived, he swaggered a little, wearing his Buster Brown suit and his Buster Brown boots home to show to the family.

Though Sam's laundry business grew so rapidly that soon he could buy out his partner, some of his customers were often so slow in paying their bills that he could not meet his own payments to Beaumont. When he approached Charlie for help, Charlie gave him the stock answer. "With new baby Phebe now on the scene — " He shook his head lamely.

Fearful and trembling, Sam took his troubles to the Tyler County State Bank. "I only need enough to cover my bills," he told the bank president Emmett Dismuke. "I'll be all right once my customers pay me."[15]

Dismuke listened carefully. "I'd like to help, son, but how much would you need?"

"Uh, well, I" — the amount seemed gigantic — "fifty dollars?"

Dismuke nodded soberly. "Sam, I can stake you for that, but you'd need to find somebody to co-sign your note. Kind of carry the load, along with you. Could you do that?"

Clenching his fists, Sam dredged up the name of Woodville's leading storekeeper. Mr. Sam Reid might help, especially since it was from Reid that he rented his steam-pressing space.

Reid reached for the loan paper. "Of course, Sam, I've been watching you. I'm glad I can give you some help."

Reid's co-signing that note and Dismuke's extending the cash were small moments, but in that early encounter with the responsible ways of a lender, Sam at age fifteen began entertaining big dreams. Glad and relieved, he settled his bills, then paid off his note. His good credit established, the next time his collections slowed down, he felt no fear in approaching Dismuke again.

"This time, could you let me have, maybe, one hundred dollars?"

This time, solely on Sam's signature, Dismuke wrote out the note.

At the telephone company, another enterprise soon began paying off when an operator needed a substitute on Saturdays. "I can pay you fifteen dollars a month," said Mr. Patton. With Tyler County now "dry," the operator's responsibilities on Saturday nights often included calling up certain parties on behalf of thirsty folks around town and slipping the bootlegger his pay when he delivered the goods.

Glad for the extra money but all too certain what Fanny would say if she ever found out, Sam knew in a few months that he was fed up with his Saturday job, and he was also fed up with too many unpaid laundry accounts in Beaumont. The only solution was to sell out the whole enterprise.

By 1911 Daughtie had died and Uncle Bronson had moved with his daughters Willie and Bird up to New York where he was now Court of Claims Judge for the U. S. Customs Service. Alone in Beaumont, Sam's lawyer cousin Bronson Jr. (whom the family called "Bubber") invited Sam to come on down and share the big house while he looked for a good summer job.

At Bubber's Sam had time now in the evenings to put up his feet and savor the books that lined the wood panelled walls of Uncle Bronson's study. For the first time in his life, he could read for sheer fun. One Horatio Alger story excited him especially. Feverishly turning its pages, he stopped and reread a whole chapter, wishing he was riding "that motorcycle that just jumped over that creek."[16]

The summer job Sam landed was night clerk at the Fields Hotel. In this much larger hotel (it had 150 rooms) in a city boasting paved streets and electric streetcars, the friendly bell boys had a lucrative sideline. Their delivering "girls" up to lonely guests' rooms embarrassed Sam's conscience, but the manager seemed not to care and, conscience aside, he was making fifty dollars a month. He had a quiet room all to himself, and his breakfast of bacon and eggs and coffee each morning cost only fifteen cents.

By September, with most of his summer cash in his pocket, Sam was back in Woodville again, working long hours at the Gillespie Hotel and going to school. But after Beaumont, he found it hard to take school seriously. Especially with Tyler High's rowdies playing practical jokes. When "Toughie" Wright pulled a prank on one teacher, the teacher hauled Toughie up front. "Straighten up now. Or leave school," Mr. Stevens demanded.

The offender jutted his chin out. But Stevens meant business. "Quit"—from his desk drawer he pulled out a pistol and aimed it straight at him—"or quit school!"

"Who says?" Toughie objected. But when he heard the sharp click of Stevens cocking his gun, Toughie headed straight for the door.

By 1913, Sam was making high grades, but he often considered quitting school too. Charlie was having more and more trouble making ends meet, and Sam was convinced that he himself was getting nowhere at the Gillespie. More than once he discussed that notion with Mr. Brown, the teacher he most respected. Each time, however, Brown stood firmly against it. "Nobody just quits. Nobody doing so well as you are."

But early in March in Sam's last semester, with his hotel job bringing in only forty dollars a month, he listened carefully when Uncle Bronson telephoned him. "Sambo, I understand that Beaumont's biggest bank, the Gulf National, needs a runner. I'll put in a good word with the bank's president," Uncle told him, "if you think you'd be interested."

"*Interested?* You bet!" Sam cried.

The next morning, Sam had more than one reason for wanting to take Uncle's suggestion, when Brown reached for his hand and gave it a shake. "I've just figured your rank in the senior class. And I'm happy to tell you right now that at commencement in May Samuel Doak Young is due to be honored. As salutatorian, you'll deliver a major speech on the program."

"Me?" Sam recoiled. "Make a speech?"

Make a real speech in front of a crowd? Sam may have inherited Fanny's own shyness. The thought of making that speech terrified him. In a rush, he told Brown about his big chance in Beaumont. "It can't wait. And... and neither can I. I have to go *now*."

When Sam told his parents his plan to move to Beaumont, they had no objections, but before he packed his few clothes at the hotel, he paid another visit to Brown. Not at all comprehending Sam's full reasons for quitting his classes, Brown shook his head. "Leave school? So near to finishing? Without a diploma? Sam, you can't do it!"[17]

Fleeing through the door of Brown's dusty classroom, Sam glanced back as Brown leaped to his feet. "You're ruining your life!" he cried. "You'll always regret what you are doing!"

2

HE'S IN THE ARMY NOW

WITH HIS TEACHER'S WARNING RINGING LOUD in his ears—"Quit school? Without a diploma?"—Sam hopped another free train ride to Beaumont. Arriving with nothing much more than the clothes he was wearing, he did have free room and board with his cousin Bubber. And the next day, he signed on at the Gulf National Bank as a runner.

Ranging through every department, Sam quickly learned the role that each officer—Paul Tullos, J. T. Shelby, Mr. Wynn, Mr. Pritchard, and the young bachelors John and Hughes Petkosek[1]—played at his desk and the function each teller served in his cage. Through this on-the-job training on the lowest rung of the ladder, Sam learned little by little the responsibilites involved in the banking business.

Though his job entailed nothing much more than dashing on errands, delivering bank forms and the mail, at times it also entailed learning to grin when old hands played tricks on the rookie. His second morning, a teller beckoned him. "Dammit, young fellow, I've got this long line of folks waiting here at my window, and I can't find my check stretcher. Somebody must have borrowed it. So"—Sam listened alertly—"so hop over to Bill's window. Number 1, there by the door. Tell him I need it and quick!"

At window Number 1 Bill shook his head. "Not me. But ask Preston Doty. As vice president, he knows everything."

Doty looked thoughtful, then nodded. "Oh, now I remember. One of those bandits at the First National came crying to us. They should have brought it back yesterday. Tell them I said so. They're just down the street."

Nobody at First had seen the check stretcher. But one teller suggested, "Lost and Found over at Texas Bank and Trust might give you some clue."

Lost and Found tried to keep a straight face, but the game was too good to hide. "We haven't seen it," that teller chuckled at last. "And neither has anybody there at the zoo where you work. There's no such thing as a check stretcher. Somebody sent you off on a snipe hunt. But before you tear him to pieces, tell him we've got his left-handed screw driver. If he can describe it, he can have it today."[2]

Back at Gulf, Sam grinned at their laughter, then rushed to tend to his chores. At night, with free run of Uncle Bronson's big house, Sam often curled up with a James Fenimore Cooper novel or more Horatio Algers, his imagination throwing him into an Indian fight or the struggles of a poor country boy clawing to come out on top in the city. Any word he did not understand, he looked up. Then to plant it firmly in his head, he used it as soon as he could, especially in letters to Woodville.[3]

After meeting a "right likely" girl at the bank named Sara Keith, he wrote her a tender letter, including some new expressions he had, well, sort of borrowed from a Robert Burns poem. "O my love is like a red, red rose," he grandly wrote Sara. But the jig was up when Sara calmly wrote back, "I read Robert Burns too."[4]

Now, with a forty dollar paycheck per month, Sam bade a grateful goodbye to cousin Bubber's free hospitality. "By taking a room at the YMCA, maybe I can make some new friends," he explained to Bubber.[5] There, he briefly shared a small room[6] then moved to a boarding house. But with rent at ten dollars a month and meals at least thirty-five dollars, he soon had to borrow survival money from Bubber until he got a small raise at the bank.

Sam's money struggles were soon compensated, however, by a friendship he formed with a middle-aged bachelor, Courtney Marshall. A top official with the Magnolia Petroleum Company who relished the boarding house's good table, Marshall enjoyed the conversations he could strike up with the other boarders. Soon he especially enjoyed his talks with the seventeen-year-old bank runner from Woodville. During their strolls downtown after supper, the talk flowed till suddenly, after delivering some weighty opinion, Marshall paused.

"Are you there, Sam? Do you follow my thinking?"

"Oh, sure, sir. I was just thinking about all you just said."

The conversations were mostly one-sided until Sam came to know Marshall as a warm-hearted adult who had never forgotten his own youthful hopes to make good. After work at the bank, when something new had caught his attention – some customer-banker negotiation, perhaps, some complicated transaction he had overheard – Sam took the gist of the story to Marshall. Marshall delivered his studied judgment, then smiled. "Do you follow my line? Are you there, Sam?"[7]

Noting a "For Sale" sign on a building, Marshall often asked, "Sam, what's it worth, would you guess?" Sam stated a figure, Marshall gave his own estimate, then noted the guesses in a little black book. After some days, when they walked along the same street again, they noticed the properties that had sold in the meantime.

"I just learned today that this property here brought" – Marshall stated the amount – "and let's see now, you figured it ought to bring – " He checked his written figures. They discussed the final sale price, pondering how close each had come to it. From such games, Sam quickly learned how to make sharp appraisals. He quickly sensed, too, that in playing those games, Marshall was sharing his own rich experience.[8]

Among Marshall's many firm opinions, Sam noted especially one simple bit of advice. "Set aside some money each month," Marshall told him. "Put it where it will start earning more."

Within three months, Sam had proved his mettle enough at the bank to merit a raise to fifty-five dollars; in six months he was up to seventy-five. Then he was able at last to enjoy some Saturday afternoon larks down at the beach, to swim and clown around in a long-legged bathing suit with the Petkosek brothers, wink at the girls, and jauntily puff a big black cigar.[9]

As his pay scale increased, Sam knew by early 1914 that with so little schooling behind him, his best chance to succeed on this job, landing a desk in the lobby, lay in careful study at night. Feeding that dream, Sam wrote to LaSalle University for a correspondence course in accounting, but when Mr. Wynn learned about that, he called him in. "Put that aside. Here on the job, I can teach you all the accounting there is."[10]

In a similar manner, Mr. Pritchard, a mathematics whiz who could add up a column of six figures in his head, soon had Sam adding up three-digit columns himself.[11]

One payday when his check was less than the amount he had promised he would try to send home, Sam went to Vice President Doty. "I need to send my folks some money, but I'm short just a little. Could you lend me — ?"

Making the loan, Doty paused. "Young, I've been watching you close. You've got everything it takes to hit the ball right, and I think you're going to hit it. But I want to tell you this about handling your personal money. When you're in debt, never miss a payment-due date. Reduce the principal by whatever you can afford, but be sure you pay something. Using that system, you can always renew your note and keep up your good credit record."[12]

Indirectly, Sam picked up another bit of important information from the steady procession of customers in and out of the bank. The posture of confidence he saw in Beaumont's big rich — men exuding power and influence like W. W. Kyle, Henry Weiss, W. P. Dunlap, D. E. Broussard, and T. S. Reed — displayed in themselves Beaumont's rapid rise to eminence since Captain A. F. Lucas, drilling for oil in a local rice field in 1901, brought in Spindletop, "the greatest gusher of all time."[13] Ever since, "Spindletop" had been a word on the tongues of the nation.

As a place for Sam to get his feet on the ground in the work force, as a chance to "try on for size" the suitability of a banking career, the city of Beaumont with all its new wealth was ideal. So too was the big state of Texas. At the Texas Bankers Association convention in 1906, its president, J. L. White, had voiced a heady prediction. "Texas, now being the fifth state in the confederation of states, financially speaking, would become in but a few years the rival in population and wealth of New York, now 'the empire state' of the nation."[14]

Like the place, the times too afforded valuable training for an alert beginner slowly perceiving himself in a world far larger than Woodville. During the fall of Sam's first year in Beaumont, important changes had occurred in the nation's manner of banking. Theodore Roosevelt, the Bull-Moose Republican, campaigning the year before for a return to the White House, had declared, "There must be a revision of our currency laws, because to leave them as they are means to incur liability of business disaster." His Democratic opponent, Woodrow Wilson, said much the same. "The question of currency is very near to the pros-

Sam (with cigar) and two of his Gulf National Bank friends, John and Hughes Petkosek, on the beach at Beaumont, about 1913.

perity of the country. We suffer from crises because of our unscientific system of currency."

In Texas, The Texas Bankers Association firmly concurred. "We are all agreed that our currency and banking laws are defective and that some remedial financial legislation is demanded, but like all God-fearing people we are somewhat divided on the plan of salvation."[15] One effort to relieve such concerns was the Federal Reserve Act, which created on December 23, 1913, a new national banking system.

Sam was too low on Gulf's totem pole to share in its officers' varied reactions to the Act's program of dividing the nation into twelve banking districts and establishing in each a "Federal Reserve Bank." For the district including Texas the Federal Reserve Bank would be located in Dallas. Sam did see, however, the Gulf officers' enthusiasm for the idea that if the new system worked, it would create a greater elasticity in the nation's credit, a sounder distribution of banking facilities, and new safeguards against dangerous speculation.[16]

Though a grown-up young man now, Sam always realized on his visits back home that he had not fully outgrown his need for his mother's straight thinking. Each time Fanny questioned him about his life in the big city, Sam shuffled his feet.

"No, Mama, I guess I'm not going to church like I should. It's just that I'm — I'm so busy and all."[17]

By the spring of 1914, the Gulf Bank knew that in Sam Young it had found a "comer." When Mahan made him a teller at ninety dollars a month, John Petkosek quickly taught him how to detect forgeries: "Note the major strokes in your regular customers' handwriting," and how to spot counterfeit bills: "Check for the red and blue threads in the paper, for the loops in the key on the face of the bill."[18]

The promotion to teller also brought Sam a broadened view of Beaumont's other interesting possibilities. Jingling his extra cash, if at one time his best use for fifteen dollars was buying a bicycle, he could now afford to take an admiring glance at Thelma Carroll, Marjorie Broussard, Grace Reed, and Fay Wise, each of whom readily accepted the streetcar rides he could offer her now to dances and parties all over town.

Yet there were times, counting the cash flow through his window, when Sam felt an itch for even more cash of his own, especially the morning a customer presented a handful of greenbacks and a deposit slip for two hundred dollars. Sam tallied the bills and accepted the indicated amount. Only as the man was turning to leave, however, did Sam notice that one of the "tens" was in fact a "hundred." He stiffened, seeing his error. But one second later he tensed, seeing the client's.

He swallowed. Here was a ninety-dollar mistake, and he had caught it in time. A warming tingle flowed through him. Here, to his personal advantage, was a mistake as big as his pay for a month of hard work. Sweating, he swallowed again.

But then he squared his shoulders and called the man back. When he had pointed out the big discrepancy, the man swore his deposit was two hundred dollars, no more.

Again, a tingle flowed through him. If the customer still would not claim that hundred, Sam himself could innocently slip it into his own pocket. But – ? Now a chill gripped him. What if, using that hundred, an officer was slyly testing his character? His job, not to mention his future, was riding on his doing the straight, honest thing. Quickly, he dashed off a deposit slip for the two hundred and ninety dollars and made the man take it. Watching the man leave the bank, he sighed in relief,[19] remembering the chill of that wicked one hundred skulking inside that stack of innocent tens.

As Sam grew in worth to the bank, his merits at his window were soon apparent to his regular customers. Ben Feinberg, a rising young shirt merchant in town, soon became one of the "regulars" willing to wait in line for a chat with Sam, the efficient young teller, even though other windows were open. So too did William Pettus Hobby, the jovial editor of *The Enterprise*, Beaumont's major newspaper. Before long, eighteen-year-old Sam looked forward to a daily visit with the thirty-six-year-old transplant from Moscow, Texas. Grinning in through the bars, Hobby told him how his own career had actually started in 1895, when at age seventeen, he had landed a job on the *Houston Post* paying eight dollars a week.[20] Soon during his visits the editor began mentioning his growing interest in Uncle Bronson's daughter, Miss Willie Cooper.

At home in Woodville, Charlie and Fanny's family grew once again when number nine child, Jack, arrived in February 1914. Sam still kept his own counsel about this endless family procession, but he tightened his belt and sent home the cash he could spare. Fanny's spirits seemed never to flag; her energies seemed never to weaken as her duties as family manager steadily grew. Teah wrote Sam about Mama's recent big scene with Cooper and William (whom the family called "Pete").

One morning when they refused to stop fighting, little Fanny ordered them out of the house. "Go bring me a peachtree switch, this minute!" While she was switching the one, then the other, they both laughed, they were so much bigger than she was.[21]

At his teller window, Sam tasted the sweet sense of his own growth as Mahan increased his responsibilities – and added another few welcome dollars to his pay. Within a few months, Mahan gave him another promotion. At the exchange window his good penmanship proved especially valuable in writing out drafts and transfers.[22] Nevertheless, during slack times at his window, Sam taught himself typewriting. Watching him hunt-and-peck, the lady secretaries smiled at him kindly.

"No man around here does his own typing," they told him.

But as he gained speed, Sam only smiled back.

Hard at work, Sam barely noticed the news that broke in Bill Hobby's *Enterprise* in late July 1914. Austria-Hungary had declared war on Serbia for harboring, that nation alleged, the assassins of Austria's Archduke Franz Ferdinand. Germany immediately backed Austria, and within a few days Russia called out her troops to protect Serbia. On August 1, Germany declared war on Russia and France. But here at home, President Woodrow Wilson quickly announced, "The United States must be neutral in fact as well as in name. We must be impartial in thought as well as in action."[23]

Seeming more to the moment just now, Sam shared the excitement that Hobby mentioned again and again at his window. "I've decided to run for lieutenant governor of Texas, sharing the Democratic ticket with James E. Ferguson, a banker from Temple." Also, he confessed with a bit of a blush, he had decided to marry Sam's cousin, Miss Willie Cooper. His mind and his heart, he told Sam, were crystal clear about the gifted helpmate Willie would make.

About that, Sam agreed. Daughtie had been indispensable to Uncle Bronson in his campaigns for Congress and the good statesman's life in Washington. Now, "Sis Willie" could add her own drive and intelligence to Hobby's ambitions.[24]

In the November primaries, Ferguson and Hobby achieved the greatest proportionate victory yet seen in Texas politics: 236,952 votes for them, 191,952 for former Congressman Thomas H. Ball. In the general election that followed, their ticket won by a landslide: only 39,000 votes had been cast against them.[25] And on January 19, 1915, Ferguson and Hobby took their oaths of office in Austin on the Capitol steps. Within a few weeks, the new lieutenant governor married Miss Willie Cooper. Soon after that, a letter arrived from the Capitol. "As soon as you can, come see us, Sam." The note was signed, "Governor."[26]

In early 1916, Sam took on new duties as collection teller. Preparing and processing real estate transfers and extension agreements,[27] helping clients with their out-of-town business, he gained an expanding sense of sophisticated finance.[28] But excited as he was with his broadening prospects, Sam recognized his growing new role as a dutiful son. From Beaumont, he could look back at Charlie's own limitations, but he saw them now in a new light. Whether he wished it or not, the good of the family—Fanny and Papa and the seven children younger than he—was partly his responsibility. With the family always looking to him, he had to make good.[29]

On quick visits home, Sam saw the family now as across a vast gulf. Little Phebe, at six, did bring a smile to his face when she told him about riding horseback to the mill, delivering a sack of Papa's field corn to be ground into meal. She showed him the fistful of arrows and the hunting bow an Alabama Coushatta Indian from out in the woods had given her lately. "You hold the bow flat in front of you whenever you need to kill a big bear or something else scary."[30]

The following spring, on April 6, 1917, the dread fears that had troubled all Americans for nearly four years came true when Woodrow Wilson declared war on Germany. Large cantonments were established in Fort Worth, Houston, Waco, Dallas, Austin, and Wichita Falls. When the two regular Texas posts—Fort Sam Houston in San Antonio and Fort Bliss in El Paso—were greatly expanded, Sam tried to imagine how such world conditions might soon involve him.

In the meantime, in the Capitol and in the Governor's Mansion, Governor Jim Ferguson had made a brilliant beginning as a leader bent on positive action. Soon after his second inauguration, however, impeachable charges were brought against him. They included misappropriation of state funds, falsifying records, depositing state monies in his own Temple bank instead of in the state treasury, attempting to influence state officials by personal loans, interfering with the control of the University of Texas, and refusing to divulge the source of a personal loan of some $156,000. After a twenty-one day hearing, the House of Representatives impeached Ferguson and found him guilty as charged.[31]

As a result, on August 25, 1917, William P. Hobby became the new Texas Governor – at age thirty-nine the youngest ever to hold that office

By now, as Sam's teller role suited him more and more comfortably,[33] the last thing he wanted to do was disrupt his career and his on-the-job schooling for military service. Yet, like most other young men in Beaumont and Woodville, he knew too that practical sense advised him to volunteer for some attractive branch of the military before the draft stuck him into an inappropriate hole. In September, he made a quick trip to Woodville to tell the family what he had decided to do.

Hearing him out, Fanny's fears loomed large on her face. "All right, Sambo, if that is how it must be. But *please* go to church. You *must* not neglect the Good Lord. Especially now."

Sam acknowledged her admonitions; he shook hands stiffly with Charlie; he hugged the whole sober-faced crowd on the porch steps, then dashed for the train. Back at Gulf, he gripped hands all around, and headed – two months shy of age twenty-one – for Fort Sam Houston in San Antonio.

There, in Signal Corps basic training, Sam quickly learned the dit-dot of the Morse code and the wig-wag of semaphore flags, then found himself transferred across town to Kelly Field for training in the Aeronautical Service. Assigned to a tent with no heat, he spent his first night wrapped in his overcoat in a makeshift "bed" of newspapers. Breakfast was liver and onions, but when he pulled latrine duty later that morning, he could only mutter along with the other raw troops, "I'm in the Army now." Before noon, however, his day brightened when a second lieutenant gave him a tap on the shoulder.

"Your name Young?"

"Yes, sir," he replied fearfully.

"It says here you worked in a bank. So pack up your gear. You're moving back to Fort Sam, Headquarters, Aeronautical Squadron No. 366."

Assigned to a desk and warm quarters at last, Sam stood at attention, facing his new boss.

"I want you to be happy here if you can," Sergeant Major Davis told him. "I'm assigning you to cut company orders. Personnel transfers – the brass, the non-coms, the enlisted – all clear through this office. Colonel Brandt tells Captain Hyman what he wants done. Hyman tells me. I pass it to you, you write it up. You better bone up on the forms. A couple of lady stenographers handle the typing."

Watching Sam's quick comprehension, Davis soon told him, "Captain Hyman's putting you in for corporal. Keep your nose clean, and hang on."

Month by month, Sam moved up through the ranks: sergeant, first sergeant, sergeant major. When he reached master signal electrician, Davis suggested, "If you want, I can get you commutation of quarters, permission to live downtown. Eighty-five dollars to cover your costs."

With that and his base pay of eighty-five dollars, Sam settled for comfort in San Antonio's top hotel, the St. Anthony. With its grand staircases and potted palm trees in the lobby, Sam blinked in surprise at the rise he had made since his old job as Mrs. Steward's night clerk in Woodville. Though such special treatment was more than enough to help Sam "be happy," Davis soon threw in a motorcycle equipped with a sidecar and a driver.

Sam was established so firmly now in the "orders" routine that Captain Hyman rarely questioned any of the papers he cut. Routinely, Hyman bucked them on up the chain of command. One order Sam cut sent a contingent of guards to Wichita Falls to protect its big new oil field from possible German sabotage. His good luck continued when a local car dealer named Ayres lent him a second-hand Chevrolet. "Use it as long as you're here," Ayres told him.[34] "I want to do what I can for you boys in the service."

In spite of the perks involved in his job, Sam's daily routine never let him forget there was a war going on. Like everyone else on the post, each morning he had to "fall out" for calisthenics. Sometimes, to his great discomfort, he had to take turns barking commands during drill practice.

"Left face! Right face! Forward, *'harch!'*"

Seeing the force of authority in the officers, Sam confessed to himself that he could happily handle deskwork, but he never would be "officer material."

Nevertheless, there were other ways through which he could gain appreciative grins from "the troops." When they told him they were tired of eating chow in a cold, drafty tent, Sam located an engineer "going to waste" in some other squadron. He cut the appropriate transfer orders. Hyman approved, and soon the new engineer arrived "to build us a mess hall."

Recognizing a good thing when they saw it, the troops next mentioned to Sam that the fine new mess hall was, well, useless on Saturday nights without an orchestra to play for some dances.

Master Signal Electrician Sam (at left) with the Army brass at Fort Sam Houston, 1917.

Sam nodded. "Over at Kelly, I hear they've got a pretty good band. Why don't you guys look around? Give me those names. Maybe I can get them for us."

The newly arrived "orchestra" had played for dances a time or two when Colonel Chitty, the Kelly Field commandant, came storming to Sam's colonel. "Brandt, what the hell do you mean, tearing up my whole band? Picking out all my good players!"

Colonel Brandt pled innocent. "Why — why, Chitty, I'm not familiar with this. But I'll certainly look into it."

Reporting on the double to Brandt, Sam stood stiff at attention and told the facts in the case. "Colonel, my captain okayed the whole list."[35]

Sam came out clean from his first encounter with higher-up brass, but a few weeks later, from out of the blue he was summoned to the commanding general's office. Fearfully, he entered that august door; stiffly, he saluted the general. But his fears quickly vanished when, from across the room Sis Willie and Governor Hobby hailed him, all smiles.

Sam dashed straight for Sis Willie, gave her a kiss, shook hands with the governor, and the group settled down for a chat. The Hobbys soon finished their courtesy call on the general, and Sam walked with them out to their shiny black limousine bearing the governor's star-studded flags and waved as their chauffeur drove them slowly away. No sooner had the governor's Cadillac passed through the gates, however, than he was summoned again to the general.

When Sam showed up at last back at his office, Captain Hyman stared at him. "My god, Young, what happened to you?"

"That general," Sam gulped, "damn him, he chewed my ass. Said I'd broken the cardinal rule of military courtesy: kissing my cousin before he gave me, 'At ease.'"[36]

When Sam could get leaves from the post, he took full advantage of having a governor cousin. Once on a three-day pass, he took Captain Hyman along up to Austin to relax in the Governor's Mansion. At other times, he went up alone, to read or lounge around upstairs, enjoying the quiet, polished routine that Sis Willie maintained as Texas' First Lady. But in August, Sis Willie sent him sad news. Uncle Bronson had just died in Beaumont and the family wanted Sam in his uniform to stand at attention with his brother Cooper beside the casket during the funeral.[37]

For weeks now, scuttlebutt at Fort Sam had been spreading the word that a big contingent of troops would soon be shipping out for Fort Dix in New Jersey, then France. If true, Sam was sure he should have known as much as anybody else on the post, but the matter troubled his sleep. In late October 1918 when official word came that his squadron would prepare for shipment overseas, bitter fears shot through the whole office. "What the hell's going on?" an orderly cried. "Not a damn one of us office guys is trained for combat."

Slowly, Sam nodded.

For more than two weeks, the rumors kept mounting up, but suddenly on November 11 the brightest possible news swept through the post and San Antonio. Hearing the shouting, Sam rushed to his window at the St. Anthony.

Down in the street, men were dancing in circles and singing, grabbing up children and tossing them high over head. Women were hugging and cheering. Through the shouts, Sam could make out the words. "*Armistice!* Armistice signed! The war's over!"

The next mail from Beaumont brought Sam an urgent request from Preston Doty at Gulf. "Try to get an early discharge. With so many of you boys tied up for so long in the service, we need you as soon as you get here."

On December 13, 1918, fresh with his new rank of second lieutenant in the Air Corps Reserve, Sam sought out San Antonio's best tailor. To celebrate his discharge, he ordered two suits, one a black serge with silver stripes, the other a khaki uniform complete with shiny puttees.[38] Resplendent in the clothes befitting his rank, Sam smiled in the mirror and squared his shoulders. Gripping his honorable discharge papers, he caught the next train for Beaumont.

3

YOUNG MAN GOING PLACES

THE TIME IN THE ARMY HAD BEEN MOSTLY PROFIT. Sam had done his job well, he had had a fairly good time, and he had learned much from his contact with new people, people he might never have met otherwise. Now, it was good to move back into his old digs at Bubber's, to slip again into a decent white shirt and a red tie, to greet the "welcome back" smiles at his old teller window.[1]

However, shaking hands with the team that had kept the show running while he was away in the Army, Sam sensed in himself a discomfort. A current song summed up his restlessness. "How you gonna keep 'em down on the farm, after they've seen Paree?" Now that he had seen San Antonio, by Christmas time his teller cage that had once seemed like the peak of success seemed more like a jail. When he mentioned the matter to Courtney Marshall, his old confidante asked, "Well, then what *would* you like to do?"

Sam thought a moment. "I'd like to help people. I might have liked being a minister, or a lawyer, or doctor. But" – he shook his head – "I can't afford to go back to school. My family needs every cent I can spare."

Marshall nodded. "Then down at the bank, tell them straight how you feel."

Preston Doty, Gulf's new CEO, understood Sam's dilemma. "Nobody can tell you a teller's job is the most promising career in the world. But later on, you might think about a phase of banking that would give you real freedom to rise. You might enjoy being a bank examiner."[2]

"Bank examiner?"

"The next qualifying exam for bank examiner is in February, up in Austin."

At home that night, Bubber agreed with Doty. "Give it a try, Sam. You'll need to bone up on commercial law. I'll lend you the books."[3]

The next morning, Sam's speaking straight out to Doty about his plan seemed the fair thing to do, but Doty surprised him. "I can't argue you into staying with us when your future here is so uncertain. But, Sam, you need time to prepare for the test, and we need time to find a replacement if your plan does work out, so you might as well resign as of the fifteenth of this month."

Doty gave him a friendly pat on the back. But leaving Doty's office, Sam was filled with dismay. Weeks before he was ready to quit, he was unemployed and unprepared for the future. To tide himself over the days till the big trip up to Austin, he took a substitute job as cashier at Duck Swan's Alamo Cafe, free meals included. Between rush hours there, he spread out his law books on the counter.

While he was in Austin taking the test, Sis Willie and Governor insisted he stay with them at the Mansion.[4] And Sis Willie gave her cousin a piece of advice. "Sam, the train conductor let you ride free down to Beaumont. Well, there's a point you need to remember. To be a successful businessman, if that's what you eventually decide to do with yourself, try to take on a job that gives you free railroad passes. That's a distinction I hope will come to you early in life."

At the moment, with the big test uppermost on his mind, Sam only nodded his head, but he did promise Sis Willie to keep her suggestion in mind.

After two full days of fast writing, Sam left the testing room in the State Banking Commissioner's office downhearted. And he endured a nervous week before W. R. Squires, the deputy commissioner, phoned him the verdict. "You only passed by the skin of your teeth, but you passed. So you're now an official bank examiner. Annual salary, $3,000 plus travel. Living allowance, $6 a day."[5] He could start work the next week in Dallas. "Stanley Longmoor, one of our most seasoned people, is examining the Central State Bank now. Report to him up there."

In Dallas, when Sam, hat in hand, stated his mission – "I'm here, but I'm a greenhorn at this" – Longmoor only glanced up from his ledger. "So I'd kind of appreciate it if you'd – " He handed Longmoor his papers.

Longmoor shot a look at the papers, then shrugged. "This shows you're a bank examiner, so you know as much as I do." He motioned over his shoulder. "The note drawers are open."

Sam was taken aback at the old pro's cool manner, but Longmoor did have a point. Taking his seat at a cluttered desk in a corner, Sam stared at the mountain of papers. Passing a qualifying test for a job was one thing, knowing how to start work was quite something else. Tempted again to ask Longmoor for help, he glanced up a couple of times, but each time Longmoor only seemed more engrossed with his pencil and paper. Sam loosened his collar.

The business at hand had nothing to do with commercial law or the regular in-and-out flow he was familiar with back at Gulf. But by the next afternoon he was onto a system that might in time justify his fat new salary and that generous living allowance. Within a week, he felt like an old pro himself. After a short stint of scrutinizing several small banks around Dallas, Longmoor – considerably friendlier now – wished Sam a hearty "good luck" on his three-month assignment out in the field.

That train trip to El Paso at the far western tip of the nation's biggest state was as far west in Texas as a young man from Woodville could go. Fairly at ease, he stopped off to examine a small bank in Sierra Blanca. That job should take half a day and he could catch the next train. But the hour grew late, and he needed a bed for the night. Sierra Blanca's little Palace Hotel was already full, but the clerk's face suddenly brightened. "In one room, we're holding a corpse till the funeral tomorrow. I could curtain it off. You'd get a good bed in a room that shore would be quiet."

"Oh, well now, I" – half grinning, Sam glanced at the long leather sofa near the pot-bellied stove – "thanks anyway. With a pillow and some blankets, I'd be just fine on that couch."[6] Next morning, fresh and rested, he caught the westbound Texas and Pacific train for El Paso.[7]

As the train came to a stop, the porter told him, "It's a hour sooner out here than where you been coming from. Watch yo' step, suh."

When his foot touched the shiny brass stool, Sam peered around at a sight a boy from the swamps of East Texas could have hardly imagined. Mountains as bony and poor as a starving cow stretched like grey walls around him. When he took a deep breath, the dry air prickled his nose. Worst of all, there were no trees to stop the dusty March wind that shrieked at his ears. Yet as he picked up his suitcase, this El Paso was obviously more than a woebegone whistle stop on a railroad. Within three or four blocks towered a goodly number of six and eight story buildings. In some incredible fashion, people here in this desolate land had managed to put down their roots and prosper.

It took Sam a few days to decide what to write home. "Out here, there's a spark in the air like electricity, a lightness." For Fanny, he could not really describe his own pep and energy – "a brightness all over this place."[8]

For living quarters, Sam's office had recommended the inexpensive little Hotel McCoy, but when he found he could stay at the town's top hotel – room and three meals only six dollars – he gladly moved into the grandly ornate Paso del Norte. Reading his *El Paso Herald* by the bright sunlight filtering down through the lobby's blue and gold dome of Tiffany glass, he missed, but not greatly, the softer glow over Beaumont and the big Piney Woods of old Tyler County.

On his own now as a fully fledged bank examiner, Sam reported for work the next morning. At the Texas Bank and Trust Company, Lee Orndorff, one of the officers, hoped he would enjoy his stay. "As an international town cut through the middle by the big Rio Grande, this place is pretty special. The American folks living here, we're about half-Mexican. The Mexican folks over there in Ciudad Juarez, they're about half-Texan."

Sam got a full sense of the community's cultural blend his first afternoon on the job when he found a $200,000 discrepancy in a Mexican checking account. On his desk lay solid proof that somebody had pulled a mountainous draft from the account of one Luis Terrazas. Yet there was no cancelled check to show who had made away with his cash.

It was good luck in timing that Sam met the aged Luis Terrazas in the bank lobby that afternoon. In his silver-studded *pantalones* and scoop-brimmed sombrero, Terrazas seemed clearly surprised when Sam, with the help of an interpreter, reported the shortage. Stroking his flowing mustache, he could not explain the loss, in Mexican money, of 800,000 pesos. Only later, when Sam confronted Orndorff and Bank President Frank Murchison with his discovery, did another officer admit that he had made "a mistake." To correct it, he deposited a cashier's check for the full $200,000.

The next time General Terrazas was in town, he accepted the matter as settled, and the major result for Sam was a pleasant lobby conversation. With the help of an English-speaking aide, the general mentioned his pastures and mountainous timberlands south of the river.[9]

"Someday, señor, you must see Mexico for yourself."

As Terrazas was leaving the bank, a teller motioned Sam over. "I suppose you know who that was."

Sam nodded. "Terrazas, a Mexican rancher."

The teller grinned. "The fact is his ranch is nearly the whole damn State of Chihuahua, seven million acres of gratitude from the Mexican government for his help in getting rid of Emperor Maximilian. He's the Terrazas who got a cattle order from the Swift Packing Plant in Chicago. 'Send us 5,000 head.' And Terrazas wired back, 'What color?'"[10]

Sam glanced though the window. Past the river beyond the barren grey hills might be an interesting place to look into, when and if he ever found time.

Unfortunately for the Texas Bank and Trust's guilty officer, Sam had not quite finished his examining chores. After Terrazas had left for home the next morning, Sam discovered that the cashier's check supposedly squaring matters with Terrazas was bogus. The culprit had drawn it as another offsetting entry against the Terrazas checking account.

Evenings around on the loose, Sam struck up an acquaintance with a young insurance salesman, Leo Schuster, who was "aggrieved," he said with a grin, that Sam had not already learned the ropes, so to speak, across the river in Ciudad Juarez. "Tomorrow, we're having lunch over there at the Central. They dish out a mighty mean plate of tacos and beans."

At a table outside in a courtyard, Sam found no reason to doubt the Central's mean tacos or its bartender's "gin bucks." But heading back over the bridge to El Paso, Sam felt his drinks begin to complain. To steady his friend before his afternoon's work, Leo drove him up to a rocky ridge overlooking El Paso.

"Take it easy, Sam." Leo told him, parking his car. "Take some deep breaths. Enjoy the view."

But sliding lower and lower down in his seat, Sam felt steadily worse. His stomach churning, he lay still till he made a sudden leap out the door. Mission accomplished, he settled back for a silent car ride back down to work.[11]

Like any good friend, Leo also made certain that Sam met some of El Paso's attractive young ladies. Several times, Sam borrowed a car and drove one girl, Mary Gates Redmond, for long Sunday drives down along the Rio Grande through the lush cotton farms. One afternoon he was helping her into her seat when he asked her pleasantly, "What's in the big bag you're bringing along?"

"It's my knitting," Mary sweetly replied, "in case I get bored."

For his date with her the next week, Sam showed up on time, but Mary kept him waiting in the living room. Through the half-open dining room door, Sam eventually discovered that she was chatting with another young man. Sam cooled his heels a half hour, then left.

Next morning one of Mary's girl friends phoned and apologized for her, but Sam tossed the matter aside. "I don't care. It was all over for her and me anyway."[12]

The fact was that he was ripe for a meaningful friendship, but given his very short stays in any one place, the chances were against such a hope. When he mentioned his problem to Leo and another good friend, Tom Mayfield, both shook their heads. "Someday," Tom told him, "you'll have to quit this roving bank-examiner life. How 'bout it, Sam? Why don't you face facts and settle down here?"

Sam nodded, but the way to do that was hard to imagine, given his lack of training for anything else.

Shortly before Sam finished examining El Paso's six state banks – its national banks were not a part of his job – he was chatting with a young banker friend, Robert T. Hoover, in the Paso del Norte lobby when Hoover turned suddenly grave. "I know you're examining us tomorrow, so I'm saving you time and effort by letting you know, right from the start, there's trouble all over our books."[13]

By the time Sam had finished the American Trust and Savings Bank that day, he had seen proof that Hoover was right. Bank troubles in El Paso in 1919, however, were only local symptoms of America's money difficulties in general. After the joyous word "armistice" had rung through the nation's streets only the past November, peace had brought with it perilous times for farmers, cattle ranchers, oil producers, and business men throughout the country. Bankers who had extended too much credit in support of any one war-time commodity were now in deep trouble.

That fact above all else occupied Sam's careful scrutiny as he pored over El Paso's shaky bank books. Though excitements across the river did at times attract his attention, at least once they attracted his profound disapproval. Pancho Villa, the Mexican revolutionary, had established a profitable sideline involving more than one El Paso bank. Using carloads of cotton he had stolen in Mexico as collateral, Villa gained good dollar credit with several local bankers, even though official Washington policy strongly questioned Villa's intentions along the border. In June 1919 when his attacks on Ciudad Juarez caused distress on the American side of the river, Sam heard the thunder of guns as Fort Bliss artillerymen lobbed shells at the Juarez race track where Villa's forces were camped.[14]

By June, when Sam had closed his books in El Paso, he felt fully at home at the Paso del Norte Hotel, and he had found a good friend in its owner, Zach White. Over lunch several times, White had reminisced about his childhood in Amherst County, Virginia. One of twenty-one children in the family, he had left home to better his chances "out west," and had come to El Paso by stagecoach in 1881 shortly before the first railroad reached town. At age thirty-one, sensing the area's bright future, he had devoted his energies ever since to the community's growth. Incidentally, he had reaped a personal fortune from his brick factory, his coal gas works, his mule-drawn streetcars, his electric company, his downtown real estate investments, his bridge connecting El Paso and Juarez, and especially his eight thousand acres of rich valley farmland.[15]

On that basis, White made a point of encouraging Sam to remain in El Paso. For an energetic young man, he said, willing to think in big terms — as he himself had done here — the town was wide open.

"I appreciate your telling me this," Sam responded, "but I'm a long way from knowing where I'm liable to settle. The business I'm in sends me packing just when I'm getting easy and comfortable."

White raised his brows. "Sounds like a mighty hard life, with too little profit. Later on, young fellow, don't forget what I told you."

Leaving El Paso, Sam journeyed by train to Austin to a meeting of the state's bank examiners. Afterwards, he enjoyed a chat with J. B. Herndon, Jr., a native of Albuquerque, New Mexico. While Herndon saw the "far west" as a wide empty country that suffered from too little rain, to Sam El Paso offered high hopes, he told Herndon, for anybody with creative vision.[16]

With this on-the-road experience under his belt, Sam was ready now, at age twenty-three, to face the big time, Houston and the banks in its district. In Humble, Texas, however, he felt a fearful timidity when he discovered that the Humble State Bank was "busted." He phoned George W. Briggs, the banking commissioner, that surely a more experienced man ought to come down and convey the bad news. Briggs disagreed. "You're a fully-fledged bank examiner. You know your duties, and I have faith in your judgment. So, proceed, if you will, with that duty."[17]

Quavering inside, Sam posted a sign on the locked doors: Bank Closed By Reason Of Insolvency. In The Hands Of The Bank Examiner.

That crisis behind him, Sam soon butted heads with one of Houston's strongest financiers. Ruling his lumber/real estate/construction empire, Jesse Jones was also deeply involved in trust companies and banks. At age forty-five, he was already the largest stockholder of the National Bank of Commerce.[18] Nevertheless, after examining one of Jones's trust companies, Sam felt duty bound to express a grim judgment. "I'm new at this business, you understand, Mr. Jones, but it does seem to me that you ought to diversify." For this enterprise, Jones's assets were almost entirely coastal lands near Victoria, Texas. "It looks to me like you're land poor."

"Well, young man," Jesse replied. "That's about right. But if I ever need money, I can borrow it."

"I'm sure you can, Mr. Jones," said Sam, "but I'm not looking at what you can do. I'm looking at what you have done. So, I have to report this to the commissioner and say that this is improper. It's not according to law. There's a lot to complain about here."

At that, Jones threw back his shoulders. "Is that so? You're mighty young, aren't you, to be telling me how to run my business?"

"I'm not telling you how you should run your business," Sam countered, "but you do need to know how the law says you should." Sam stood his ground while Jones pondered the greenhorn's report.

"Well, yes, I know," Jones grumbled. "Go ahead. File your report."[19]

By the fall of 1919, Sam felt secure enough in his job to take on a deeper involvement at home. Things were not going well with Charlie, the storekeeper. After trying to make sense out of Charlie's bookkeeping system, Sam appealed to his old Beaumont friend, Courtney Marshall. Through Courtney, Charlie got a nightwatchman's job at the Magnolia Refinery in Beaumont. He sold his store and packed up his family: Pete with his coon, Mike with his rabbits, Jack with his dog, and Margaret and Phebe cuddling their dolls. Along with some money from Sam, he traded the Woodville house as down payment for a family home in Beaumont. Now Fanny had electric lights and running water and much better schools for the children.[20]

About that, Sam sensed a bright new day in his family's own fortunes. For himself, however, there were times when his job hung heavy upon him: living full-time out of a suitcase, eating alone every night. In San Antonio he mentioned his loneliness to a friend, Joe Jennings.

"The only cure for a fellow with troubles like yours," replied Jennings, "is – " He hauled out his University of Texas yearbook and flipped to a page full of pictures. "Here, Young," he grinned, "feast your eyes." Sam whistled, then pointed at a beautiful blonde, the most attractive girl on the page. Jennings nodded. "That's Betty Goodman from Corsicana, a good friend of mine. You ought to meet her."

"I'd like to. But *how?*" Sam wanted to know. At the time, there seemed no possible hope, but Sam thumbed again through the yearbook.[21]

Back on the road, often wishing for a full-time assistant to keep him company, Sam occasionally deputized an aide from whatever bank he was working. "Most of the time, however, I'm a lone wolf," he wrote Fanny. Especially after learning the hard way that a bank examiner, with his freedom to gloss over bank shortages, had to be careful with afterwork sociability. In Laredo, Sam was already in bed one night when a burst of men's voices down in the street stirred him awake. Some of the boys from the Merchant State Bank were serenading him. "We're heading across the border to Nuevo Laredo," one called. "Come on, let's have some fun."

Sam joined the group for several rounds of *cerveza*, but heading back toward the bridge about midnight, he put his foot down when the assistant cashier at the bank tugged his sleeve toward a doorway glowing bright red. "Hell, no," Sam told him. "If the commissioner ever found out, I'd lose my job."[22]

Sam only learned the next day that the good time had had a sober, ulterior purpose.[23] He had just entered the bank's men's room when, in a stall, he happened to look up at a shelf holding spare rolls of toilet paper. On top of those rolls lay a stack of checks and deposit slips that, he quickly discovered, had never been entered on the bank's books. Back at his desk, he also found that the bank's "due from" account was short by some $275,000. Immediately, Sam notified the bank president. "The shortage impairs your capital structure."

Ill at ease with the responsibility that he was about to shoulder again, Sam called Commissioner Briggs in Austin. "Wouldn't you like to send out an examiner more experienced in matters like this?"

"No, Mr. Young," Briggs replied calmly, "you did the right thing in Humble. You'll know the right course in Laredo."[24]

Flexing his "muscle," Sam gave the Laredo bank president till noon the next day to restore his capital structure. When the time came, the president had not raised the money and, interestingly enough, the assistant cashier in charge of the "due from" account had left town. Sam now learned from one of the young bloods on that beer trip the evening before that the assistant cashier was hiding in Nuevo Laredo. Out of concern for the fellow's "mistake," Sam took another teller along to help him locate the culprit.

When their long search paid off, Sam tried to talk sense to the cashier. "My job didn't require me to come over here. I'm only trying to save you from worse trouble. If you come back and confess, you'll put yourself in position for leniency under the law."

Bowing his neck a bit, the cashier agreed to go back with Sam to Laredo to prove he was innocent. But on the bridge, at the yellow line marking the international boundary, the cashier let out a cry. "Help me!" he shouted. "They're kidnapping me!"

Dumbfounded, Sam showed his credentials to the Mexican guards on the bridge. After explaining what he was trying to do, the officers let him proceed to Laredo. By then, however, the cashier had whirled and fled down an alley.

Weeks later, at the bank culprit's trial, the verdict read, "Prison."[25]

In a Pullman car headed for Dallas, Sam soon fell afoul of more theft. In the warm night, he had opened his window, but when he woke up in Fort Worth, he found that a robber had reached in before daylight, apparently, and taken his wallet with all of his money, his tailor-made uniform, his Army discharge papers, and most of his clothes.

Later, a troubled friend questioned him. "Sam, why in the world were you wagging all that valuable stuff around with you?"

Sam shook his head sadly. "Moving around all the time, I didn't have any home place to leave it."[26]

In the spring of 1920 Sam interrupted his lonely days on the road with another visit to the Hobbys in Austin. One afternoon, Sis Willie was guiding the Zeta Tau Alpha sorority girls from the University of Texas on a tour of the Governor's Mansion when, leading them along an upstairs corrider, she pointed toward a polished doorknob. "But we can't open that door. My cousin Sam Young is napping in there."

"Sam Young!" cried one of the Zetas, "I know him from Beaumont. He won't mind."

With that, Fay Wise pushed open Sam's door. Sam roused up, blushing at Fay and the giggling cluster peering in at him. Half-smiling, Sis Willie herded her charges away, then shut Sam's door behind her.[27]

Still blushing from that sudden visit, Sam was watching the famous Battle of Flowers in San Antonio a few weeks later when his heart skipped a beat. There, scarcely an arm's length away, came the stunning blond college girl he had seen in Joe Jennings's yearbook. Tonight, in that grand beauty pageant, Betty Goodman was gliding along on the arm of a prominent young banker, Franz Groos. Tongue-tied and uncertain how he could ever hope to meet that young lady, Sam trudged back to his hotel. But Betty Goodman was never far from his thoughts during the fall of 1920 while he was working banks in West Texas again.

He did make a new friend just then, a clerk at the El Paso branch of the Federal Reserve Bank. Eloy Vallina was the son of a Spanish immigrant who ran a small grocery on the corner of Piedras and San Antonio streets. When Vallina told him about learning his banking job partly by correspondence from LaSalle University,[28] Sam mentioned that he had thought about the same course until a banker in Beaumont had saved him the trouble. The encounter with Eloy Vallina was brief, but Sam long remembered the awe he felt for this amiable young Spaniard whose fluent English made him totally at ease in this American bank.

On the road again, Sam soon locked horns in Big Spring with the town's major banker, T. S. Currie, at the First State Bank. After working through a drawer of loan notes all one morning and posting it shut with a government seal, he came alert after lunch when he found that that seal had been broken. Immediately, Sam confronted Banker Currie.

"Oh, well, now," Currie grinned, "I had to review some of those notes with a customer. But don't worry" – Currie nodded toward the bank's board room – "those notes are in there with him right now. With us," he winked, "the customer always comes first."

Sam might have been confronting Jesse Jones again. "The customer doesn't come first with me," he shot back, "and you don't come first with me either. Now, I'm going to list all of those notes again. And I'm charging you an extra fifteen-dollar fee for doing it. Then I'm sealing this drawer once again. If you break *this* government seal, I'm calling a Texas Ranger!"[29]

Currie smiled coolly, then walked away.

Next day, needing transportation to a bank thirty miles away in Garden City and finding no bus going in that direction, Sam mentioned his problem to Currie. "Oh, well, now, Mr. Young." Currie said jovially, "I guess I could drive you myself."

The ride went along well enough, Currie dropped Sam at the bank right on time. But when Sam got back to district headquarters in Dallas and opened his mail, he found a note from Currie. "For services rendered. Car ride Big Spring/Garden City. $15.00."[30]

Sam studied the bill, then chuckled. Currie had finessed him out of the extra fee he had charged him.

4

HOME BASE AT LAST

By October of 1920, Sam knew he had had enough of the road. In his district's small banks he had heard too many sad stories: bankruptcies, crop failures, short markets for beef, dwindling prices for oil. And he sorely missed his visits with the family. A letter from Fanny had mentioned that Jack was more and more the family clown now. Teah never tried to make a cake without keeping one eye cocked for Jack, lest he swoop through the kitchen, poke a finger into the icing, and run away, laughing.[1]

Always unsettled, Sam also figured that his $4,000 salary now was not quite all he was worth. To supplement his earnings, he began a little sideline business in Dallas with Governor's former secretary John McCall, dealing in city and county warrants and bonds. McCall kept him posted about upcoming bond issues, and when Sam could afford to follow the tips, in some months he cleared as much as $500 – once or twice even $1,000.[2]

In Dallas one morning after he had finished examining the Guaranty Bank and Trust Company, he dropped in for a visit with its vice president, Fred Florence. "I'm not exactly looking for work," he told Florence, "but it would be mighty nice to unpack my gear for a change."

The long nosed, slender banker already knew of Sam's work in the field but, he asked, "What kind of training, Sam, could you bring to a desk job?"

Back in February of 1919, nervously leaving the examiner test, Sam had had little hope of landing any job that demanded much formal schooling. But now, to Florence, Sam was quick and specific. "Being a state bank examiner, I've met just about every banker in Texas. From every state bank I've looked at, I've learned the ropes about banking. If you'd like to ask me some questions, fire away."[3]

Florence smiled and gave him a nod. In a moment, when he offered Sam a vice presidency at $6,000, Sam said he would give the matter some thought overnight.

Passing the Commonwealth National Bank, Sam dropped in on its Executive Vice President Ed Hobby (Governor's brother), to chat about Florence's offer. Hobby took a slow pull on his black cigar. "Sam, I can do better than that. We've got a vice presidency too, and it can pay $7,500. But" – Hobby leaned forward – "before we could sign you onto our Dallas team, we have to tackle a problem with the City National Bank in Eastland. They're into us for $500,000 on some oil loans, and we need one of our people to take charge as interim president awhile and straighten it out."[4]

If Sam had felt a bit cocky discussing his merits with Florence, he now felt decidedly humble. A bank presidency, in an oil town sick like every other oil town in Texas? After he paid a visit to Eastland, Sam saw no way to reassure Hobby about the little bank's prospects. But if he turned its fortunes around he did see a slim chance to come out – at age twenty-four – looking shiny and bright.

Taking that risk seemed urgent when Sam got word from Beaumont that after a long siege of flu and homesickness, Charlie was moving the family back home "where we belong." What Charlie did not immediately point out was the fact that in breaking his purchase contract on the nice house in Beaumont, he had forfeited all of the equity Sam had put into the place. Now there was no money for a decent house back in Woodville.[5]

With that heavy concern on his mind, Sam settled into his new desk job in Eastland in early 1921. After studying the gloomy ledgers before him, he fired all the bank officers except one, a former railroad postman. "I'm keeping him on," Sam told Ed Hobby, "because he knows everybody in this part of the country."[6] To shore up the bank's chance to revive, he persuaded Hobby to put in a new money-transfusion of $165,000. To make good with that new lease on life, in the second-hand Cadillac he bought for himself he made it a point to get acquainted all over town, explaining his plans for pumping life back into the bank. After all – he emphasized in his conversations – the City National Bank still had deposits totalling over $4 million.[7]

The new scheme Sam devised involved recapitalizing the old national bank under a new State of Texas charter and a new name, The Security State Bank and Trust Company. Once he had that institution's accounts protected under the State depositor guaranty fund, Sam had reason to hope that his bank might soon be "out of the woods," though Eastland's economy grew steadily worse as oil prices soon bottomed out at ten cents a barrel.

To take a quick break from his troubles, he drove down to check on Fanny and Charlie. After making a down payment on the best house the family had ever lived in, he took a sort of bemused pleasure as Charlie squired him around, showing off this biggest son who, Charlie told all the old-timers, was making good out in the world.[8]

Yet if asked for specifics, Sam could have given little support for his father's pride in him or much reason to feel any self-confidence. At a luncheon the Eastland Chamber of Commerce gave for ex-President William Howard Taft while he was touring the Texas oil fields, Sam sat tongue-tied and shy while the other young men bantered jokes with the portly guest of honor.[9] Since nothing came up about banking, he could think of nothing to say.

Some weeks later, when he mentioned his shyness to George W. Briggs, now a Dallas banker, Briggs tried to settle his fears. "Don't ever think that I don't have the same trouble. Whenever I have to stand up facing a crowd, I try to hide it, but it's bad."[10]

Likewise, when his old friend, Joe Jennings, showed up in Eastland one afternoon and told Sam he was attending a party that night at Frank Funderburk's home, Sam hesitated a moment before he nodded, "He's the bank's lawyer. I'm invited, but I'm not too eager to go."[11]

"But you've got to," Jennings insisted. "That beauteous blonde in that yearbook, that Frances Elizabeth Goodman from Corsicana, she's supposed to be there."

"In Eastland?"

At Funderburk's party the honey-blonde beauty whom Sam had admired from afar in San Antonio looked up as Funderburk introduced them. "Oh, yes," she smiled. "I remember you." Then she laughed. "In a sense, we've already met."

"You and me? Where?"

"In Austin. Mrs. Hobby was showing us Zetas through the Governor's Mansion," Betty explained, "and that silly Fay Wise pushed open your door."

Sam gave a weak laugh. "I guess it could have been worse," he said limply.[12]

But before the evening was over, Sam felt fully at ease with this elegant twenty-year-old college girl who told him she had come to Eastland to visit her cousins, Jack and Effie Lewis. A few nights later, when Sam escorted Betty to a local carnival and into a fortune teller's dark tent, the wrinkled old gypsy studied Betty's palm. "Ah, yes" – she smiled mysteriously – "it's here in your heart line. An engagement ring, very soon."

After bank hours, Betty and Sam brought each other up-to-date about themselves. Betty soon knew all about Woodville and a bank examiner's monotonous routine. Sam knew all about Betty's family in Corsicana – her mother, the widow of a prosperous wholesale grocer who had died in 1910 at age fifty; her brother Robert Jr.; her two younger sisters Martha and Jo.

Three weeks after they met, Sam was so sure about his feelings for Betty that he drove into Dallas and made a $900 purchase. The next night, in his open-topped car in the moonlight, he stated his case to Betty. "If I gave you an engagement ring, would you marry me?"

Betty replied just as directly, "Well, yes, Sam, I would," she smiled.

Sam slipped his glittering purchase with its Tiffany mounting onto her finger. But then he said, "That little ring doesn't do you justice. I'm taking it back and getting one bigger. All right?"

Betty hesitated. "Sam, I – "

But after a pause, she smiled. "Well, Sam if you really want to, that would be lovely."[13]

By May, 1921, Sam knew the worst about his sick bank. Despite three urgent trips to Chicago on behalf of Eastland's hopes to float some road bonds, despite his best efforts to protect both his stockholders and his depositors, he knew that his bank was a strangling pawn in the grip of forces he could not pry loose. Not even a magician could draw new capital out of a "busted oil field" like Eastland.

Heading for Dallas to report the worst to Ed Hobby, Sam was sick with a deep sense of failure. Though he had stepped into a hopeless dilemma, his chance to distinguish himself against heavy odds had come to nothing. In Hobby's office, he was in for worse news. The vice presidency that had been waiting for him in Dallas had died on the same vine. Ed Hobby himself was out of a job. The Commonwealth National itself was awash in red ink.

For a young swain with a bride on his mind, a sobering truth laid him low. Too long now he had ignored the old comfort that Fanny had tried to instill in him early. "When you're lost in the dark and can't see your way clear, get down on your knees." In his mind's eye, Sam could see her glaring up at him. "And you pray for His guidance to light up your path."

After many sessions down on his knees, he renewed a commitment. "I will forever look to Thee for my guidance," he prayed, "and I promise that whatever success I may achieve, I will give Thee the credit. I will confess it before all the people through the passing of time."[14]

Special light may have guided Sam's path to a City Hall office in Dallas when he thought of opening a brokerage dealing in bonds. After presenting his case to the necessary city officials, he met a Judge John Henry. The judge thought well of his plans, and Sam left that brief conversation with a new spring in his step.

Mostly on faith and a slice of his meager Eastland savings, Sam opened an office in the Southwestern Life Building, Room 1307. Superstition might have questioned his tempting fate with such an unlucky number, but practical fact won the debate. After buying Betty a little new car, thus adding weight to his engagement ring on her finger, that square little office was the best he could hope to afford.

The next day, a drop-in visit surprised him. "I'm John Lane Henry," the visitor announced. "My uncle, the judge you met yesterday, said I ought to look you up. He said that you and I might see our way clear to run this business together. My uncle told me, 'That young man is going places.'"[15] In the resulting partnership with John Lane, John concentrated on running the office, Sam became the go-getter[16] agent for bond dealers in Denver and Chicago, concentrating on municipal bonds.[17]

While Sam kept his happiest thoughts sharply focused toward Corsicana, the business at Henry and Young only slowly developed. The partners eked out a living; but about the bills mounting up, Sam was strictly candid in his visits to Betty in Corsicana. By late summer, his heart was still singing what he wanted to hear, but his head was preaching cold logic. Seated beside Betty in her mother's porch swing, Sam laid out the facts as he saw them. Eastland had failed, and now his Dallas bond business was barely paying the rent. "I don't know any right way to say this" – he took a deep swallow – "but the fact is, this may not be the right time for you to think about marrying me."

Betty took both his hands. "About Eastland, you didn't do anything wrong. None of that Dallas trouble makes any difference to me." She paused. "Anyhow, Sam, I'm *going* to marry you."[18]

Not trusting his voice, Sam looked away. But when he could look at Betty again, he knew that he did not have to say anything else. "You mean that?" he said at last. "You'd still go along, knowing the worst?"

"Things would only be worse for us both if I didn't," Betty replied.

Sam took a long time to say what he said next. "Then I guess we can start thinking about setting the date."

"The sooner the better," Betty answered, "so long as it isn't Friday the Thirteenth."

Sam threw back his head, laughing. "Do you really believe all that nonsense?"

"I most certainly do, and you yourself need to be very careful."[19]

On October 26, 1921, Betty made good on that declaration. At Westminster Presbyterian Church in Corsicana when she said, "I do," Sam's world took on bright new dimensions. Sis Willie and Governor (actually "ex-Governor" since January 18, when Pat Neff succeeded him into office)[20] were there. Bubber stood up as best man, and Teah represented the family from Woodville. But at the end of the minister's charge to them both, as he and Betty turned and faced the crowd smiling up at them, Sam pondered this church full of Goodmans. Could he ever make their Betty a decent living?

When the new bride and groom caught the noon train up to Dallas and on to Washington and New York, history repeated itself just a bit. By now, Henderson Jacoway, who had given Sam the silver dollar, had been elected to Congress, and the Jacoways were all smiles at

Washington's Union Depot when, stepping down from the Pullman, Sam introduced them to "Mrs. Sam Young." Their first night at the Jacoways ended a little more abruptly than planned when four-year-old Margaret came bounding in without knocking and planted herself between the sleepy young bride and the bridegroom.[21]

At breakfast that morning Henderson asked them, "Where are you young folks planning to live?"

Sam smiled across the table at Betty. "We're not sure. But on the train somewhere east of St. Louis, Betty motioned out the window at a tree-covered hill and asked if I had any idea where we'd live, when we could just settle down. I told her we'd have to think hard about that, but if I had my druthers, it would be in El Paso, out in the sun country, in Texas."

Later that day, Congressman Jacoway ushered his guests up the columned front steps of the White House and into the Blue Room where the President of the United States was receiving a long line of guests. Silver-haired President Harding in his frock coat bowed grandly over Betty's hand when Henderson explained the couple's presence in Washington. "Ah, yes, my dear," he told Betty, "if I were getting married again, I myself would select Washington for a honeymoon. Surely, it's the most beautiful city on earth."[22] Outside just then the maples along Pennsylvania Avenue were glowing deep red and gold.

There was no time for real conversation, but Sam later recalled Harding's quick comment to Jacoway when he learned that Sam had recently worked in banking. America needed more likely young business men. As a matter of fact, said the Republican President, the good of the nation demanded a freer deal for American business.

Pleasantries aside, Sam knew that his and Betty's life back in Texas, or wherever fortune might send them, depended on his keeping his eyes trained for openings. With Jacoway's help, Sam made a call the next day on the comptroller of the currency, Henry Dawes. "I want a job as either a national bank examiner or as a receiver of failed national banks. Preferably the latter, Mr. Dawes, because now that I'm married, I want to establish a home." Sam mentioned his work as a state bank examiner and his valiant attempts in Eastland. "Oh, yes—" Dawes studied a moment—"our examiners have told me all about your good efforts in the oil fields." With that, Dawes summoned the head of his insolvency division. "I want to recommend this young man for a receiver appointment. Whenever an opening occurs."[23]

Later that day, bidding the newlyweds a happy time in New York, Jacoway asked Sam his old question. "Sambo, have you still got that silver dollar?"

Sam reached in his pocket. "You bet. Right here. Just in case."

By the time the week's honeymoon in New York was over, Sam had put them up at the elegant Pennsylvania Hotel; he had squired Betty around to good shows and expensive restaurants; and she had asked several times, "But, Sam, can we afford this?"

"We can. At least for right now," he assured her.

But by train time, his budget was "busted." He did have their return tickets and just enough cash – not counting his silver dollar – to settle them back down to earth in Dallas.

The minute he checked in at Henry and Young, however, a Washington telegram changed all his plans. A national bank had just failed in Hastings, Oklahoma. If Young was still interested, he could sign on as its receiver.

Hastings was a mighty long trip from honeymoon land. The little farming town was very close, however, to the heartbreak that Sam had already learned all about in Eastland. Along with dwindling oil markets, widespread drouth throughout the summer had sown its own evil seeds. Reporting for work in Hastings, Sam quickly discovered the farmers' sad plight: after pledging all their farm assets on big bank loans, now they could only stand sullen and itching to fight while Sam as the bank's receiver directed the task of driving their cattle, their wagons and plows away to the auction yard.

Life was scarely easier at home, such as "home" was in Hastings. The best quarters he and Betty could rent was a bedroom in nearby Waurika, across the street from a boarding house. For a recent belle in a San Antonio pageant, the only rewards were the pleasure of cheering Sam off each morning, ready to face whatever troubles arose, and the joy of welcoming him home each evening. Between times, Betty "made do" with chats with the boardinghouse ladies and writing long letters to Corsicana.

Neither Betty nor Sam regretted the change in 1922 when the comptroller transferred Sam to central Texas, much closer home.

Llano, Texas, forty miles northwest of Johnson City, was suffering through much the same ills that had plagued Eastland and Hastings. Its

Llano National Bank had already failed; Sam took it over and then the Home National, when it soon followed suit.

For Betty and Sam, Llano itself was a bright, happy change. Under oaks hung with gray Spanish moss, the Llano river ran through the town and Betty fell in love with fishing its pools for blue catfish and bass. At least twice a week she gathered a group of new friends to go fishing upstream. After work other days, Sam happily joined her and hauled out the cane pole and fish hooks he kept in his car. Oftentimes, if they had caught a sackful of "keepers," he built a small fire near the stream, and Betty fried the day's catch for their supper.[24]

In a house owned by the bank, Sam and Betty set up their first real housekeeping. Now, with four bedrooms and all the other necessary amenities for large-family living, Sam cheerfully invited Betty's mother and sisters to move in with them. With her brother Robert a freshman at Texas A&M College, there seemed no need to keep their own house in Corsicana. Investing Mrs. Goodman's ready cash resources, $24,000, Sam established a monthly income for her and the girls.

Over coffee visits around Llano and drives in his Oakland coupe out in the field, Sam evolved a strategy to save Llano from more of the troubles that had wrecked both its banks. To his calls for new capital, Llano dug deep in its pocket, and Sam knew the satisfaction at last — after Eastland — of seeing the healthy result of his efforts take solid shape, the new Citizens National Bank. Quickly, he sold it the collectable assets of the two others, thus making available to their worried depositors their cash that had been tied up in the failures.

Unfortunately, all was not peaceful, however. In cases where he could not avoid foreclosures, Sam soon knew that he needed a bodyguard. "That's an appalling idea," Betty shuddered. But the fact remained that out in the county — when a farmer yelled at him, "Why can't you fat bankers face the same risks as us? You and us both is gambling on the hope of good weather" — a bodyguard's pistol strapped to his hip afforded the best protection.

The guard that Sam hired, an ex-rancher named Moseley, stated his system. "First off," he said, "I'm driving my car behind yours. When you step out to face facts with the boys, I'm backing you up, more or less out of sight."[25]

To get away from his chores and his worries one weekend, Sam piled his women into Betty's little sedan and drove them to San Antonio. The shopping trip had gone well, but Sunday afternoon, driving home, Sam was fording a stream near Fredericksburg when the high water drowned his engine. At that moment he heard a clap of thunder and an ominous roar from upstream. Leaping out of the car, he saw a headrise of water "at least a yard high," rushing straight for them. Sam whirled and yelled to the women. "Get out of the car! Run for dry land!"

When Mrs. Goodman did not quite grasp the crisis – "But we'll get ourselves wet!" Sam yelled all the louder, "All of you, run!"

Sam splashed around to the trunk and hurled all the luggage onto high ground; he had just got his ladies up out of harm's way when the headrise sent the car tumbling downstream.

Under flashes of lightning, the family was standing huddled together when a new Ford sedan drove up and stopped. In his black suit and string tie, the driver looked like a preacher. "Can you let us into your car," Sam yelled, "out of this rain?"

Turning to leave, the driver only called though the window, "Course not. I don't want you getting my new car all sloppy."

Fortunately for all, after an hour or so an old man in a wagon drove up and waved. "Everybody load up," he called. "My place ain't but a mile down the road."

Though the man's German wife spoke no English, she clearly knew what to do. After turning down the beds for the women and drying their clothes in front of the stove, she served them all a big supper while the lightning kept playing outside. The next day the farmer drove the family on in to Llano.

A week later, when Betty's car was fished out of the river, its engine was clogged with rust, its fenders dangling, its upholstery hanging in shreds. Sam sold the wreck for one hundred dollars.[26]

After eighteen months in Llano, Sam was in his barber's chair one morning when a call came from the comptroller. The First National Bank in Carlsbad, New Mexico, had just failed after a long drouth and low prices for beef. Sam was to take it on as receiver immediately.[27]

Leaving his brood in Llano till he could rent a big enough house in Carlsbad, Sam faced the grim task before him. Happily, the new house did have a fine kitchen, which Sam himself put to good use. By the time the ladies awoke each morning, he had their bacon and eggs all ready. Betty and Mrs. Goodman mildly protested; but Sam only grinned. "I like to," he told them, serving their plates.[28]

At his new post, Sam ran into the same sad dilemma he had already confronted too often: the chore of foreclosing on cattle and sheep men obliged to come again and again to the bank for loans to feed their livestock, and having no possible hopes to clear up those debts.

Sam respected their frustration. But by the time he arrived on the scene, it was too late to talk terms. The First National had already failed: hard-working depositors in town were just as irate over losing their money – perhaps their life savings – as the ranchers and farmers their livestock and goods.

At his locked gate, one angry rancher spoke for all the stockmen crowded shoulder to shoulder behind him. "I'm warning you, banker; my only livelihood is my cattle. I can't let you take the food out of my family's kitchen. So, don't you come aiming to drive off *my* cows!"

"But your cows are starving!" Sam countered. "Pretty soon all the cattle you've got will be dead. You don't have any more money for feed, and you'll still owe the bank."

After more feeble attempts to make himself heard over their jeers, Sam knew he had no way to talk reason to them. Nor could he fight them alone. Back in town, he called his old bodyguard in Llano. "Come on out and back me up as before."[29]

Yet despite the slim comfort Sam found in Moseley's guns behind him, at home he soon faced Betty's worries. "Why, oh why, Sam, do you keep doing all that?" she demanded. "Facing those dangerous people?"

Slowly, Sam tried to explain. "It's what I signed on to do." He took a deep swallow. "For better or worse, it's my duty."

"Your duty! It may be your duty – as long as you work for the bank. But, Sam, before somebody shoots your stubborn head off, why can't you just quit?"

Sam's answer did not come easy. "I just can't. Who knows how many hungry town children are looking to me just as fairly as any hungry ranch children. Suppose the money I'm bound to protect belonged to us or, let's say, your mother?"[30]

To play fair with all parties, Sam approached several large banks in Chicago, Kansas City, and New York that had earlier bought some of the ranchers' overlines of credit. Though those efforts failed to clear up the troubles that now were more and more urgent throughout the whole state of New Mexico, Hugo Anderson of the First National Bank in Chicago was especially concerned. Anderson could offer no solid help, but that friendly contact reassured Sam that he had done his best.

In October 1924, nearing the end of his efforts to effect some kind of peace in Carlsbad, Sam was en route to Washington for a conference with the comptroller when, between trains in Dallas, he stopped by to see R. H. Collier, chief national bank examiner. Collier was on the phone, but he motioned Sam in. "Why, here he is now," Collier said to the phone. Hanging up, Collier asked, "Sam, where are you headed?"[31]

Sam had barely said "Washington" when Collier shook his head. "We've had another bank failure. It may take you one year, it may take you two, to settle all the affairs of the National Border Bank in El Paso."

"El Paso!" Sam's eager answer came straight from fond memories. "Ever since my first stint out there, I've been in love with that sunny country."[32]

When he phoned Betty the news, her reaction was open relief.

To make the long move, Betty and Sam loaded the family and their total possessions in two cars, Betty driving one, Sam the other. Using the only passable roads, they headed first for Roswell, seventy miles north, and west through pine-covered mountains to Alamogordo, then south eighty-five miles along a road that was mostly deep ruts and soft sand.

From Sam, Betty already knew that El Paso sprawled like an oasis in an empty desert where Apache Indians as recently as 1881, only forty-three years before, had once run amok. What he had not told her was that here where three states and two nations joined, two cities flourished in ways at once characteristic of all cities and also in ways quite unique. "El Paso and Juarez won't look a thing like Corsicana or Dallas, but in time I think —"

Unloading their bags at the steps of his old friendly hotel, the Paso del Norte, Sam did not try to describe anything more. Back in 1919, a few days had been plenty of time to make him fall in love with this place. Now, for Betty as well, time might be the best teacher.

5

GO WEST, YOUNG MAN

EXCEPT FOR HIS HAPPY RECOLLECTIONS OF EL PASO five years before, Sam returned now a changed man. No longer a young blood on the loose after work hours, he was a twenty-eight-year-old man of position – a receiver authorized to liquidate one of the town's erstwhile most solid houses, the National Border Bank. Happily now, he also had a focus on home and loving companionship.

For both Sam and Betty their change in scene could not have been more distinct from the wooded Old South they had left. Together, they had reached an open frontier along which two ways of life had grown up and adopted traits from each other. When Sam introduced his family to his old friend, Leo Schuster, Leo neatly characterized the international community for them. "The friendly folks over there" – he motioned away past the river toward Juarez – "the friendly folks here" – he gestured around him – "we do have our ways. Living as neighbors, the whole 100,000 can't be too wrong."

As for family quarters, Sam and Betty knew there was no point in buying a house: a receivership was always at best a temporary assignment. For their family of five adults, they first rented a three-bedroom house at 504 Cincinnati, after three months another at 1307 Cincinnati. But choosing the latter was no simple decision. For all her big change,

Betty had not left behind her a set of old superstitions that stretched backward in time before Corsicana and the Civil War. As a child born just after that war, Betty's mother Martha Goodman, a member of the Blair family of Virginia, had come west with her parents in a covered wagon. Brought up by former slaves, Martha (whom the family called "Mimi") had been instilled early with their superstitions. Black cats were beasts to be dreaded; all Fridays were bad, but Thirteenth was the worst; green clothes must never be worn in a wedding. Betty and her sisters had grown up with those same convictions.[1] Now, though hundreds of miles separated them from their deep family roots, the Goodmans' hated old fears still plagued them.

The house on Cincinnati looked comfortable; the street of new lawns and saplings curved pleasantly upwards toward a jumble of rocky foothills. But to live in a house numbered 1307? For Betty, that number posed a fearsome obstruction.[2] For Sam, on the other hand, the number 13 foreboded nothing at all: "1307" on the door of Henry and Young in Dallas, after a difficult start, had not jinxed it to failure. Nor, once they moved in, did it trouble him that he and Betty could not afford to furnish it fully. "When people drop in and we don't have enough furniture yet," Sam told the family, "if they get upset, well, we can't help it."[3]

Only a few blocks from their home, Scenic Drive led up and around the brow of the Franklin Mountains, the jagged 7,000-foot southern end of the Rockies. Its view extended a hundred miles south into Old Mexico, a hundred miles westward and north into New Mexico. Between the two nations, the Rio Grande wound its leisurely pace through the irrigated green valley that stretched upstream and down as far as the eye could see. Among the foothills to the west nestled the five red-roofed structures of the Texas College of Mines, a branch of the University of Texas. Directly below, El Paso's downtown buildings defined its grid plan of streets. Farther out, neighborhoods climbed the cactus-covered gray hills. The place might lack easy charm; but as a site to make a home in – however briefly, Sam told Betty one afternoon – El Paso certainly extended its arms.

More and more, Sam appreciated that sentiment each time he made the long drive uphill and parked at the lookout. One afternoon he and Leo Schuster were sizing up the broad scene below when Sam gave a low chuckle. "I'll tell you one thing, my friend. I sure as hell feel a lot better now than I did my first time, when you drove me up here 'to settle my stomach!'"[4] As a vagabond receiver now, Sam was sure it was not in his cards to put down his roots here. Nevertheless, the big scene became more attractive each time he took in that view.

As for the crisis that had brought Sam so far west, shortly before he arrived the troubled City National Bank of El Paso had sought to merge with the Border National Bank. Such a run of withdrawals had resulted at the Border's own windows, however, that Charles Milton Harvey, the Border's highly respected president, mounted a box in the lobby. In his gold-rimmed spectacles, he urged the crowd, "Rest assured. Your deposits are safe. This bank is sound."[5]

For all of Harvey's good cheer, his words lacked conviction, however. The Border National had already lost the confidence of its worried depositors; regretfully, Harvey resigned. Under a new president Crawford Harvie and a new name, the "National Border Bank" hoped to accomplish miracles. Unfortunately, after an officer's defalcation of $57,000, and summer weather so dry that it doomed the fall cotton crop, the National Border Bank admitted defeat.[6] The time had come for one of the U. S. Comptroller's experienced men to take over.

No amateur now at dealing with outraged customers and frantic stockholders, Sam necessarily trod on a few toes. When his secretary Dora Lee McRay informed him on a Monday that she could not work the following Saturday, Sam was direct. "Why can't you?"

"I've got a date."

"With all this mountain of work?" Sam bristled. "To hell with your date!"

The liberated females of the 1960s may have stemmed from a long line of forebears like Dora Lee. "Then to hell with your bank," Dora calmly replied and walked out.[7]

Outside the bank worse hazards dogged Sam's footsteps. When the owner of the Mulligan Building could not keep up his payments and Sam had to foreclose, the disgruntled owner began following Sam all over town. "I don't have any money," he begged. "When are you going to give me some money?"

On the golf course, Sam had hoped for relief from his old burden, "duty," but the debtor trailed him the full eighteen holes. "When are you going to give me some money?"

Sam finished his drive. "You and I both are stuck with the terms of your loan." The agreement had not been met. "I can't mark it off."

The debtor now altered his tactics. On the phone several times after midnight, he begged, "You have to give me some money. You took my property away from me."

Again, Sam stated his position. "I can't give you any money. So don't call me anymore." Still unconvinced, the debtor established a camp at Sam's office door. For a week, he repeated his plea. Sam was about to request a peace bond from the court when the debtor finally drifted away.[8]

To recover some of the notes on debt-ridden farm lands down the river, Sam sold several first liens on them to the Federal Land Bank, but still the results were painful. To the farmers, their pleas were reasonable. "Can't you just give us till the market turns around, the weather gets good again, and prices go up?"[9]

Sam tried to be equally reasonable. "But nobody knows when that may be. We're trapped in the same boat as you people. Nobody likes it."

By early 1925, Sam had liquidated the National Border Bank so effectively that the U. S. comptroller, J. W. McIntosh, came out to El Paso to see if anything newsworthy might be done – he spoke frankly – to mollify the newspapers blaming his office in Washington for so many bank failures in West Texas. "Sam, you did a fine job down in Llano. How about staying on in El Paso awhile and organizing a new bank for us here? El Paso is down to only four banks now, so it certainly has room for one more."[10]

McIntosh promised his fullest cooperation; as comptroller he would issue the new national charter as soon as Sam organized the new bank. Once it had bought the old assets of the National Border Bank, its depositors could quickly recover their money.

The feasibility of the McIntosh plan struck Sam well. Immediately, he broached the matter to some of the major business people in town. He had just arrived home from a conference with C. M. Harvey, former head of the National Border Bank, when Betty informed him that a matter at least as important to them as any new bank was in process at home. The doctor had just confirmed their high hopes that the family was due to welcome a tiny new member the last week in June.

About the McIntosh plan, Sam had first buttonholed one of El Paso's wealthiest men. "Mr. Harvey, the comptroller has put me on orders to organize a new bank out here. As you realize, the problem is urgent, but to do it I need the support of solid people like you."

C. M. Harvey drew back in his chair. "Well, Mr. Young, you know I've been embarrassed," he said, "in this Border Bank trouble and frankly, at age fifty-five, I'm tired."

"The Border Bank failed due to a lot of mismanagement," Sam countered. "But I'm convinced it wasn't due strictly to you as an officer." Sam detailed his own role in the comptroller's plan.

"That's commendable, of course," Harvey replied, "but in that plan I don't see myself as important."

Delicately, Sam continued. "As I say, you and the directors did nothing wrong, but the fact is, you could be in trouble with your unhappy stockholders. If you helped me organize this new bank with you as a director, Mr. Harvey, I can't promise you legal immunity, but I can recommend it."

Harvey asked for time to think out the matter. "Till then, you know I've got a young wife. She doesn't want me in any more banking. You'd better talk to Maude about this."[11]

Several afternoons after work, Sam took Maude Harvey for drives down the river, explaining the good to be served for the people who had suffered when Harvey's other bank closed and for the Harvey family as well.

"Mr. Harvey may face trouble if we don't get this thing started. As one of the old bank's directors, he might well be sued."

Sam had met a shrewd lady.

"On what grounds, Mr. Young?" asked Maude Harvey.

"Negligence of duty. While I've been working through the NBB's troubles, your husband has been my good friend. It's just that this is the best way for him – bearing your interests and" – Sam mentioned the Harvey children, Paul and C. M. Jr. and Rufus and one-year-old Phil – "to dispose of this matter."

Maude Harvey replied that she needed some time to consider the factors involved,[12] and so too, did Paul Harvey. As a director of the strong First National Bank, Paul at age twenty- seven had no wish to involve his father, himself, and the family in another expensive struggle.

To an outsider, one who had known the grim story of American banking since 1920, El Paso's need of a truly stable bank and Sam's chances for meeting that need might have looked naive. Back in 1920, the nation had had 30,000 banks. Every year since, that figure had severely eroded. Yet here in this sunny young town, a large clientele needed safe, custodial care for its wealth. As the comptroller's man, it was Sam's job to help it.

Once Mrs. Harvey approved, C. M. Harvey himself talked specifics. "Who else would you get for your board?"

"Who else would you like?" Sam asked him.

"John C. Hayes?" Harvey suggested. "As former manager of William Randolph Hearst's ranch down in Chihuahua for more than twenty years he would bring us good connections in Mexico." Sam nodded approval.

"And Adolph Schwartz? As El Paso's biggest merchant and owner of the Popular Dry Goods Company, he's respected by everybody. We need his good business sense."[13] Sam nodded again.

"G. P. Putnam? As superintendent of schools, he could help us land those payroll accounts. Besides" – Harvey looked thoughtful – "for this new bank to succeed, we've got to put ourselves in the hands of the Lord. Putnam prays a good prayer."[14]

"My sentiments exactly," Sam agreed. "W. P. B. McSain? As a former tax collector, he knows property values."[15]

Finally persuaded himself, Harvey exacted a strict condition: Adolph Schwartz must be on the board.

Sam's case to Schwartz, however, struck a snag. As a director of the failed City National Bank, Schwartz objected that he had already suffered too much criticism. Sam countered that point with specifics. In an American city numbering 100,000 people, where two big banks had failed lately, El Paso – money-wise – was almost in chaos. "Mr. Schwartz, you and your thousands of customers need a sound bank. It's to your interest too."[16]

At that, Schwartz agreed to associate himself with the new organization but only on certain conditions: he would invest in some stock; his partner in the Popular Dry Goods Company, I. Weiss, would represent him on the board of directors; his nephew, Maurice, would sign the charter as one of the original incorporators; his attorney, A. H. Goldstein, would serve as the bank's attorney.

Schwartz's strong stand came from long experience. Born in a Czechoslovakian village in 1866, Schwartz had come to America at age sixteen to avoid his country's compulsory military service and its strong anti-Semitism. Since then his pioneer zeal in Mexico and in El Paso had paid off in wealth and benevolent influence: by 1925 he was the head of an ever-expanding department store business. His name and his practical sense were both vital to Sam.[17]

As to C. M. Harvey's own community stature there was likewise no question. A teetotalling Methodist born in 1869 in Trezvant, Tennessee, Harvey grew up in Bloomfield, Missouri, and in Booneville, Arkansas, where his father was county judge. In the career that lay behind him now, Harvey had been a small-town newspaper man: editor, copywriter, typesetter, business manager. One winter when he was forced to accept a wagonload of sweet potatoes as pay for a bill, he and his printer had lived on potatoes till spring. In Indian Territory, before Oklahoma became a state in 1907, Harvey ran a general store selling gunpowder and shot to the Indians.

Harvey had made additional money as agent for Indians willing to lease their tillable lands to white squatters. Harvey's biggest money, however, had come from his enterprise as a mining developer in northeastern Oklahoma. Drilling into a large ore body of zinc, his drill test had come up bright yellow—"the color of turkey fat"—sure proof of high grade zinc, as Harvey liked to point out.

From that "Turkey Fat Mine" and his Commerce Mining and Royalty Company, Harvey had become a rich man by the time his wife, Bess, fell prey to tuberculosis in 1910 and needed a dry climate. Harvey brought her and their three sons to El Paso. By 1916 when Bess died, Harvey owned rich spreads of ranch land in New Mexico: 10,000 acres near Cloudcroft, 12,000 acres near Alamogordo, and sizable sheep country north of Carrizozo. All the while, his income from his mining enterprises in Oklahoma increased.[18]

In 1923, when Harvey remarried, his new wife Maude Phillips had been a practical-minded school teacher and, in the two years since, had become Harvey's devoted helpmate and most able adviser.[19]

By the late spring of 1925, Sam's day-and-night efforts to found a new bank had borne fruit. The new bank charter, Number 12769, had been fully approved in Washington, and capital stock totalling $200,000 had been collected, plus a surplus of $20,000.[20] C. M. Harvey alone had subscribed 51 percent of its stock. The remaining shares had been divided among the directors and officers and a few small outside investors.[21]

Handpicked, the founding board of this new "El Paso National Bank" read as Harvey and Sam had wished: Charles M. Harvey, I. Weiss, John C. Hayes, G. P. Putnam, A. H. Goldstein, W. P. B. McSain, and Sam D. Young.

At the organizational meeting, Adolph Schwartz asked, "Now that we're founded, just who is to be our general manager?"

From the background, Sam suggested, "That's for you gentlemen to decide, but I've got a competent friend I'd recommend."

Schwartz waved that offer aside. "All along I've been thinking that you yourself, Mr. Young, are the proper party. With your long experience, with your firm knowledge of the risky banking conditions just now, surely no other bank person in Texas is more qualified." Schwartz paused, then made a telling remark. "Putting it bluntly, gentlemen, unless Sam Young agrees to be our chief executive officer, I wish to have no part in this organization."

Schwartz's stand was flattering, but for Sam it posed a possible problem in his wearing two hats. Still the active receiver of the National Border Bank, his officially heading the fledgling El Paso National might pose a legal question.

To that fear, A. H. Goldstein, the board's lawyer, spoke up. "If the comptroller approves, Sam Young can certainly take charge to everyone else's approval."[22]

Betty tried to share Sam's excitement, but by the time the new bank's table of organization was set — making it a reality on paper at least — morning sickness made her barely able to raise her head off the pillow when Sam bade her goodbye before leaving for work each day.[23] She could only smile weakly when Sam told her that Comptroller McIntosh had written him a "hold harmless" letter absolving him of any apparent conflict of interest.

Now clear to proceed as the directors had stated, the board unanimously elected C. M. Harvey president and chairman of the board. As active vice president and chief executive officer, Sam Young would *de facto* chair the command. Those weighty steps taken, one director spoke for them all. "That ought to secure the public's confidence. Now it's up to us, the directors, to support Harvey and Young in every possible way."[24]

Still, Sam expressed some concern. As an official, he would function as responsibly as his title implied. He wanted, nevertheless, a place in the new enterprise that assured the public of his sincere commitment.

"To head this bank in every meaningful sense, I myself want to own at least 300 shares."

Wholeheartedly, the board approved the idea, but Mr. Young himself would have to come up with the cash. With shares at $100 each, Sam scraped together $3,000, enough to buy the first 30 shares, but the cash for the remaining 270 would have to come from outside. Sam thought immediately of George W. Briggs, now a trust officer of the City National Bank in Dallas.

The morning that Sam was approaching Briggs' Dallas office, he happened to pass the open door of J. A. Pondrum, the City National's chairman of the board. Pondrum motioned him in. "Mr. Young, sit down. I understand you're about to open a new bank in El Paso. I've been watching you for the last couple of years, and frankly, I'm impressed with your abilities. If you need any money to buy some of that bank stock yourself, I'll lend you the cash."[25]

At that offer, Sam leaped to his feet. "For me, this comes at the best possible time. I need to borrow $27,000 against a pledge of $30,000 worth of our stock."

Immediately, Pondrum wrote out the note. "Now, Mr. Young, how many shares may I buy?"

The question took Sam by surprise.

"Unfortunately, Mr. Pondrum, all our shares are subscribed. But" – he did some quick figuring – "for a man of your standing, I think I can get my board to release some of their shares in your favor."

When Sam returned to El Paso, the board found Pondrum's good will "inspirational." Out of their pockets, they gladly sold him a full twenty shares.

On the new Bank's founding day, the founders' net worth totalled $3,535,000. Most of that, as local El Paso money, represented the community's own confidence in its new bank. It represented as well its confidence in its twenty-nine-year-old executive vice president.

When the board at its first official meeting on June 22 deliberated overall policy, Harvey made the first motion. "Gentlemen, I hope that as long as this bank shall last, we can always begin our deliberations with a minute of silent prayer."

Similarly, Sam made plain his own hopes for the Bank's foundation policy. "No customer, no matter how large or how small, no transaction no matter what size, will ever be dealt with in any light other than the rules of Christian fair play."[26]

Its policies set, the board then put pencil to paper to determine the operating costs it could afford. After Harvey himself, who volunteered to serve without pay, Vice President Sam Young headed the annual salary list at $7,500. Cashier McSain followed at $6,000, Assistant Cashier Howard L. Moore at $2,700, and Second Assistant Cashier H. Silberberg at $2,000. A $3,000 expense account, Sam was to use as he saw fit in the Bank's interest. Goldstein, the Bank's lawyer, would receive a $600 retainer. For staff salaries, the board put a limit of $150 per month per employee. For rent on its space in the Muir Building at the corner of Mills and Mesa, it would pay $600 per month.[27]

Though the ground floor of that little three-story building was ample for the new institution, some might have suggested that a new bank occupying the National Border Bank's old quarters might have chosen healthier soil to put down its roots. Superstitions aside, the site's central location facing San Jacinto Plaza was ideal. The flurry of opening for business was mostly a matter of changing the faces at the desks and the cage windows and of installing a tall, shiny sign over the entrance: *El Paso National Bank.*

Anticipating that ceremonial day when his new Bank could officially open its doors – firm and determined never to close – Sam would have been calmer and happier if Betty's doctor only last week had not told him in private, "I may be able to save the baby and I may not. It's nip and tuck for the next several days." That night, after Betty was soundly asleep, he had spent an extra-long time on his knees.[28]

As the Bank opening's details molded into a program, for Sam there was also the matter of a proper new suit to wear. To Max Fischbein, the tailor, he was precise. But taking Sam's measure, Fischbein chuckled a bit. "Don't worry. Like I tell everybody, for outfitting big dignitaries I've got a pretty good record. When I still had my shop down in Chihuahua City –" Fischbein chuckled again. "As a matter of fact, you're looking at the only man who ever took the pistols off of that swaggering bandit, Pancho Villa. For his uniforms, I had to, to measure him."

On June 29, 1925, Sam was knotting his tie when Betty shook her head weakly. "I wanted so much to be on hand for your big day this morning. I know everything will be lovely, but, Sam, you won't have to make a speech, will you?"

Sam frowned at her as his old fear of addressing a crowd took him straight back to his old teacher Brown. "No speech, no sir-ree. I've got enough on my mind as it is."[29]

Shortly before 10 A.M. when the doors of the new Bank were scheduled to open, C. M. Harvey stood a little aside and out of the limelight, but Sam Young—by far the youngest banker in town—moved briskly about, checking supplies on the counters: deposit slips, pen staffs, ink wells. Were the desks lined up straight? Were the window shades raised to just the right level?

Then Mayor H. P. Jackson was whacking his ceremonial scissors through the red ribbon spanning the entrance. With that, the crowd clapped and rushed in, most of them intent on recovering their funds from the old NBB. And most of them, Sam was pleased to observe throughout the morning, were happy enough to leave their cash on deposit as new accounts in the El Paso National.

Flowers had come from the Citizens National Bank of Los Angeles, the Mercantile Trust of St. Louis, South Texas Commercial National of Houston, and Fred Florence's Republic National Bank in Dallas. Shaking his hand, one old lady beamed up at him. "It's all so wonderful, what you and all of you folks"—she gestured around—"are doing. I just know how elated you feel."

Sam returned her bright smile, but he did not feel elated. At age twenty-nine and $27,000 in debt, with a sick wife at home and a baby due in one week, his own name was on the line as executive vice president. In a town where bank failures were almost a norm in the business, his job would be hard and he knew that Betty knew it would, too.[30]

Chief national bank examiner, R. H. Collier, from Dallas was on hand representing the comptroller. "I never saw a bank open under more auspicious circumstances," Collier told Sam. "You've made a mighty fine start."[31]

"I can thank you for that," Sam replied. "The last time I saw you, Betty and I figured that about now we'd be heading on, maybe to Denver."[32]

For its maiden voyage into the unknown waters of the 1920s, the new Bank had Harvey and Sam and its full complement of officers and crew. If photographs had been taken that morning, the captions would have included seventeen names: C. M. Harvey, Sam D. Young, A. H. Goldstein, W. P. B. McSain, C. L. Ezell, Howard Moore, Marie Halleran,

A new little bank determined to grow and prosper, the El Paso National in its first quarters, the Muir Building, on the corner of Texas and Mills, June 1925.

Sam (fourth from right) and the El Paso National's first bank family, 1925.

Bertha Bull, S. O. Potorff, Dorothy Smith, Nida Collier, Howard Clayton, Herman Silberberg, Norman Pitchford, Tommy Thompson, and J. F. Jenkins.[33] On their good works and their unified hopes, the new Bank sounded its whistle. "Anchors aweigh."

When 2 P.M. closing time came and Sam and Harvey could settle back and reflect, they had reason to feel that all signs had been right. The day's take in deposits: $1,226,719. Clearly, this new game in town was loaded with hope.

Bright as the day was, Sam only learned later about one little oversight. Days before the opening, tellers and secretaries had worked feverishly transferring by hand the NBB accounts onto the new ledgers. They had written out hundreds of checks to the old bank's depositors who wanted the reassurance of solid cash in their hands. When the new Bank opened for business, Sam had meant for all the Bank's "inherited" clients to be told that 65 percent of their NBB balance had already been entered in their new accounts, and the check that each was receiving that day was for 10 percent of their balance still due. The rest would be paid to them as soon as possible.

Sam's secretary Marie Halleran and Bertha Bull, the bookkeeper, overheard, however, an irate lady who had misunderstood the Bank's explanation. "This check ain't but 10 percent of the cash I *know* I got coming," she complained to a friend in the lobby. "I never was no madder."[34] Carefully, that friend spelled out the details.

The next day when Sam was asked about the opening, his smile was much easier. "I never witnessed such a display of faith and loyalty in a new institution. It encouraged me to believe that the people of El Paso appreciate our efforts to be of service to the community."[35]

The Bank's first published statement, dated June 30, 1925, when the Bank was one day old read as follows:

RESOURCES

Loans and discounts	$476,744.29
Stock in Federal Reserve Bank	6,600.00
Stocks, bonds and other securities	7,329.00
Furniture and fixtures	10,000.00
Other real estate	14,100.00
Expenses paid	192.66
Cash, exchange, Liberty Bonds	931,753.21
	$1,446,719.16

LIABILITIES

Capital stock (common)	$200,000.00
Surplus	20,000.00
Total deposits	1,226,719.16
	$1,446,719.16

Home at last and weary from all the excitement downtown, Sam brightened when he found Betty propped up on pillows. "Tell me, quick. About everything, Sam. How did it go?"

"Everything went off just fine," he told her. "We had a real flood of folks in and out of the lobby all day. Mr. Harvey and Maude and the boys—we all missed you." Then he chuckled. "I told you about that skirmish I had with old T. S. Currie over in Big Spring, when I charged him fifteen dollars for re-examining a note drawer and he charged me the same for a ride to Garden City. Well, among the congratulatory letters I opened today was a sizable check and a note from T. S. Currie. 'I want our State National Bank in Big Spring to be the first correspondent bank to open an account with you. Wishing you well!'"[36]

Sam patted her hand. "We needed you there," he said, "but you were here where you needed to be, just as much as I was, down at the bank shaking hands."[37]

Next day, when a newspaper reporter asked, "Who was the first depositor in your new bank? The first borrower?" Sam shook his head.

"It isn't easy to say, since we brought along so many from the old Border Bank. But you wouldn't be wrong to mention Leslie Levy of the Angelus Cleaners. That little go-getter was here bright and early. The account he opened with us was as 'first' as anyone else's."[38]

6

THE FOUNDING FATHER

A WEEK AFTER CO-FOUNDING A BANK, Sam knew with Betty the joy of co-founding a family. On July 6, 1925, their splendidly healthy Frances Elizabeth weighed in at eight-and-a-half pounds. When the doctor let Sam into the room, he took Betty's limp hand. "Nothing else in my lifetime," he whispered close to her ear, "can ever make me feel so important."[1]

Passing out cigars down at the Bank the next morning, he beamed to everybody that asked, "Mother and baby just fine, thanks. I'll be showing both of them off just as soon as the little new mama out at the house tells me I can."

Later when he could look back at that week's two big events in his life, Sam expressed his full sentiment. "I looked upon both as my babies."

The new Bank's opening day over and done with, Sam addressed his new board a bit tensely. "We all know these are troublous times for banks here, but beginning now, I promise to try to measure up to your expectations. I hope this bank will never knowingly grant any loan that will hurt the El Paso community. If a loan application looks good for the town we all live in, I hope we go along with it. I trust too that, given our competition, we will always be courteous, and, gentlemen, since service is all we have to sell, we offer service with a smile. Otherwise, we stand no better chance to grow strong that did the old failures."[2]

Sam paused while the board nodded approval. "I want to say clearly too that, judging from my observing them all over Texas, legitimate banks are conservative. They never allow their ratio of loans to capital surplus to go above about 50 percent." Again, they nodded approval. "And I hope we'll be especially careful with farmers and ranchers. I've already seen too many griefs in those faces. Gentlemen, I never want to have to foreclose on a farmer or rancher again."[3]

"Only one other thing seems important to say. To make your chore as easy as possible, I will try to solve all the little problems myself. I will bring to these meetings only the major problems, when and if they arise."

The next day at his first meeting with the Bank staff, Sam spelled out the policies he had already cleared with the board. For its code of ethics, the Bank would follow the rules of Christian fair play. The fact that the Bank stood genteel and ready for business, however, guaranteed in no way that new customers would come rushing in. To survive in a town that still had four other banks – the First National, the State National, the City National, and the American Trust and Savings – "we must all roll up our sleeves."

Within a few days Sam ran across Isadore Feinberg, a former Gulf National client in Beaumont and now president of the El Paso Pipe and Supply Co. Head down, Feinberg was charging briskly along Mills Street, gripping a fat money pouch under his arm.

"Good morning, Izzy," Sam called. "Where are you going with all that cash?"

Feinberg looked up. "To the State National, to make a deposit."

"Why not to us, at our place, the new El Paso National?"

"Well, Sam, my brother Ben and I haven't got an account with you folks."

Grabbing the money pouch, Sam whirled on his heel.

"You do now. Follow me."

Grinning, Feinberg followed Sam into the Bank.[4]

Leading that brand new customer straight through the lobby and back to his desk, Sam was seeing himself as he wished to appear to his staff: the aggressive salesman hot on the job.

To that end, at the outset Sam established a scheme for himself. If he could not run the whole operation himself, he could keep alert to what everybody else should be doing.[5] He could also make it his job to involve himself, as a person, all over town. Unlike a merchant, a banker never could feature "push items" to bring in the trade. He could, however, shake hands with every new prospect; he could know everybody by name. "I kind of like hearing folks call me by name," he told his Bank people, "and I figure it's probably the same way for them."[6]

Playing that role sincerely, shaking hands with every newcomer, Sam often seemed more like a host at a party than a money man adept at his job in the lobby. "Are you being taken good care of? Can we do anything that will help?" he asked all and sundry.[7]

While the staff were to be on their toes at all times, Sam made it clear that they must look neat and professional: the men in coats and ties, the women in ladylike dresses. "Slouchy bank people never did inspire confidence in a bank's customers," he explained.

On his banker's outreach around town, when somebody asked him if he enjoyed mixing business with pleasure, meeting every merchant in town and every farmer out in the county, Sam's answer came easy. "Sure, I like to chew the rag with them. You've got to enjoy your work to be successful."[8]

He liked to drop in on car dealers like Sam Watkins and Harvey Wilcox; laundry men and dry cleaners like Frank Fletcher and Paul Heisig; department store merchants like Jake Miller; train men who ran the Southern Pacific, the Santa Fe, and the Texas & Pacific; cotton buyers like Robert T. Hoover; produce men; hardware men; wholesalers like Albert Mathias; men who ran the county's little outlying banks like Alex Gonzalez down the valley in Fabens.

From his 1919 days at the Paso del Norte, Sam already knew that for "chewing the rag," its lobby was the favorite hangout for the area's leather-faced cattlemen and *caballeros*. From north and south of the Rio Grande, they propped their feet up and swapped stories. Sam often made it a point to show up among them just before noon, to chat about prices and weather and anything else the booted-and-spurred old regulars had on their minds.[9]

He also came to know well the hotel's owner, Zach White, who had become an El Paso legend for his high-balling zeal for buying up the sandy bottom lands and hillsides that local smart money knew "would never be worth a damn." Shrugging aside such "small thinking," White mentioned to Sam one morning that he was donating 120 acres of raw valley land for the new El Paso Country Club to use for a golf course: a little recreation never hurt anybody.

Now that he was in El Paso and meaning to stay, Sam got in touch with Eloy Vallina, the Spanish friend he had made at the El Paso

Federal Reserve Bank back in 1920. "Eloy, I hear your brother Rafael has opened a new bank down in Chihuahua City, the Banco Mercantil,[10] and that you're into it too. I do wish you folks well with your bank and, to tell you the truth, I'm hoping you'll open a correspondent account here with us."

Eloy shook his head. "Sam," he explained, "Rafael has already opened a correspondent account with the State National."

"Oh? Well, that's fine," Sam told him. "Just keep us in mind if the folks over there ever don't treat you right."[11]

It was fine too if friendships could flourish within the Bank staff, but between himself as CEO and the rest of the team, Sam drew a line which, for the good of the institution, they early learned to respect. There were exceptions, however. One morning when Sam was passing the desk of Cashier McSain's red-headed secretary, Bertha Bull, he remarked that she was getting a bit gray in the temples. "Humph, look who's talking," she tartly replied.[12]

As soon as he could get to a mirror, Sam checked his own hair. It was true; his shock of brown hair was turning quite gray.

Though Sam's early professional style was, for the most part, smoothness itself, at times it did include a hot temper. "I'm not easy to get along with, momentarily," he often confessed. But the point was, he explained, he wanted "everybody working efficiently, everybody working together as a family. I'm sort of a perfectionist."[13] Clear to his meaning, most of the Bank employees called him "Mr. Young"—not "Sam."

But after hours, Sam's personal friendships early stretched to include the mayor, C. E. "Uncle Henry" Kelly, a wholesale druggist, who liked to throw political rallies on his farm down the valley near Clint. There, to his visitors' delight, "General Barleycorn held sway over the meetings at times,"[14] and along with the barbecue and all the trimmings, political talk quickly gave way to salty stories. Observing it all, noting the game as played by the political heads more "savvy" than his, Sam noted especially one bit of political wisdom as played by more than one businessman at those parties. Since politics related to any good citizen's hopes for good government and since the whole process cost money, Sam quickly perceived a role for himself as a responsible citizen keen on helping good men, whether Democrat or Republican, achieve office: he would contribute as much as he could afford to *both* political parties.

For both Sam and Betty, the circle of friends that soon opened included names from his bachelor days: Leo Schuster, Tom Mayfield, the Robert T. Hoovers. Bob had left banking and now owned a cotton finance and trading company. Betty was flattered when the El Paso Junior League urged her to be their new president. But practicality argued against that honor: "Little Betty" needed her mama at home, Sam told her.[15]

Still, Grandmother "Mimi" Goodman was a highly convenient baby-sitter on those regular occasions now when sociability attracted Betty and Sam away from home in the evening. Betty was never inclined toward being the star of the party, but her sense of humor and her ability to rip off an appropriate joke helped make a place all her own in their circle.

Among the pleasures of forming new friendships, Sam never forgot one particular fact in his life as a banker. "Nobody wants anybody mad at him," Sam reminded himself again and again. But along with being a friendly professional, his role included his explaining the facts of an overdue note. "But, sir, you haven't made us a payment in months. The time has more than run out."

Watching the disgruntled debtor trudging away, Sam knew how the story would go when that customer explained his loss to his friends. "I only needed a little more time. But that s.o.b. at the El Paso National laughed in my face."[16]

That risk was inherent, of course, in the charge that Sam had fully accepted. Cleaning up the debris after a poorly run bank had gone bust, he meant to make its replacement a bank that everybody could trust. To do that, he had to stand tough.[17]

By year's end the progress that the new Bank showed to its shareholders reflected hard work and friendly community outreach. The Bank's assets had risen to $1,891,531.[18] An ad in the *Herald* on January 19, 1926, described the people with whom the Bank sincerely wished to do business:

"The little money owned by a poor man is just as important to him as the big money owned by the rich man." To both parties, The El Paso National guaranteed "the same courtesy, the same service, and the same safety." The El Paso National Bank knew very well, it declared frankly, that other banks were competing for their same business. "To succeed, this bank depends entirely on its customers."

Toward that end, Sam decreed that no customer would ever have reason to consider himself a lonely sheep, prey to the wolves. For his Bank to be "person to person" with all its customers, every individual account would have an officer personally in charge of it.

Now, a man with a growing family himself, Sam knew the circumstances of most of his customers when they came, hat in hand, seeking loans. Since J. A. Pondrum's generosity the preceding spring, Sam was a debtor himself, deeply so now, given his annual draw as the Bank's executive vice president. Unable to make large payments to Pondrum immediately, he remembered Preston Doty's advice back at Gulf National. "When you must borrow money, make some kind of payment every time one comes due. It won't matter too much if you can't pay the set figure. Just be sure you pay something."[19]

For that reason, Sam felt at ease with his $27,000 debt to Pondrum. Each time he sent "something," Pondrum never pressed him for more.[20]

Likewise, with the Bank's broader growth all up to him, Sam had to think of himself when he considered the larger, "good business" world beyond El Paso in Texas and farther afield. Each time he went down to Houston, Governor, who now owned the *Houston Post*, chatted with him about "making contacts." Hobby's taking him to lunch with the great Jesse Jones was sociability only in part. Jones remembered his brief encounter with Sam when Sam was a lowly examiner. Over cigars, Jones listened when Sam mentioned this or that scheme he was "thinking to start, out there in the wild west where I come from."

When Sam told Hobby he planned soon to go to New York to seek some national accounts, especially one with the Texas Company, Governor patted his back. "Let me go with you, Sam. For whatever good my name might do. Those Texaco boys from Houston, they know me."[21] To make good his offer, Hobby arranged an appointment for Sam in New York with Texaco's treasurer. But after Hobby went on upstairs for a chat with the company president, Treasurer Woodbridge was puzzled why Sam had brought along an ex-governor of Texas. "No particular reason," Sam told him. "He's just a friend."

By the time the appointment was over, Sam had Woodbridge's firm commitment. "We'll send all our West Texas business through you," he said, shaking hands.

Back at his desk at the Bank, Sam set up the account, but after many weeks passed and no deposits showed up from Texaco, Sam was pursuing more national accounts in New York when he dropped in on

Woodbridge again. "I thought we had an agreement. Why didn't you send us your El Paso business?"

Woodbridge was vague, but soon after Sam was back home a Texaco deposit of $50,000 came through. A year later, the Texas Company funds for all of West Texas began clearing through the El Paso National. Telling his officers about that account, Sam made a strong point. "This bank won't grow and it won't make a profit if we don't go after the chances – hot and heavy. That's my challenge to you; that's my challenge to me."[22]

The next week the Federal Reserve Board authorized the Bank to open a Trust Department. Reading the scrolled letters on the official certificate, Sam smiled. As one man, he was that total "department."

By the fall of 1926, when Sam needed additional help in running his "store," it was a matter of luck that a former employee of the defunct City National whom he knew well was looking for work.

"What are your plans?" he asked Homer Jacobs.

The thirty-year-old thought a minute.

"Well, Sam, I've got the prospect of a job with the Valley Bank in Phoenix."

"What salary would you need to stay here? With me?"

When Jacobs named his figure, Sam settled him into a desk as assistant cashier.[23]

A native of Rock Valley, Iowa, Jacobs brought to the Bank a welcome, quiet efficiency. Jake's shy smile that could broaden into a grin when at times the going got rough – perhaps Sam's impatience when an employee took more time with a task than he had expected – a quick joke from Jacobs could ease the tension. Within a few months, Jacobs became a director.

Jacobs may have attempted to smooth out a tiff that developed one afternoon in Sam's office. Because his own secretary, Nida Collier, had gone to a party out at Fort Bliss, Sam summoned McSain's secretary. Bertha Bull showed up with pencil and pad, and Sam dictated a lengthy letter. At quitting time, Bertha returned to her desk, put away her note pad, and left.

The first thing the next morning, Bertha typed out the letter. When she took it to Sam, he glared at her. "Why didn't you type this letter yesterday? It should have gone straight into the mail."

Replying, the anger in red-headed Bertha exploded. "So where was Nida?" she asked hotly.

In the face of Sam's anger, Bertha charged back to her typewriter, ripped the little rubber cushions off of its keys – "They're mine," she announced to everybody in earshot, "I bought them myself to protect my fingernails" – and quit.[24]

Tiffs aside, a wave of good cheer flowed through the bank on November 5, 1926, when Sam announced that as of that day, the individual (personal) deposits had reached above the one-million mark, to be exact $1,003,965.86.[25] Representing customer confidence, that statement was both a figure to smile about and a benchmark for measuring all future growth. The board added another nice touch to that drama on December 23, 1926 when it increased the Bank's capital stock by 1,000 new bank shares at $150 per share. Within a few minutes, Sam and the other stockholders present bought up the lot, increasing the Bank's capital to $300,000 and adding $50,000 to surplus.

To the newspaper, Sam expressed his pride. The stockholders "have shown in no uncertain manner their faith in the continued growth, progress and permanence of El Paso as a commercial center." Proudly, he added "The new capital provides additional money to care for the increasing financial requirements of a rapidly growing clientele."[26]

Saluting their CEO's aggressive salesmanship, the board on January 11, 1927, raised Sam's salary to $10,000. That raise was welcome – given his growing family – but it afforded Sam no significant increase in his own financial range. On a visit to Dallas, Sam broached a plan to Fred Florence, now a top man at the Republic National. From the opening day of his new Bank in El Paso, Sam told Florence, Mexican borrowers had besieged him for loans significantly larger than his Bank's capital allowed it to lend. However, Sam pointed out, if he could work out a line of personal credit with Florence – one bearing a low enough interest – Sam could borrow those dollars, then lend them to the Mexicans as the sizable funds they required. The result: a healthy advantage to them and Sam both. His board of directors had already approved such a plan.

Though the plan involved risks in international credit, Florence willingly gambled on Sam's best judgment. In short order, Sam was buying Mexican "commodity paper" covering rice and flour and corn meal. Soon he was into bills of lading, offering short-term loans on rail shipments enroute north to Ciudad Juarez and El Paso. As his personal profits steadily mounted, Sam could smile. At long last, he was free from worries about his "duty" to any stockholders and depositors. In his new enterprise, he was risking nobody's grief but his own.

Again in 1927, Governor expressed confidence in Sam. Although the thirty-five shares of bank stock he now bought were small in number, Sam recognized that in yet another nice manner Governor and Sis Willie were wishing him well.[27]

With his growing affairs, Sam found it hard now to get back to Woodville whenever he liked. The best he and Betty could manage was an occasional run over to Woodville during business trips down to Houston. Charlie and Fanny were gratefully able to live on the money their children together sent them each month. Content with her house and her flowers and the farflung affairs of her offspring, Fanny seemed never to age. Her whole family knew she never would change. Teah and Margaret caused Sam to smile when they shrugged at their efforts to help Fanny start wearing some color, instead of her usual navy or black. When Margaret settled a little black hat with a pink rose on Fanny's head, Fanny threw up her hands.

"Now, Mama — just wait," Margaret objected. "Oh, Mama, you do look so pretty."

"We want you to wear it to church," Teah begged.

"To church!" Fanny turned pale. "I *couldn't* do that."

"Mama," said Margaret, patting her cheek, "just this once, wear something pretty. It isn't a sin."

To please them, Fanny did wear the new hat, but after the service, Fanny was shaking the minister's hand when he brightly remarked, "Mrs. Young, you look so pretty today. I do like that pink rose on your hat."

Fanny blushed scarlet.

When she got home, she put the hat firmly away. Her strong morals had won the day against decoration.[28]

As for Sam's brothers, Mike now lived in El Paso himself, running two grocery stores in El Paso, and selling real estate in nearby Ysleta. Cooper was still living at home, helping Fanny and Charlie. As for Pete, he was their "problem brother," as Margaret expressed it.[29] Pete could have been a good salesman, the whole family agreed. At age twenty-four he was lighthearted, he mixed well with people, but in spite of repeated promises to change and "do better," alcohol could turn him ugly and mean.

As for Sam's Bank "family," C. M. Harvey was content to be president in name only. By 1927, both understood that Sam was the responsible judge in every decision. "Mr. Harvey takes my word about banking," Sam told Betty one night, "like I'm the Bible."[30]

But Harvey's jovial disposition could pose problems. Holding court in the lobby, Harvey chatted with the customers flooding in past his desk. Much as Sam appreciated Harvey's skill in the role of banker as friend, Sam had to remind his co-founder that other concerns were more urgent. Harvey often sauntered into Sam's office just to tell him a good fishing story or to report on his silver fox farm near Cloudcroft. Sam played along with the stories, but at last, he did have to say, "Mr. Harvey, I wish I could visit all day. But the fact is" – he came to his feet – "I've got to get down to work."

Also, Harvey's generous nature occasionally created other problems. When an out-of-town check for $300 came back, Sam called Harvey in. "It's me that's got this bum check to deal with, but it's your 'okay' on the back. Mr. Harvey, you're not supposed to do that, you know."

Looking puzzled, Harvey examined the check. "Oh, yes," he said after a pause. "That fellow was in a big hurry, and he was wearing a Shriner pin on his lapel, and well, I could have sworn he was all right."

Sam lifted an eyebrow. "If you okay any more checks and they bounce, you're going to pay them yourself."[31]

Harvey grinned. "Maude said I was all through with banking, and by golly, I am."[32]

By April 1927 Sam and the board faced up to a problem with the Bank's quarters. While the little Muir Building had been a good place to start, the Bank's growth in employees – twenty-eight of them now – its increasing business, its rising prominence in the community now demanded more room. Its December 31, 1927, Statement of Condition[33] showed solid evidence of the Bank's growth.

Loans and discounts:	$1,229.630
Capital stock:	300,000
Surplus:	100,000
Undivided profits:	24,483
Deposits:	2,582,235

With the City National Bank's recent failure, its space in the Two Republics Building on Texas at Stanton was available. That eight-story structure appeared to meet Sam's every need for more space. So, again tempting fate by moving into a building that had witnessed disaster, after Sam signed a ten-year lease at $259,000, he told the staff to pack up.

In its new quarters the Bank occupied one half of the main floor and a part of the basement level. Throughout, the space was more convenient for work, better arranged, and much more attractive to business. The mezzanine added tone to the place, the polished stone floor and the curving row of tellers' windows stood ready that bright morning as another phase of the Bank's young story began.

Within the next work day or so, however, that mezzanine had become more than a treat for the eye. From it, if Sam discovered too many teller lines stretching too long, he could shout down, "Get the rest of those windows open! These good people can't wait here all day."[34]

In typed bulletins, Sam was equally firm in instructing his tellers. "All checks cashed or deposits received by a teller should be placed face down. This is to prevent giving confidential information to outsiders who may see the deposit in the teller's cage."[35]

About business from across the river in Mexico, Sam was equally clear to all parties. "Please see that all letters coming into the Bank from the Republic of Mexico are translated from Spanish into English." Likewise, any letter in Spanish leaving the Bank was to be signed by the officer or by the employee who had written it.[36]

As a command post, Sam's personal office on the mezzanine represented a rather grand rise for a young man from Woodville. The walls were paneled in dark acacia; the two desks he had had built to his special design were lined up as he meant them to stay. Together those desks covered both halves of his daily routine. Facing the front one, he could do business with clients. Rotating his chair and facing the other, he tackled his paper work.[37]

By late summer, the captain's commands were hauling his crew alert and onto their toes. Any staff member in touch with a person inquiring about opening an account should "keep his interest centered upon that person until contact is made with the New Accounts desk." If that prospect appeared to be leaving the Bank without having been served, the employee must notify an officer or wait upon the customer himself. All personnel should see that "everyone is served in a polite and courteous manner."[38]

The Bank's second home, the Two Republics Building, on Texas Street at Stanton, 1927.

For a whole staff to function in such a manner, Sam searched for top-quality help in his own office; his secretaries must give their full strength to the job. On that score, the secretaries who in due time threw up their hands and walked out pretty much agreed on the problem.

"Mr. Young is so good at his job, he is so enthusiastic about everything that he does, that that excitement ought to rub off on us. And a lot of it does." But when the boss was about to leave town on a business trip, "everything has to be ready and waiting. All his last minute letters have to be on his desk for his signature. We try hard to keep up, but after awhile, we can't do it."

Now, suddenly without a secretary again, Sam remembered Bertha Bull, the saucepot who had quit him two years before, the secretary who always acknowledged having processed a paper by penciling "B Bull" on its top. Sam located her in the Southern Pacific's El Paso office. "B Bull, I need a secretary. Get on down here."

There was a pause. "But, Mr. Young, I'm happy here." After Sam urged her again, B Bull told him, "Well, I'll come, but I don't know if I'm interested."[39]

While Bertha was now so well set with the SP that free railroad passes took her wherever she wanted to go, she signed on again with Sam when he gave her a sizable raise. And she learned in due time to keep calm, even when his orders came thick and fast and sometimes conflicting. "Go get me this. Go get me that. Go get what I said."[40]

For Sam himself, the larger world of the banking business opened its arms shortly thereafter when one of his correspondent bankers, Joe Williams of the Commerce Trust Company of Kansas City, proposed him for membership in the Reserve City Bankers Association. Sam stated frankly that he could not imagine being elected to a national membership of only 400 top bankers, but Williams reassured him. "You are young, that's true, but I'm going to get you into it."[41]

At Sam's first Reserve City annual meeting, the older heads scarcely noticed him. But hoping to profit in time, he kept his ears open if for no other reason than to give simple good luck a chance to find him. Whether it would or would not, the talks at those meetings and the manner of the other members fueled young Sam's vision of what he himself might hope one day to become.

On his own turf, running his bank, Sam usually trusted his own best judgment, but there were times, he was frank to confess, when he needed a sounding board before he made big commitments. That best sounding board was Homer Jacobs. If Jake raised serious questions about any proposal he was about to present to the board, that proposal went back to his "paperwork" desk for more study.[42]

Likewise, Sam perceived in Katherine Dorrian another team member who possessed special abilities. It surprised him a little, given the prevailing doubts about a female's skill with money, how quickly Katherine gained special regard with her customers. Waiting in the long line at her window, one client commented, "If I stepped to another window, I could get service quicker, but it's worth my time here. When I get to her window, I know I'll get a big smile."

In time, when Sam settled Katherine into a desk in the lobby, her smiling good nature soon became one of the Bank's appreciable assets. "Women have a tremendous advantage in banking," she explained to an *El Paso Times* reporter, "because they are more sympathetic about the small, everyday problems which bother people, and they can take the time to listen and to help."

About her smile, well, Katherine said, it came easy. "The main attribute for a successful career in banking for women is a genuine interest in people."[43]

To the same degree, John C. Hayes was proving his worth as a director. For his dedication to banking in general and for his familiarity with business affairs in Mexico, Hayes's "yea" or "nay" demonstrated his special talents again and again. It came as no surprise to Sam one evening when at Hayes's invitation, Betty and he were guests for a dinner in a lavish private railroad car parked at the depot. Newspaper tycoon William Randolph Hearst and his Hollywood friend Marion Davies were making an overnight stop to visit Hayes, former manager of Hearst's Mexican ranch.

Over drinks and the spectacular dinner, Sam and Hearst and his former manager ranged though a long list of mutual interests: politics, the world economy, most especially Mexico. Hearst was as enthusiastic as he ever had been, he said proudly, about his 875,000 acre Babicora ranch in western Chihuahua, about his cattle that sometimes numbered as many as 20,000 head.[44] By the end of the evening Sam had hit it off so well with Hearst that he left the party convinced anew that El Paso National's hopes profoundly involved its concentration beyond the Rio Grande.

On that note in July 1928, Sam brought aboard another very special assistant. As a Mexican-American, thirty-two-year-old Manny Escajeda immediately filled a vital spot in the Bank's operation stemming from Sam's own lack of Spanish. With Manny's smooth ease in both English and Spanish, the Bank extended its reach into the growing city across the bridge, a market as such that no other bank in El Paso took seriously. Manny had hardly signed on when his good humor began spreading light over the Bank's daily routines. Glimpsing Sam coming in from a trip, Manny's stage whisper alerted the lobby. "Everybody, quick! On the job! Big Storm coming in from the west." Or the east, or wherever *El Jefe* had been.

Big Storm soon learned about this, but the first time or two he refused to notice. Up in his office, he was still laughing one day, however, when he called Manny in. "If you don't stop that," he grinned, "I'm going to pull every hair out of your head."

Next morning, when Manny came to work with a very close crew cut, Sam again summoned Manny. "Why are you coming to work with your hair looking like that?"

Manny did not blink. "So you can't pull it out," he explained.[45]

About a month after Escajeda joined the Bank, Sam was tackling his paperwork when B Bull ushered in three visitors from Houston. Each in his early thirties, Paul Kayser, H. G. Frost, and J. W. Colvin had dropped by to chat with Sam about their hopes to build a gas pipeline into El Paso. With abundant natural gas now available in the new fields in Winkler County, Texas and Lea County, New Mexico, Kayser explained, El Paso was an obvious market. Later on they might extend their system to points farther west, but for now they needed only an official permit from Mayor R. E. Thomason to buy the right-of-way, start digging the ditch, and laying the pipe.

Frost was an oil man and rancher, Colvin headed the Southwest Gas Utilities Co. and Kayser was a member of the Houston law firm, Huggins, Kayser, Liddell, Benbow, and Butler. While they had not come to Sam for a loan — they expected to finance their project through the State National — they wanted to know how their plan looked to him.

To Sam, the project looked splendid. While his visitors talked more details, he recognized in each one a spark of his own creative energy. Theirs was a vision writ large: they were sizing up the financial potential of a vast part of the nation as surely as he himself saw it.

Sam wished them every success in their venture; before the visit was over, he also perceived the good they could do for El Paso, still only feebly supplied as it was with artificial gas manufactured from coal. More than that, he had made some new friends, especially Kayser, who told him that back home in Houston he was chief counsel for Jesse Jones, long associated with Houston's National Bank of Commerce. Perhaps Sam had met him? Sam grinned that he certainly had, on one crucial occasion while examining Jesse's own books.

As Sam was extending his influence into the El Paso community, he was expanding a team to support his own long range plans. In September 1928 when Sheley Warnock signed on as assistant cashier and assistant trust officer,[46] the thirty-one-year-old native of Gonzalez, Texas quickly established himself along with Jacobs and Escajeda as one of Sam's squad of essential "right hands."

Now, with a cadre of hand-picked assistants, Sam found time after work for another heart-warming friendship. Soon after twenty-eight-year-old Dorrance Roderick arrived from Lubbock, Texas in December 1928 to negotiate with—and then buy—El Paso's major newspaper, the *Times*, the young banker and the young publisher were sharing their opinions of what "this place can become if we dig in our toes and start pushing." "Hell, man," cried Roderick, "just look! Think about it!"[47]

Sam now sensed another identical creative excitement in an old acquaintance dating from 1920. Since the opening of the El Paso National, Sam and Eloy Vallina had occasionally crossed paths in El Paso, and Sam had followed Eloy's rapid rise in the Banco Mercantil down in Chihuahua City. Each time, Sam and Eloy shook hands and wished each other good luck. But late one afternoon in 1928, Eloy popped his head through Sam's door, suitcase in hand. "I've been standing in line over there at the State National for an hour, but nobody would bother to wait on me. Finally, when I got up to the fellow's counter to make a deposit, he hardly looked up. All he said was, 'Can't you see I'm busy?'" Eloy shrugged. "So, after that, here I am, Sam. Let's do business."

Eloy laid his suitcase on Sam's desk. When he opened it, Sam gasped. "My god, Eloy. How much are you carrying?" The large suitcase was stacked full of U. S. greenbacks.

"Fifty thousand. And I'm transferring the rest over here with this deposit." Eloy reached in his pocket and wrote out a check for $400,000.

If at that moment Sam did not quite rub his hands together in glee, a few days later he gave a very warm chuckle when he told his board about that sudden windfall. "Being friendly and helpful is a policy we set for this bank at the start. Eloy Vallina is proof that it pays."[48]

Another warm friendship surfaced again in the late fall of 1928 when his old bank examiner friend, J. B. Herndon, Jr. of Albuquerque, got in touch with him during a banker trip to Dallas. J. B. was full of enthusiasm for his new job as an assistant hotel keeper. "When you've got some free time, I want you to meet my new boss. He started out helping his folks run a little roadside hotel out in San Antonio, New Mexico – our part of the country. This Conrad Hilton has got an itch to go far.[49] Let me know when you've got the time to meet him."

"I've got the time now," Sam announced, "for somebody with that kind of itch."

The meeting in a hotel cafe was brief. Hilton and Sam and Herndon talked about the stock market and the economy; they laughed about their days in the Army. Sipping his coffee, the tall, forty-one-year-old New Mexico man waxed expansive about his hotels; the Mobley in Cisco, the Melba in Fort Worth, and this little Dallas hotel with the grandiose name, the Waldorf. "I kind of think of these three" – Hilton crinkled his nose when he grinned – "as my 'chain.'"

Pleasantries aside, there was an urgent matter of business that Hilton wished to discuss. A bit short of funds at the moment, Hilton said his friend "J. B., here" had suggested that Sam might be willing to listen. Partly out of respect for J. B.'s warm regard for the innkeeper, partly out of his own intuitive grasp of this Hilton's potential, Sam wrote out a note for $15,000. "I'm taking a chance, you understand," he told Hilton. "But you have made me a mighty big promise. You will repay this, *come what may*. On those grounds, I think you and I have struck a pretty good deal."[50]

They shook hands; J. B. gave Sam a quick nod; and Sam moved on to the rest of his business appointments knowing that he had just met, in this host of oil operators and cattle buyers and traveling salesmen working the big Texas scene, another young dynamo of ambition. As in the case of his first encounter with the Houston trio bringing their natural gas line into El Paso, Sam savored the creative fire he had sensed in that eager New Mexican. Talking hotels, that Hilton man did have a sparkling eye.[51]

Sam's thoughts sobered quickly soon after when Governor wired him on January 14, 1929, that Sis Willie had died.[52] To his good friend, there was no adequate sympathy Sam could express. Sis Willie had been one of those special people – by now, Sam could make a long list of them – whose early interest had helped him envision his goals.

On a trip to New York in May 1929 Sam was playing the "go-getter" again, pursuing the accounts of National Biscuit, Otis Elevator, and J. C. Penney. Armed with their full credit ratings[53] – and his friendships with their El Paso managers – he had barely arrived in the big city before he sensed an ominous tension in everybody he talked to. In Wall Street, stocks were selling for prices far beyond their profit potentials; speculators were buying on margin and covering their shares with hardly much more than pennies.[54]

"All the signs are predicting a major bust in the stock market," Randolf Cutten, president of E. F. Hutton, told Sam.[55] Gerald Loeb, the famous financial counsellor, was equally pessimistic. "Mr. Young, the market's going too wild. It can't continue this way."[56] All over New York, Sam encountered the same dire story.

Sam came home deeply distressed. Immediately, he called a board meeting. "Gentlemen, the frenzy up there in New York was terrible. There's no value behind anything. Judging by what I've just seen, I'm fearful: a boom bigger than ever, then bust! We've got to make it plain to our customers what's in store for this country. I've got to advise them to sell their stocks now, before prices collapse."[57]

To his startled directors, Sam delivered a personal warning. "As for ourselves, our little bank should be very cautious in lending money. In particular, we should lend no money at all for purchasing stocks."

The next day, Sam butted horns with one of El Paso's most substantial business men. Portly "Uncle Gus" Momsen wanted to borrow $15,000, a figure the Bank would ordinarily have granted him on his signature. But today, Sam asked him how he would use the money. Hotly, Momsen replied, "Mr. Young, that's none of your business. I can throw it in the Rio Grande if I want to. But if you must know, I mean to buy stock."

Sam felt his face flush. "Uncle Gus, we expect a big bust in the stock market. Just yesterday we adopted a policy that we should not lend money to anyone to buy stock."

Momsen stuck out his chin. "With my line of credit, I'm entitled to borrow $15,000 or more whenever I like and for whatever reason. I don't propose for you to tell me how to handle my affairs."

"Yes, sir, I know, and you have every right to that opinion," Sam countered. "But at the same time—" If the Bank broke its rule for Momsen, its other prime customers would expect the same risky support. "So it must stand as we've said. No. And I hope you'll forgive me."[58]

Fuming, Momsen charged out of the Bank. A few days later when the papers carried the news that Sam's Bank had been the successful bidder for some El Paso city bonds, Momsen grumbled all over town. "That fellow Young is no banker. He's a bond buyer."[59]

"It's true, I did buy some bonds," Sam explained when the word of Momsen's anger reached him. "But old Uncle Gus may be thanking me later, for telling him 'No.'"

7

ROUGH TIMES ON THE BORDER

BANKER SAM NEVER WAS BORED when a customer with a gleam in his eye came in and rolled out his big plans, then later came in with his "mission accomplished," or at least well in sight. With Dorrance Roderick at his rapidly growing *El Paso Times,* the talks were always bursting with hope. And further good talks with Paul Kayser and "Tif" Frost foretold the thrill that Sam felt whenever a customer's struggles turned into general good for the town. Just as Dorrance Roderick's wish to buy out the *Times* owners had come true in February 1929, it was similar good news when Kayser and Frost's new El Paso Natural Gas Company made good their promise to El Paso on the night of June 18, 1929.

That summer evening hundreds of excited people gathered at El Paso Natural Gas Company's city gate, six miles east of the city limits, to watch Paul Kayser open a valve on his new pipeline. While a band played, Mayor R. E. Thomason fired a Roman candle at a huge jet pointed straight up, and the happy crowd burst into cheers when, roaring before them, a giant blue flame shot skyward. From two hundred miles away in eastern New Mexico, across sand dunes and rocky arroyos, a sixteen-inch pipeline began at that moment delivering abundant, cheap natural gas into town.[1]

Sam was away at the time, but for him like every other El Pasoan sensitive to his city's practical needs, the arrival of unlimited gas brought with it boundless hopes of wonders ahead. Like the oldtimers who had seen the Southern Pacific's first train puff into town in 1881, new-timers were witnessing now a moment of similar untold promise.[2]

By the summer of 1929 when Conrad Hilton, now comfortably out of the red and fully paid up with Sam, received a letter postmarked "El Paso," he had already slapped his brand on – or taken charge of – hotels in Dallas, Fort Worth, Abilene, Waco, Marlin, Plainview, San Angelo, and Lubbock. That letter from his widowed mother Mary Laufersweiler Hilton carried bad news. Her younger son August ("Boy" to the family) had just entered a tuberculosis sanatorium in El Paso; no doctor could firmly predict the outcome; he would be in bed indefinitely.

Between his visits to Boy, and following Boy's death soon afterwards, Conrad had let his sharp entrepreneurial eye wander around over the city. By September he was sure he knew a gold mine when he saw it: the empty downtown lot on the corner of Mills and Oregon Street facing San Jacinto Plaza. Quickly he spread the word around town and then over Texas that he planned to build a modern, skyscraper hotel in El Paso.

With Hilton, Sam recognized the building site's good location. Now that Conrad had made good on his El Paso National Bank note, Sam bought for himself and Betty a fistful of shares in the venture, and he also encouraged two local investors, Douglas Crowell and William Banner, to come in along with him.[3] After taking a lease on the site, Hilton announced on October 5, 1929, his plans to build there a hotel to cost $1,750,000. Unfortunately, nineteen days later came the twenty-fourth of October and a stricken nation's outcries.[4]

Roderick's front page grimly detailed the crisis: "Wealth of New York banks is unable to check a wave of liquidation in stocks. Values were pared down another $10,000,000,000 or more in the worst break in history.... Millionaires saw their holdings reduced and many a man who could figure his fortune in six figures yesterday was today in the ranks of actual paupers so far as funds were concerned."[5]

At his desk when the long-dreaded stock market crash came, Sam whispered a prayer of thanksgiving that he had managed a little to forestall the worst in El Paso. With the restraints he had placed on his loan people, not a single El Paso National customer had overextended himself with new stocks. Yet the news in the *Times* carried ominous warnings.

For Hilton, the predictions were clear. Despite the dark prospects, Hilton proceeded apace with his elegantly ornate El Paso Hilton Hotel: its architecture would embrace "the best of the town's Spanish and western legacy."[6]

Locally, though the facts in the El Paso papers clearly said "doom in the East," there was no immediate frenzy at the Pass of the North. One up-and-coming young business man, Chris Fox, at age thirty-one knew the stock market had broken, but with "most of us already living on beans and cornbread, it just didn't make a great splash," he said later.[7] Likewise, over at the State National, Sam's major competitor now, that bank's thirty-one-year-old assistant cashier, George C. Matkin, sensed little local heartache. While "the stock market break was a very exciting thing," there was only "a very limited amount of stock owned by local people."[8] For that reason, it was more a thing to talk about than worry about how to solve.

But Sam, glued to his desk and his balance sheets, could not smile. If fortunes were being wiped out overnight in Wall Street, if the losers were diving out of skyscraper windows, what might those events come to mean in El Paso? Could a little four-year-old bank, no matter how ambitious and courteous, withstand the rough seas ahead? Could a thirty-four-year-old banker, no matter how alert and hardworking, survive the tidal waves of a national money crisis?

At the Bank, it was business as usual, though at Sam's firm instructions the loan people again shined up their caution. All applications for long-term loans, they explained to their clients, would require extra special study. As always, however, the loan people would abide by the Bank's loan guidelines in an effort to be fair to all: "The good credit risk is the man who has a steady cash flow; he is the man who is clearly dedicated to his goal; he is the man who can pledge significant collateral. We are not interested, however, in his collateral as such. We don't want his cattle, his business, or his goods. We do want his *concern* for his cattle, that is, his concern for repaying his loan. That man, we will lend money to."[9]

For his staff's special notice, Sam added one weighty word. Glancing ahead at the uncertain future, "we will adhere to our 'cash on demand' policy. Whenever a client at one of our windows wants all his money, we will cheerfully give it all to him, right then. No 'if,' 'and,' or 'later.' To fail to do so would spread the wild rumor, 'that bank is broke.'"[10]

On that note, Hilliard Bryan, the head teller, witnessed a scene that may have come from taking Sam's orders a bit too literally. One morning a face appeared at the window of a new teller. "I want two packs of five-dollar bills," the customer told her.

Smiling her "friendly bank" smile, the teller reached under the counter, laid out the first pack before him, and bent down again for the rest. When she stood up, the man was dashing away for the door. "Oh, sir," she called toward him, "don't you want the rest of your money?"

Only then did it occur to her that the "client" was a robber making his getaway. After cries alerted the guards in the lobby, an El Paso policeman captured the robber just as he was boarding a bus to skip town.[11]

Hearing that, Sam could manage a smile; but he did not relax his intentions. In his next round of guidelines to the staff he wanted all the Bank people, including himself, to maintain their zeal in giving their clients informed financial advice, especially now in view of the crash.

In spite of that, Sam saw total ruin descend on a customer, a newcomer from St. Louis, who had ignored his firmest counsel. That client had come in with a portfolio of municipal bonds and stocks and had exchanged it all for downtown real estate. Within days, the worth of that investment had dropped "to ten cents on the dollar." Helpless, Sam watched the client, now absolutely broke, shaking his head.[12]

Unfortunately, stock-owner Sam did not quite heed his own advice. As the market declined, Sam watched his ten shares of National City Bank of New York – his personal profits from some of his "commodity paper" in Mexico – fall from $1,380 per share to $380. Holding that shrunken paper, a clear loss of $10,000, Sam felt profound sympathy for all other victims.[13]

In the local economic downturn, when Zach White's own fortune turned suddenly grim, Sam often got a jovial call inviting him over for lunch. At the Paso del Norte, the conversation always flowed casually until after dessert. "Mr. Young," – White cleared his throat – "you know I'm into many kinds of endeavors but the fact is, with the economy getting steadily worse, I need the right man to manage my estate."

Sometimes White's invitations also meant picnic drives through his apple orchards and cotton fields up the valley near Berino and Vado. But always the talk concluded, "Mr. Young," — with White gesturing around him — "I need your *help* in running all this."

Each time, Sam explained carefully. "I'm up to my neck, Mr. White. Just running my bank, I haven't got time to tackle such a major account."[14]

Nor, Sam might have added, did he have much inclination just now to involve himself away from Betty. Her good news of another child on the way was never far from Sam's thoughts. Happily for them both, the months of waiting went much more safely for Betty this time. On March 15, 1930, Sam gave a joyous cry when the doctor reported, "Betty's just fine, no complications at all. It's a boy."

Sam rushed to the phone to call Woodville. He rushed home to tell Little Betty and Grandmother Mimi. That afternoon, down at the Bank, when somebody asked him just how he felt, Sam sobered a moment. "Mrs. Young and I" — he took a deep swallow — "feel like we're the new king and queen."[15]

"So what have you named the young prince?" everybody wanted to know.

A broad grin lit up Sam's face. "Sam Jr., of course. He's my boy."

Though the *Post* newspaper story on March 18 was true to Sam's mood, it decorated the facts just a bit. "Sam D. Young, vice president of the El Paso National Bank, was arranging 'his' desk at the bank Tuesday. 'His' happens to be Sam D. Young, Jr., newest eight-pound member of the Young family."

It took five months for the Wall Street collapse to impact on El Paso in a truly significant way, but when it hit, everybody took the full blow, especially bankers and business people. Property values staggered and tumbled, home values fell. Businesses stagnated, tenants in general defaulted on their rent payments.[16] Breadlines formed all over town; soup kitchens were packed. In whatever direction one looked, he saw hunger and fear.[17]

Though Sam and Betty's household was filled now with the healthy cries of a new infant son and the laughter of a four-year-old daughter, they were not wholly apart from the shrinking fortunes around over town. Every night Sam came home troubled and not really hungry, worried for the sad depositors trudging in and out of his lobby. In a sense he was personally more fortunate than most, his salary did hold steady and regular. Most importantly, his enterprise in Mexican commercial paper and bills of lading helped him escape the worst infections rampant on Wall Street. And small though it was, that Mexican resource helped him help others a bit when they turned to him for personal financing. At home, ever the frugal half of the team, Betty helped the family live within their means through careful shopping and tight control over household expenses.

In the grim times, Mrs. Frank Feuille, Jr. typified the people who knew adversity but who learned through sheer grit to withstand the worst onslaughts of the Depression. Some years before, she and her lawyer husband and their six young children were living in Caracas, Venezuela, when Feuille died suddenly of a tropical fever. His grieving widow managed to get herself and the children safely home to El Paso, and for a time her insurance proceeds and a few other resources took care of their needs. After that, she turned to school teaching. Unfortunately, her $200 monthly salary could not feed her large family.

At that point, Sam lent Mrs. Feuille the money she asked for, but in a few months she had to approach him again. "Mr. Young, I hate to say this, but I just don't know how I can repay you as much as I should and on time."

Sam listened carefully, then told her what she most needed to hear. "I know how things are with you, and I don't want you to worry. If you can't pay me now, well, that's all right. Things are bound to get better. And I do understand."[18]

At no point in Sam's personal story, however, did the Depression center more fortuitously than in the havoc it played with that sunburned New Mexico man who had confessed to Sam one morning in Dallas that, well, he had a kind of a yen for leasing and/or buying and/or building hotels. On November 5, 1930, when the new El Paso Hilton Hotel threw open its doors, Conrad Hilton and his local manager, Sam's former bank examiner colleague J. B. Herndon, welcomed some 15,000 El Pasoans to an "Open House." Touring the building, they marveled at its tiled lobby, its grand ballroom with space enough to banquet 500 people, its 300 brightly lit rooms, its richly appointed "exclusive suites on the roof," as Hilton called them. Above the city's despair, that nineteen-story new building waved like a battle flag "in the face of adversity."[19]

That night, Hilton hosted a dinner to celebrate his hotel's completion and, not incidentally, to publicize its virtues to 500 of El Paso's top dignitaries. Two of those dignitaries, Betty and Sam, arrived late for the party because they had mislaid their invitation. When the doorman refused to admit them and Sam irately called Hilton on the house phone, Hilton sprinted downstairs – "My god, Sam, I'm sorry as hell" – smoothed down the feathers, and escorted them up to the party.[20]

Sipping Hilton's champagne, Sam felt anew a small thrill of pleasure recalling himself at age twelve. Tonight, looking around in a hotel built with a bit of his money, he realized that his job at Mrs. Steward's hotel in Woodville had been a step into this very business.

During the weeks that followed, watching Conrad Hilton skillfully operating his business, Sam felt increasingly sure that though this Hilton hotel was no guaranteed winner in the competitive world of inn-keeping, this Conrad Hilton himself was a mighty good bet. His Texas chain already included 1,800 hotel rooms. Also, it soon came to pass that this Connie Hilton would make a good friend, at a time when Hilton needed a friend in his banker. Hilton's new hostelry had grandly opened for business, but hardly more than a trickle of paying guests had actually checked in.

Yet dark as the prospects appeared for Hilton and for the city, life's finer amenities were still within reach of a fortunate few. In 1930 Dorrance Roderick revitalized the El Paso Symphony Orchestra. Sam, partly as simple good business, agreed to serve as secretary for the El Paso Country Club.[21] And, he told the *Times* when they asked him about his pet hobby,[22] Sam firmly nurtured a wish that some day he could afford to travel, not just on business, but to encounter the world with Betty, to meet the world's peoples.

Hope for that kind of travel opened up rather out of the blue in 1930 when the Texas and New Mexico Railroad Co. asked Sam to join its board of directors. Running between Monahans, Texas and Lovington, New Mexico, the little ninety-five-mile line was a feeder branch of the much larger Texas and Pacific. Attending its monthly board meetings, Sam found the agenda mostly cut-and-dried managerial matters where he gained, for the most part, in perceiving "the other fellows'" viewpoints on the West Texas economy. But his chair at that table did bring him one solid benefit. Years ago, Sis Willie had commented, "Sam, to be a successful business man, you must have railroad passes." Now, as a T&NM director at age thirty-four, his T&NM passes were valid on all the other railroad lines in America.[23]

Nevertheless, given his long hours of stress at the Bank, Sam's only true getaway time was a weekly golf game. One afternoon, he had just sunk an uphill putt when the caddie master came running. "A call for you from Houston."

On the phone, Governor's voice sounded strained. "Sam, I know I'm interrupting your game, but I'm in distress down here at the *Houston Post*."

"I'm mighty sorry to hear that, Governor. What's up?"

"Well, as president of this paper, I've got to meet my payroll by next Friday and I can't do it. I need $40,000." Hobby paused. "Could you help me?"

"Forty thousand?" It was Sam's turn to pause. "Governor, I guess so, but I sure hope you can pay it back promptly."

"Oh, yes. Sure, I can."

Luckily, friendship and good business could play hand in hand. "Then, all right," Sam told him. "Go ahead, draw your check on your account here for the $40,000."[24]

Though the conversation was brief, it said a great deal to Sam; from far out west on the border, he could rescue a friend down in the big city who had already invested hard cash in his bank as a gesture of confidence strictly in him.

Sam's highly intuitive one-on-one style of banking, dealing oftentimes on a customer's good name alone, the Bank board itself might have questioned. But as Sam often explained when a loan application came under review, "I know the man. I have faith in the man. I'd just as willingly let that man have $100,000 on his name alone as on his security. He will repay his loan."[25] Hobby's quickly settling his own note typified the means through which the directors had long ago learned the style of their executive vice president. If they were astonished sometimes at his trusting "the man," Sam's own record proved that they could in turn as safely trust him, their man Sam.[26]

Occasionally, sour loans that could be handled without undue difficulties, Sam himself quietly absorbed. Leslie Levy, the Angelus Cleaners man, had co-signed a note with a relative, but the $150 was due and the relative was unable to pay. Hesitantly, Les explained. But Sam was already ahead of him. "Les, from the beginning you have trusted me as your banker. So this cancelled note is between you and me – personally."[27] Sam paid the $150 himself.

Around the same time, Sam received an urgent phone call from "Tif" Frost in New York. "Sam? Paul Kayser and I are in a tight spot." Their El Paso Natural Gas Company needed $750,000 but, given the country's shaky condition, no bank in New York would make them the loan. "I've called the State National, but Charlie Bassett will swing us only one half, and only that half if you will lend us the rest."

Sam had to think only a moment. Extending their line to Arizona and into Mexico, their gas company was certainly sound: it was that vast region's only supplier. Knowing he could cooperate happily with his friend Charlie Bassett, Sam lent Frost and Kayser the $375,000.[28]

Sam had other ways too of playing along with the State National. The venerable George Flory, the State's ruggedly solid vice president, was slowly relaxing his hold on his bank's affairs, but he still kept an amiable eye out for fresh talent, even if it occupied the EVP's chair at a competitor bank. Sometimes on Sundays, he telephoned Sam. "I'm lonesome. Come on over here and tell me some lies."

Puzzled, Sam went. But the second time he "came over," Sam knew why Flory had called him. The old pro "picked my mind to see just what he could get," he told Betty after that visit.[29]

"So why do you always go?" Betty asked him.

"Oh, I like that old fellow. Besides, rocking my chair out there with him on his porch, I pick up some leads from him too." One typical chat covered the weather, the cotton and chili crops down the valley, the market prospects, and state politics. Suddenly Flory stopped rocking.

"Where do you get all this information?" he wanted to know.

"The papers," Sam answered. "And I read *The American Banker*. Don't you?"

"I never heard of *The American Banker*."

"Well, Mr. Flory, you ought to. To stay abreast of what's going on in your correspondent banks."[30]

Flory slowly nodded, then pulled out his notepad and scribbled a note.

In El Paso's money scene, as in every other aspect of its life, a dread report hit the headlines the first week in September 1931. James McNary's First National Bank, the biggest bank in the city, had just failed. There were no plans to reopen. That afternoon, R. H. Collier, chief national bank examiner, called Sam. "To relieve the hundreds of people who'll suffer, Sam, can't you consolidate the First National's assets with yours?"

Sam did not need to think twice. For weeks rumors about the FNB's shaky condition had kept him alert. "Chief, I do wish I could," Sam replied. "That might help the FNB's people, but I can't risk hurting mine. We're in good health over here; we're solvent. And, Chief, I mean to keep us that way."[31]

After Sam's firm rejection of any plan to merge with the First National, W. H. Keller, a Los Angeles businessman who was also a heavy investor in El Paso's Globe Flour Mills, its Globe Ice Co., and its Harry Mitchell Brewing Co. made him an offer. Since the First National was beyond help, he would be glad to join Sam's board of directors, thereby bringing with him the banking business he had controlled at First National. That offer, Sam gladly approved. Those new Keller accounts – plus Keller's advisory work on the board – made a dramatic upsurge in Sam's growing profile in El Paso.[32]

To Keller, as the newest director, Sam explained the proper relationship, as he saw it, between a chief executive and his board of directors. Doing so, he was repeating a little comment he had made to Frank Fletcher when Frank came aboard on January 14, 1930.[33] "A board always goes along with management until management proves itself bad. A director on a board is there as adviser, and he gives his advice when it is timely."[34] To simplify matters for the directors as much as he could, Sam reiterated one of his policies from 1925. "I'll do my best to bring only the big decisions to you. I'll deal with the small ones myself."

When old hands on the board softly chuckled, one of them calmly explained, "Nobody's complaining, Sam, but in all my years on this board, there's never been a big decision for us to tackle. But as long as you want it that way, like I say, Sam, nobody's complaining."[35]

Regarding Zach White's troubled estate, Sam could no longer avoid White's repeated requests for his help. Knowing from the start that restoring Zach White to solvency would take time that he could ill afford from running the Bank, from his civic works, most of all from his family, he became White's official trustee. There was no rule to help him apportion his hours, but doing his best for all parties concerned now composed most of his life.

White's interests were local, but along with those complications, Sam now involved himself, both as banker and friend, in the affairs of

R. L. Ziegler, an El Paso meat packer who imported thousands of Mexican cattle each year for fattening along the river. Through Sam's financing Ziegler, other major Mexican accounts came in from Ziegler's *ranchero* associates. Similar growth proved true with Hal Bruner and Jess Burner, cattle importers who now looked to the El Paso National for big credit. As solid, satisfied customers themselves, they too spread Sam's name and the name of his bank throughout the state of Chihuahua.[36] Oftentimes now, when other American cattle buyers offered Mexican cattlemen letters of credit drawn on banks in New York, those suppliers preferred letters of credit with Sam.

With such opportunities now opening up, especially in light of the money troubles at home, Sam grew increasingly amazed at the lack of interest other bankers in Texas felt for the promise he himself so clearly perceived south of the border.

8

A TIME OF DEEP DEPRESSION

THE FLOOD OF HARRIED DEPOSITORS that stormed the only two El Paso banks now left in business, hoping those banks would still cash their First National checks, was the immediate result of the First National's demise on September 4, 1931. Since the State National stood directly across San Antonio Street from the First National, that bank took the main brunt of the torrent, but Sam's own windows three blocks away were also deluged until he adjusted his business hours, mainly to reassure his own customers.

The next day, a Saturday, though all local banks normally closed at 12:00 noon, both Sam and State stayed open till 6:00. On both days Sam kept his tellers' visible shelves piled high with greenbacks, demonstrating to his worried depositors that the money stream of "their" bank – Harvey's and Sam's and the customers' – was not about to run dry.[1]

To that end, when R. E. McKee, a prominent El Paso contractor, commented, "Well, Sam, I see people here, but they don't seem to be withdrawing their funds," Sam backed up his point with statistics.

"Mr. McKee, 85 percent of our deposits are in cash and government bonds. The other 15 percent represent the personal funds of our board. Under no circumstances would our directors withdraw their own funds." Sam gestured toward the stacks of green bills in the cages. As McKee could see plainly, the El Paso National was "fully able to pay off every deposit."[2]

The next day when Charles Bassett, president of the State National, dropped in to see Sam, the visit came as no particular surprise. Given the downfall of the First National, said Bassett, Sam and he also had reason to fear. "To prevent our own failures," Charlie said tensely, "we ought to join forces. Sam, you could be CEO of the new institution."

The State National outranked Sam's bank three to one in deposits,[3] but Sam quickly perceived disastrous consequences. "For the good of this town, Charlie, we can't do that. Competition between us will keep you and me both on our toes, and that will pay off, both for our customers and for our stockholders. Besides, you're the oldest bank in El Paso and me, I'm the youngest, but if the State and the El Paso National failed to maintain our own separate strengths, some new institution would soon spring up and cause us both trouble."[4] Reluctantly, Bassett agreed.

One especially bitter result of the First National's end was grief for many El Paso homeowners. With their money tied up in its frozen accounts, they had no choice but to default on their house payments. The result: foreclosures all over town. For some mortgage companies, as well, the shortfall proved fatal. When the First National's own affiliate, The First Mortgage Company, soon fell and was bought by Mortgage Investment Company, that company developed serious troubles, a point not lost on a rising young entrepreneur, MacIntosh Murchison.

MacIntosh came to Sam. "For $60,000," Murchison told him, "I can buy all the stock of Mortgage Investment. Can you lend me the money?"

Sam pondered the facts: the firm's name, "Mortgage Investment," in itself had value. More to the point, Murchison was known to be responsible, hard working, and solid.[5] After granting that loan, Sam took a quiet pride in watching Murchison slowly turn his new company's fortunes around.

Another caller expressed no interest in borrowing growth money; Tony Lama needed cash to survive. Though Lama had been El Paso's best bootmaker ever since 1911, the hard times had cut his cash flow so sharply that he had had to declare bankruptcy. In answer to Tony,

Sam came straight to the point. "You and I know this town needs a business like yours, Tony. To get it going again, how much do you need?"

"To clear up my debts and buy new equipment," Tony told him, "about $80,000. With a fresh start, my boys and I can go places."

Sam reached for his pen. "I think you can too."[6]

The problems of Conrad Hilton, however, were hardly so simple. By early 1931 Hilton, like Lama, had declared bankruptcy. With every one of his hotels "borrowed up" to the limit, he had depended entirely on his cash flow to keep going. But with nobody traveling, that flow had dried up, leaving his business in limbo. To have a roof over their heads, Hilton brought his wife Mary and their sons Nicky and Barron to El Paso where his mother now lived. Once again at J. B. Herndon's good urging, Sam was ready when Hilton came calling. "What I really need now, Sam, is a small personal loan till the first of next month. Can you float me?"

In no banker's judgment was Hilton "bankable." Yet, to Sam, this Hilton was now not only a friend deeply in need. Just as surely, this Hilton as a business talent looked as promising now as he had looked at his El Paso hotel's grand opening.

Consequently, with his "paper deals" in Mexico paying off well, Sam could listen when Hilton came to him again. "Honest to god, I hate this kind of showdown, but I'm telling you straight how I stand. And I won't try to argue you down if you have to say 'No.' Once again, for just a few weeks, can you float me some way?"

Out of friendship, Sam's way to float Hilton turned into two or three hundred dollars each month when Hilton stuck his head in, after asking Sam's current secretary, "Is he in a good mood today?"[7] Sam kept these small support checks going until, no longer able to afford the risk on his own, he turned to the Bank for a regular lending arrangement with Connie.[8]

Though Sam's salary had risen now to $12,000 a year, the figure seemed hardly worth crowing about, given the long day and night hours he put in to make it. On his next visit to Woodville, however, he did mention the figure to Teah.

"Twelve thousand dollars!" cried Teah. "A thousand dollars a month!" Teah dashed with the news to Charlie. Though Charlie did not say how the figure hit him, Sam saw a new cheer in his face, chatting with folks around town. As for Fanny, Sam surprised her straight out with a $500 check for her secret little "wad," as she called it, upstairs in her wardrobe.

Fanny studied the check very carefully, then looking deeply troubled, she asked him, "Sambo – son, did you come by this money honestly?"[9]

Grinning, Sam reached down and hugged her. "Mama, I didn't steal it. If I had," he grinned, "I know you'd whip me."[10] Then he stood still while Fanny shyly patted his cheek.

At home in the Bank, Sam could also bask in the satisfaction that C. M. Harvey found in his efforts, in his skill with the board and the stockholders, in his efforts for the community's good. There were occasions, however, when Harvey talked to Sam like a Dutch uncle. "I'm worried about your Saturday nights over in Juarez. I'm speaking the truth, and I know what I'm talking about. Drinking can cause terrible trouble. Sam, if you'll stop doing that, I'll give you two thousand dollars."

Sam recognized Harvey's intention. "That's tempting, Mr. Harvey. I certainly wouldn't drink over here, with Prohibition on us and all. But all I'm doing over in Juarez is just unwinding a little, sometimes after work. Besides, I can't sell my" – he chuckled – "my birthright."

Harvey did not join in the laugh. "Believe me, Sam. Stop and I'll give you two thousand dollars."[11]

Reluctantly, Sam accepted Harvey's challenge, but it took him a few more "birthright" occasions to convince himself that Harvey knew best.

In the Depression, the four-bedroom house at 1104 Cincinnati – housing two parents, two children, Grandmother Mimi and Betty's sisters, Martha and Jo – was decidedly cramped. Congenial as the whole menage was, Sam would have liked at times to lean back in his own roomy domain and put his feet up, away from the crush of – he never said so even to Betty – too many people at home, too much routine at the Bank.

And there was no good way to escape except for brief summer train runs up to Cloudcroft, New Mexico. In a cool, rented cottage at 9,000 feet above sea level, Sam and Betty relaxed at the bridge table with summer people like themselves or on picnics with people from home: Dr. and Mrs. Michael Philip Schuster, who owned and managed the thirty-bed Providence Hospital in Sunset Heights, and the James A. Dicks. There was time now for nine holes of golf on the highest course in America, time to wave with Little Betty and Sammy when the train chugged uphill every afternoon to disgorge another tired load of homefolks eager to cool off in the shade and forget their money worries at home.

Though Cloudcroft offered only temporary time off, Sam would have accepted the fact of his crowded homelife indefinitely if a sudden windfall had not appeared in a savings and loan company's listing. A repossessed house at 4520 Cumberland Circle in Austin Terrace could be bought for $12,000.[12]

From his profits in his Mexico deals, Sam already owned $3,000 worth of that company's stock. Now, shopping the open market, Sam located an additional $9,000 worth of those shares, which he managed to buy for $4,500. Those stocks in hand, he made the loan company an offer. "My stocks for your house." When the company people agreed, Sam got his $12,000 home for an actual outlay of $7,500.[13]

True, the building needed minor repairs, but the basic good deal was a case of successful, straightforward negotiation. Sam's skill in the game won the pot.

Soon, as his growing finances permitted, Sam added an upstairs sleeping porch, where Betty and he and the children all slept on hot summer nights. To cool off the rest of the house till bedtime for Mimi and Martha and Jo, he sometimes hosed down the lawn and the shrubbery. Many times, as the water evaporated, the house turned almost too cool.

For Betty, there was one flaw in the new neighborhood that she felt she must quickly address. Their neighbors the Dorrance Rodericks had a large weeping willow tree in their back yard. For their own good Betty repeatedly urged Olga Roderick to "get rid of that terrible tree. Weeping willows are very bad luck, you know."

For tough-minded Olga, there was no problem. "Betty," she countered, "we like its cool shade. As for us, we're willing to take our chances."[14]

To other friends, it seemed equally strange that Betty could be religious and superstitious at the same time. Like never walking under a ladder. Like driving out of the way to avoid a black cat crossing the road.[15]

Such fears aside, from the demise of the First National Sam inherited an account that deepened his friendship with Dorrance Roderick. With much of his capital still trapped in the First National fiasco, Roderick soon needed help to pay off his note on the *Times* and handle his day-to-day operations. Since Roderick required more than the Bank's loan limit, Sam arranged that credit with his friend Fred Florence in Dallas. As his personal finances permitted, Sam invested $12,000 in Roderick's paper.

On January 31, 1932, after only one year of managing Zach White's tangled affairs, Sam was saddened when White died at age eighty-one. Restructuring White's holdings, Sam had earned his trust fee, but hearing White's will, Sam laughed aloud. The good Mr. White had left Sam only an oaken barrel down in his cellar, safe from the law. Expecting great things from that fragrant barrel, Sam slowly removed the plug. To his dismay, the bourbon inside had evaporated by nearly a third. Telling the tragic tale to White's daughters Katharine (Mrs. Paul Harvey) and Mary (Mrs. Jess Boykin), Sam chuckled. "But I'll tell you one thing, it's beautiful whiskey, what there is of it."[16]

Quickly, life at 4520 Cumberland Circle took on a more ample style than had been possible in the houses on Cincinnati. Sammy was talking small sentences now and toddling all over the two-story house; Little Betty expected a romp each night when Sam arrived home, sometimes long after dinner, but always she scrambled up into his lap and snuggled back, happy and safe while he read his newspaper around her.[17]

Betty herself ran the house. Planning her menus a week in advance, she went every day to "market" (the old Corsicana way to say "grocery store"). She was the family secretary, she was the hostess when her turn came to entertain. Though she performed that social role gracefully, those responsibilities never came easy. While the new house was cut to the style of big parties, small dinners with friends or family each Sunday around the big dining table, watching Sam carve the roast while she ladled the soup, were the kind of social occasions Betty most enjoyed.[18]

At the Bank, the 1931 year-end Statement of Condition brought better news for all parties concerned, given the times, than they might have expected. Since the recent sudden drop by $175,000 in deposits (from $3,091,873 in 1929 to $2,917,210 in 1930) Sam could beam with relief as he shared his latest ledger details with his people. 1931 deposits were up by $1,185,062.[19]

For Sam personally just now, a letter from Governor brought good news of a quite different sort. At age fifty-three, Governor wanted to marry a lady aged twenty-six. But before he took such a step, he wanted the approval of Sis Willie's family. To represent them, could Sam come down and meet Oveta Culp? Hobby had long been impressed with Oveta's skills as parliamentarian to the Texas Legislature. At that dinner visit with Oveta and Governor at the St. Anthony Hotel in San Antonio, Sam recognized in Oveta the charm and intellectual vigor that had captivated his old friend. Shaking Governor's hand, Sam smiled at them both. "So, what are you folks waiting for? When's the big day?"[20]

The happy wedding of December and June was only a momentary diversion in the sober money scene back at the office. Since 1930, 9,102 banks had closed.[21] At year's end 1932, though, Sam's own deposits totalled $4,214,000 (a rise for the twelve months of $100,000).

Early in 1932 it was clear to Sam, like most other Texas bankers just now, that the strength of his institution – subject like any business to the ups and downs of free enterprise – forced him to take a step contrary to his policy of "serving" his customers. Because of his rising in-house expenses, he imposed a service charge on all checking accounts.[22]

In another respect, he flatly refused to serve a strangely nervous woman who applied to him for a personal loan. Since she had no account and could put up no collateral, Sam gently explained that he was unable to help her. Suddenly, the woman leaped at him in a fury. "If you don't give me the money," she screamed, "I'm spreading the word all over this town that I saw you going into a whorehouse in South El Paso!"

Sam stared at her, then shot to his feet. "Get out of my office!" he cried, shaking his finger, "Don't you ever come back!"

Sam never learned why the woman had thought her threat might pay off, though from long experience now, he knew there was no way to avoid such heedless assaults. As a responsible watchdog guarding the community's wealth, he could hope that in some better world he might reconcile the wants of the needy with the rights of the many depositors and stockholders who trusted him. In the world as it was, however, he saw no way to imagine Utopia.

Yet in November 1932, the presidential election had everything to do with Sam's personal concerns both as a banker, a family man, and a humanitarian. Protesting against the failures the nation had suffered under Republican President Herbert Hoover, Sam voted his hopes for a change in the White House, then listened intently to the inaugural broadcast from Washington on Saturday, March 4, 1933, when Democrat Franklin D. Roosevelt spelled out his policy regarding the nation. "Values have shrunken to fantastic levels; taxes have risen; our ability to pay has failed; government of all kinds is faced by serious curtailment of income; the means of exchange are frozen in the currents of trade." The savings of thousands of families were gone: a host of unemployed citizens were struggling for sheer existence, an equally gigantic number toiled for meager return. "Only a foolish optimist can deny," declared the new president, "the dark realities of the moment."[23] That being the case, Roosevelt continued, "I am prepared under my constitutional duty to recommend the measures that a stricken nation in the midst of a stricken world may require."[24]

The next afternoon, Sam was playing golf with Hilton and Paul Kayser when a messenger came running toward him on the tenth hole. "Your office needs you," he called.

Sam's office did indeed need him. FDR had just declared that, until further word, every bank in the nation was closed.[25]

Sam did not wait to pick up his ball.

9

PLAYING THE DOUBLE SIXES

When troubled El Pasoans rushed to their two banks, the State National and the El Paso National, on Monday morning, March 6, 1933, the message tacked on those doors did nothing to reassure them: "By proclamation of the President of the United States this bank, in common with all other banks in the United States, is observing the Banking Holiday."[1]

The word "holiday," as the local papers explained, meant that for the good of the people, every bank in America would stay closed until bank examiners could determine its basic health. Though Sam was appointed to serve on the examiner team in El Paso,[2] it annoyed him that his bank had to shut down due to the managerial shortcomings of banks far distant from his, especially when the examiners found the El Paso National in a firmly liquid condition.[3] Their good report did not resolve, however, the difficulties suffered by a goodly number of his own customers. During the holiday, local business could only be conducted by check or with whatever cash the customer had in his pocket. Those checks kept El Paso businesses open, yet merchants who had accepted out-of-town checks were sad indeed a few days after the holiday when Sam and his people had to explain that many such checks had bounced. Three thousand banks out of the nation's 11,000 had failed their "physicals."[4] Given such griefs, however, Sam had wholly supported the President's tough measure. "If he hadn't done it, it would have been a worse mess."[5]

Summer reunions in Woodville brought pleasant escapes, as usual. For two weeks, Sam could stretch back and relish Fanny and Charlie's ease with Little Betty and Sammy, their manner now far more relaxed than he as a child had ever known it to be. Fanny's gentle comment, "Well, now that's all right," still smoothed troubled waters,[6] and though Little Betty whispered to Sam more than once that she found Granddaddy "scary," Charlie's gruffness had softened. He took an obvious pleasure now in sweeping Little Betty up into his saddle and riding all over town, showing her off. At meal time, however, nobody found anything "scary." Fanny still loaded her table with black-eyed peas, new potatoes and tomatoes fresh from her garden, chicken and dumplings, the butter she churned every morning. When everybody was stuffed, she shyly mentioned that over there by the door, the sideboard had coconut cake – Sam's favorite – and peach and blackberry pies.

By fall, Franklin Roosevelt's promise to shore up the nation's economy bore fruit when he persuaded Congress to establish the Federal Deposit Insurance Corporation, an agency insuring bank deposits up to a fixed maximum, which guaranteed that no depositor should ever lose his whole balance. Sam readily agreed to this government change, though "deposit insurance" seemed a rather weak comfort. For one thing, the cost of that insurance premium came very high. For another, it only guaranteed to the customer the safe and responsible service he should have received from his bank all along.[7]

Later in 1933, as the nation's economy slowly improved, Conrad Hilton was still far from out of the woods: a Los Angeles insurance company had foreclosed on his beautiful El Paso hotel; he owed $30,000 back rent to Albert Mathias, the adamant party from whom he had leased the land his building stood on. At that juncture, when he appealed to a group of El Paso friends and suppliers to lend him the money, they in turn came to Sam.

Sam's reaction was a gamble based on the same trust he had always placed in the man. Only the previous May, when Rafael Vallina's Banco Mercantil in Chihuahua had asked the Bank the probable worth of Hilton stock, Homer Jacobs had expressed Sam's own opinion. "We doubt if there is any market at the present time," wrote Jacobs. Hilton's heavy mortgage involvements made it reasonable "to assume that the possibility of the stock ever having any value is rather remote."[8] Yet, with no facts to counter that judgment, Sam lent a sizable chunk of that $30,000 rent money to Hilton's small group.

Along with Hilton's mother, who gave him her check for $5,000, those El Paso backers were a disparate group. Joseph Goodell owned the Citizens Finance Company; Robert Price owned Price's Dairy; Bill Rank worked for Blatz Beer; Bill Tooley was a hotel man himself; Frank Fletcher owned the Acme Laundry. Each agreed to lend Hilton $5,000, but they were not acting on sentiment. For their cash and their confidence, Hilton made them a cheerful promise. The El Paso Hilton would serve no beer but Blatz's, no milk or ice cream but Price's, it would use no laundry but Fletcher's.[9] As Hilton's own banker, Sam lent him $5,000, explaining that his "whole interest in him developed from my personal confidence in him. I couldn't sell him to other banks anywhere."[10]

When the group all shook hands, Conrad dashed with their checks down Texas Street to Sam's bank, then on to Albert Mathias. By next morning, the El Paso Hilton was back in Conrad's own hands.[11] By the end of the year, Hilton had repaid all those lenders; he had settled his note with Sam's bank.

Now Sam could see fit as himself – no longer as Hilton's banker – to take a broad step. Until the Bank was out of the picture, Sam had not considered involving himself in Hilton's company: bank policy forbade its officers from making personal connections with its borrowers. Now, however, when Hilton made Sam a special offer of stock at $2.50 per share, Sam freely bought 2,500 shares on his own,[12] mostly to express his renewed belief that this Hilton would still make his mark.[13]

With Hilton cheerful again, a vigorous off-duty friendship reopened. Connie and Sam's golf games took on a new challenge. At a three dollar wager per hole, they revved up their shots. "Hurry up, Sam," Connie hollered when Sam was about to capture a hole.

"Dammit, Connie," Sam hollered back. "You keep shouting like that and I'm throwing this putter straight at you. To hell with your piddling three dollars."[14]

On behalf of other valued hotel customers, Sam's contacts with Jesse Jones, now heading FDR's Reconstruction Finance Corporation in

Washington, paid off when Lee and Seth Orndorff needed help with a hotel they owned in Tucson. On their behalf Sam presented himself at Jones's office. Through Jones's aid, he sent in an outline of the Orndorffs' problem. Almost immediately, the aide came back, nodding his head. "Mr. Jones tells me, 'Take care of Sam Young.' I'm to let you have what you need."[15]

The grateful Orndorffs made Sam accept a check of $3,000, but after clearing the matter with his board of directors—"It's your money," they insisted, "it doesn't belong to the bank"—he and Betty gave the full amount to the Westminster Presbyterian Church to fulfill their recent pledge to it.

Sweating behind a mule team in Charlie's corn field back in his childhood, Sam and his friend, Mayo McBride, had sworn that sun-up to sun-down hard labor was clearly not right for them. In the summer of 1933, however, a matter involving a farm twenty miles down the valley made farming come alive in Sam's mind. Back in 1924 when the National Border Bank failed, it was holding a note on those 400 acres. During Sam's receivership, the Federal Land Bank had bought the first lien on that note, and in due time, the new El Paso National Bank had bought the second.

Now, nine years later, when Sam learned that the Federal Land Bank was about to foreclose on its lien and that, thereby, the El Paso National would lose the value it owned in the second, Sam asked his friend Martin Lettunich to estimate the farm's worth. Lettunich came back eager to buy "that good piece of irrigated cotton land" himself. "Better yet," he cried, "Sam, I want you to go partners with me."

Sam shook his head. "When I left that sorry old farm back in Woodville, I said goodbye forever to that kind of life."[16]

"I'm not talking about any sorry old farm," Martin insisted. "As an investment, that irrigated cotton land is about the same thing as gold." Firmly, Sam again shook his head.

Yet the more he thought about Martin's idea, the more he liked it. Still, how would his board feel about a deal that might embarrass the Bank? Harvey and the board heard him out, then voted, "No problem." By the farmer's default on the first lien, the Federal Land Bank effectively controlled the property. "Sure, go along with it." Lettunich and Sam were as free to bid on that land as anyone else.[17]

The hot bidding at the sheriff's auction soon proved Martin's skill as an appraiser. The happy new partners got the farm for $85 an acre.[18] It soon clouded Sam's pleasure, however, that a wide rumor questioned the way he and Martin had acquired it. Adolph Schwartz mentioned the rumor to Sam. "My family has said that you foreclosed on that farm. They say that's the way you got it personally."

Sam shook his head, then explained the Federal Land Bank's role in the sale. With that, Schwartz expressed his relief. "Oh, I understand now."[19]

In late December 1933 Sam's friend Eloy Vallina made a significant rise as a financier by opening his new Banco Comercial in Chihuahua. When Eloy soon realized, however, that his major clients wanted to borrow far larger sums than he could handle, he proposed that Sam and he form their own lending agency. The plan would involve Sam's long experience in borrowing "low" from Fred Florence and lending "high" to clients in Mexico.

In the resulting partnership, there were risks to be sure, but Eloy was a well placed Mexican citizen and a business man fully accredited under Mexican law. To Sam the risks were "reasonable." On that footing, the Vallina/Young combination was soon reaping rich profits. Later, when somebody asked Sam if he enjoyed his lucrative sideline, he cried, "Yes, sir!" That game was like dominoes. "With Eloy, I learned to play the double sixes the right way."[20]

At year's end, the Bank's 1933 Statement of Condition reflected, at least in part, the turnaround in the national economy that FDR had helped bring about. Undivided profits stood at $54,342; assets stood at $5,260,372; deposits stood at an all-time high, $4,450,451.

In 1934, when eighteen-year-old James Onick signed on as a runner, a bright new face appeared among the Bank's twenty-eight other employees at forty-eight dollars a month.[21] Literally coming in on the ground floor (the basement mail room), Onick soon found himself in full charge on "bank statement nights."[22] To get out those statements, Jim and two porters, Harry Matthews and Sam Harris, developed a streamlined routine: Onick stuffing the envelopes; Harris spreading them out in a row — flaps facing up — then "licking" those flaps with one swipe of a sponge; Matthews weighing each statement to figure its postage, then feeding the lot through the postage machine. Each time, with Harris's rich bass voice singing the blues and spirituals, by 3 A.M. they loaded the statements onto a dolly and pushed it up Stanton Street to the post office. The postage averaged $200 a month.

Sam now took a Mexico jaunt with Kayser and Frost into the state of Sonora, the domain of the late Colonel William Cornell Greene. Driving south to Cananea, headquarters of Colonel Greene's mining empire, Tif Frost practiced his marksmanship from a moving automobile: shooting birds off the fence posts. Each time he scored, Paul screeched the car to a halt, and the party celebrated that shot with a "shot" from Tif's jug.[23] But celebrating aside, that trip was a fact-finding survey, and Sam came home convinced more strongly than ever that Mexico was a money field ready for harvest.

When Martin and he began turning a profit on their cotton farm, Martin scouted south of the border for places to put their money to work.[24] In due time when their investment in Mexican timber land began paying off, those profits went into more ventures, some on good tips from Eloy. The Mexico Northwestern Railroad that ran westward from Juarez through the mountains then south to Chihuahua was one.

On a matter more personal, Sam grieved along with Conrad Hilton in 1934 when he and his wife Mary divorced. Hilton's financial troubles and his long business absences had created irreconcilable problems. Mary and their three young sons, Nicky, Barron and Eric, remained in El Paso until Hilton arranged for the good of all the parties concerned. Each month, the Bank staff looked forward to a friendly chat with Mary Hilton when she and the boys came in to collect Connie's check for their monthly support.

Sam's 1934 stockholder report was distinctly more cheerful than others of late. The officers had solicited many new commercial loans and new "through the window" accounts. Cotton prices were up. For the Pima variety, growing conditions had been especially favorable; the crop yield in the valley was greater per acre than ever before. Government relief—food, clothing, and shelter for the destitute throughout the nation—had actually saved the livestock industry and many small businesses. Locally, with merchants and manufacturers making small profits again, the Bank's assets stood at $6,787,198; deposits at $5,935,193.[25] On the strength of that bright report, the board voted a grateful reward to their EVP. Henceforth, Sam Young would receive as an annual salary supplement a percentage of the Bank's profits.[26]

Perceiving the choices which that additional income gave him, Sam immediately heeded Courtney Marshall's early advice. A windfall like that was not for spending. Expressing a good deal of faith in himself and his institution, Sam invested it all in El Paso National Bank stock.

As more and more Mexican depositors became important borrowers, Manny Escajeda became more and more Sam's bilingual voice. In this happy aftermath of the Depression, with Escajeda smoothly translating the negotiations, Sam smiled with "the many beautiful cattle accounts" flowing in from across the river.[27]

To encourage that flow, Sam increased his calls on prospective clients on their home turf, always with Manny beside him. Always genial, always clear in his translations, Manny was fully at ease in the subtleties involved when men of differing cultures often expressed themselves mainly in gestures and slight overtones. Yet as Sam often pointed out, Manny was first and foremost a banker, alert to all the specifics in any discussion.

Now, in line with the Bank's outreach beyond El Paso, Sam leased an elegant suite at the Paso del Norte for the convenience of his out-of-town clientele. There, after hours, he and his people could mix business with pleasure, "get a feel for" the financial needs the guests themselves sometimes scarcely perceived.

On the home front, in 1936, six-year-old Sammy looked forward each night to the romps he could have with his dad, when work at the Bank slacked off before bedtime. Sam realized how much he too had enjoyed those romps when Sammy came down with scarlet fever. He lay in bed for three months. Late in the fall when he returned to school, listless and pale from the fever, he found himself the butt of the other boys' pranks on the playground. Too weak to fight back,[28] too dismayed to know how to tell his parents or Grandmother Mimi (his aunts Martha and Jo were married now and established in homes of their own), Sammy carried his problem locked up inside. Sam accepted Sammy's lack of spirit as an unavoidable aftermath of Sammy's long illness, but Sammy knew that at school he was mistreated and abused and he did not know why.[29]

With the country's burgeoning financial recovery, Sam foresaw a long-range success for Hilton's El Paso backers, as he himself bought more and more Hilton stock. At lunch one day with Dossie M. Wiggins, the new president of the Texas College of Mines, he mentioned FDR's conviction that no American needed an income larger than $25,000. "And I firmly agree," Wiggins declared.

With his own salary still only $12,000, Sam found that remark incredible. "Wait a minute, Dossie. Have you any idea how it would feel to have more than $25,000?"

"No," Dossie replied, "and I never expect to."

Sam thought a long moment. "I'm not sure I do either," he said firmly, "but who is to say that *nobody* needs an income larger than $25,000? Who has that right?"

Wiggins did not mince words. "I do. For *me*."

Sam shook his head. "I'm sorry to hear that, Dossie. Connie Hilton is going great guns now. Anybody willing to risk a little cash on him stands to make a real killing. Anybody, just for instance, like you."

Wiggins looked up. "Like me? Like how much cash, just for instance?"

Sam figured quickly. "Oh, maybe $25,000," he grinned.

"Twenty-five thousand!" Wiggins smiled wryly. "You already know I haven't got $25,000. I wouldn't be tempted to buy any such stock if I did."

"You do have it," Sam countered. "I'll lend it to you for practically nothing."

Dossie looked stunned. "I'd have to think about that," he said. The next day Sam's telephone rang. "Sam? Dossie. Were you kidding me yesterday?"

"Kidding you? You just give me the go-ahead and I'll get you that good Hilton stock."

Wiggins gave a low chuckle. "Go ahead. Wish me luck!"[30]

Though Betty continued to deal with her old superstitions, inside her they ticked like an alarm clock. By now it was her long-standing schedule to go for a horseback ride on Stockings, her own saddle horse, every Friday out at the Country Club. Every Friday the Thirteenth, however, gave her the shivers. Nevertheless, at breakfast one morning, she announced to the family, "Today's the Thirteenth and I *know* my old fear is silly, but to prove there really is nothing to this superstition, I'm going out and ride Stockings."[31]

While she was gone, Sammy was playing out in the front yard when a big friendly Airedale brushed against him. Falling, Sammy's forehead struck a metal yard sprinkler. When Sammy yelled, Grandmother Mimi came running, but seeing the blood, she screamed for the nearest neighbor. Together, they gathered him up and rushed him to the doctor. Fourteen stitches later, Sammy was back home and all right.

That afternoon, Betty arrived home from her ride, her old fear conquered and done with. When she saw Sammy, however, her smile faded. "On this Friday the Thirteenth, nothing ever will change my mind," she told the family, as she picked Sammy up.

Early in 1936 two developments indicated the Bank's basic good health: at its January 14 meeting the board voted Sam a salary increase to $15,000,[32] and it settled on plans to expand the Bank's floor space for a larger lobby and more office room. It added as well three new teller cages and, for women shopping downtown, an "appointment room" equipped with easy chairs, tables and writing desks, stationery, and a telephone. It also made available a special "private executives' office" for businessmen's conferences. With that expansion, the Bank now occupied the building's entire ground floor.

Announcing the changes, Sam recognized the ways his bank had altered its scope during its first ten years. Caring for customers all over "our own southwestern territory and northern Mexico," Sam told the *Times*, his deposits now stood at over $6 million. Since such increases called for more personnel and equipment, the improvements enabled the Bank to "serve our customers better and faster, with less congestion and less waiting in the lobby."[33]

His pride in the Bank's rise suffered a serious setback, however, in 1937 when out of the blue he received a note, its words crudely snipped out of a magazine and pasted on a sheet of plain paper. That note threatened to kidnap Little Betty and Sammy unless Sam responded with $50,000 in cash. Immediately, the Lindbergh tragedy of 1932 raced through Sam and Betty's minds. A few days later Sam received a second note demanding even more money. Fearing the worst, he hired a retired Texas Ranger and a retired county sheriff – Mr. Stancil and Harry Moore, Sr. – as bodyguards, driving both children to and from Coldwell School, watching them during recess, standing duty outside their bedrooms each night.[34] One night when Little Betty woke up screaming from a nightmare, she saw Harry Moore and Sam rushing into her room, hand guns at the ready. Though Sammy came to think of Stancil and Moore as "pals," his pals carried sidearms and they stood night-and-day watch for nine months.

In the end, the lost sleep and Sam's two unsuccessful attempts to pay off the kidnapper came to nothing. Sam and the El Paso police never learned who had written the notes: they never learned why, or what that person had gained.[35]

Though the Bank had always employed bilingual staff people, it enhanced its services to its Spanish-speaking clients when it added Jose M. Moreno to the Mexican Department in January 1937. Beginning as a stenographer, writing letters in Spanish and translating the replies into English, Moreno was an advantage both to Manny Escajeda and Sam. Though Sam himself had long known that to function truly effectively in the full community life, he needed to speak the tongue that 60 percent of El Paso now spoke, to learn that tongue, "I needed more time for lessons and practice than I had. That's been my loss, but I'm lucky in finding people like Joe and Manny to handle 'my Spanish for me.'" Watching Joe's skill with details, Sam soon assigned him to tasks requiring responsible judgment. Assistants like these, Sam freely confessed, made it more and more possible now for him to involve himself in civic campaigns and in meetings away from his phone and his desk.

Late in 1937, Conrad Hilton made "the big jump out of the Lone Star State and into San Francisco," as he wrote later, "to me still a jewel among cities."[36] With his credit excellent again, "I could have rested there, but I didn't enjoy resting. I enjoyed buying hotels."[37]

Sam was ill in bed with a fever when Connie called him from California. In San Francisco, the luxurious Sir Francis Drake Hotel (22 stories, 450 rooms, original cost: $4,100,000) could be bought for only $1,500,000.[38] "Sam, I tell you this hotel is a beauty. We can get if for only $275,000 down."

Sam came alert just enough to reply. "Connie, you did well in El Paso, you're doing well in Texas again. But don't you think you ought to move slow? Anyhow, come on home and let's talk it over."[39] Hilton caught the next train.

Back on his feet again, Sam called his Hilton friends and told them what Hilton had said. If the deal with Connie was not sure-fire, Sam explained, "It's superior to anything I have seen for some time."[40] At that meeting, Sam's good word raised $225,000[41] – more than enough to swing Hilton's big purchase.

True to his major commitment, his bank, Sam combined business with pleasure, however, during the summer of 1938 by calling on his correspondent bankers in West Texas and southern New Mexico. To make those trips special, he took young Sam along, partly to let Sammy see what his dad did for a living, partly to give himself a chance to know his son better.

His visits in Van Horne, Sierra Blanca, Carlsbad, Artesia, Deming, Lordsburg and other small towns had always been more than friendly fence-mending, but now, driving the narrow rough roads in his Nash, he told Sammy about his own childhood, about the time he left the lid off the coffee barrel and a new litter of kittens surprised him and Charlie the next morning. While Sam talked business over coffee or out in the field, Sammy sat mum but alert to the ways his dad garnered ideas or matched stories with men he so obviously liked.[42]

Another business relationship began ripening into a friendship in 1938 when a small San Antonio contractor came in to open a checking account. H. B. "Pat" Zachry was building stock tanks on ranches scattered over West Texas, he told Sam. The visitor's obvious confidence in his own ability struck Sam immediately, but a few weeks later, Zachry dropped in again, gravely subdued. "I don't mind telling you this, Mr. Young, I need serious help."

With his resources spread thin and his cash flow exhausted, he was fearful about meeting his payroll the next week. Sam waited while Zachry gathered his thoughts. "The fact is" – Zachry finally shrugged – "now please don't ask me for my financial statement because if you saw it, you'd turn me down."

Knowing from other reports that Zachry's project was sound, Sam answered him straight. "Pat, you're going to complete that job at a profit. Don't worry, I'm happy to lend you the money, even without your figures."

Beaming, Zachry sprang to his feet. "Hooray!" he cried, grabbing Sam's hand. "Success is in sight!"[43]

Success for Conrad Hilton took another upswing in 1939 when he learned he could buy, for a song plus some small cash, the once lavish Breakers Hotel in Long Beach, California. The building had been a pigeon roost ever since 1933 when an earthquake twisted it askew on its foundations, but Hilton sensed another "sure thing," he told Sam. "Long Beach is riding an oil boom, but it hasn't a single decent hotel. Come on out. Help me size up this wreck."

Touring the building, Sam quickly learned that once it was stabilized and restored, the whole cost would come to less than $550,000.[44] Back home, Sam once again alerted his Hilton backers. Once again they came through with the cash, and Sam bought a good block of stock for himself.[45]

Fully restored within a few months and graced now with a sumptuous cocktail lounge facing the ocean, the Breakers made money from the first day. "In no time at all, the place was so crowded you couldn't elbow your way into the bar," Sam told his El Paso people.[46]

In a similar way, Sam became a special pillar of strength for his minister, Paul N. Poling, at the First Presbyterian Church. When the church roof leaked and the pipes needed replacing, Sam led the fund drives to cover the cost. When the congregation outgrew its Sunday school space, Sam campaigned for the funds to build a three-story annex. Briefly, he served on the church's music committee, till he butted heads with his friend Jimmy Dick, Sr. "Sam Young, you don't know a thing about music."[47]

"Which is true," Sam had to confess.

Betty took charge the summer of 1940 when Sammy's health once again caused his parents serious worry. After a tonsilectomy and a recent appendectomy, Sammy at ten was still sickly. "You can't get away from your work, Sam. I know that. But I want to take him to California, settle down in an apartment with a good swimming pool, and teach the boy once and for all to take care of himself. I mean, to begin with, that he learn how to swim." Cowed by his schoolmates, unsure of his own capacities, Sammy seemed on too many occasions a little boy content to stay small.

That summer in Santa Monica, Sammy conquered his fear of the water. By fall, he was swimming a mile and feeling "like a new man." When he got back to El Paso, the neighborhood boys rushed him and started pulling their old bullying tricks. But this time, Sammy put up his fists. They all proceeded to the back alley, Sammy recalled later, "and we went the whole route. I beat the dog out of everybody in the neighborhood. What's more, my dog Friskie bit their dog. That happy day changed my life."[48]

Sam and Betty never knew of that fight, but seeing Sammy take charge of himself lifted their spirits.

10

WARFARE AND BUSINESS

THOUGH THE BANK's 1940 deposits stood at $14,633,964, the growth in accounts, the growth in the crowds that flocked in on paydays did cause problems. In spite of Sam's intention that no customer need ever stand waiting, sometimes the tellers had to play the game mostly by ear. One busy day, a savings teller summoned Hilliard Bryan. "A man has fainted at my window. Will you please get him out of the line so I can wait on my customers?"[1]

Other acts of God brought other crises. Early in 1941 when an ice storm glazed all the streets, only Sam and Hilliard and one staff member managed to show up at work. As one team, they got the doors open on time, but the fact that almost no customers could make their way into town left Sam and his aides with little to do.[2]

By May, however, Sam was writing good reports home to Woodville. Down at the farm, "we have the most perfect stand of cotton we've had in many seasons. If the worms leave us alone, we might make a little money."[3] Sam was less happy about Little Betty's outcries one afternoon at the farm while she was riding her new Arabian horse. The stable hand had warned her, "You ought to put a better bit on him, one with a rowel under the tongue. When you mean business, that'll get his attention." Refusing to use "anything so cruel," Little Betty was trotting happily alongside an irrigation ditch when Sam and his farm neighbor, Leo Schuster, drove up. Sam tapped his horn.

Immediately, the Arabian was dashing away in a panic. For more than a mile, Little Betty tried to control him. When the horse finally calmed down, she rode him slowly back to the barn, furious at the horse, even more angry at Sam. His face white, Sam helped her dismount; they made the drive back to town in silence. At home, neither mentioned Little Betty's wild ride.[4]

It was only a short time until Sam had vastly more urgent concerns. Hitler's march into Poland and Czechoslovakia in 1939 had brought war to more than just Central Europe. Daily, the war clouds beyond Europe grew more ominous.

At the Bank normal routine had to go on, but it was not at all "business as usual." Defense Savings Bonds had been selling briskly since May 1941, but nobody could silence his fears that the word "defense" in the name of those bonds predicted perils. Drastic changes were already at work in the Bank staff. As Frank Harriss and Manny Escajeda and other male personnel left for military training, females became increasingly vital in the Bank's operations. Wives of husbands in uniform were especially welcome as replacement tellers, though troop movements into and out of El Paso often meant that such women quickly resigned to move on with their men. Much to Sam's annoyance, one lady left even before she balanced her cash.[5]

In the bond department, a new employee broke down when the work flow grew too "confusing." "I told you I only came here to be with my husband," she sobbed to an officer, "and that I did not want any responsibility."[6]

Nevertheless, the skill and dependability of most of these women Sam and his officers quickly recognized. As they adapted themselves to the workplace, mothers with school-age children especially appreciated Sam's flexibility. "You can leave for the day," he told them, "as soon as you get your work done."[7]

Even with war threatening, there were smiles between Sam and his innkeeper friend in January 1941 when Sam saw fit to credit Hilton's account with $29.17. Getting that rebate, Connie wrote, was "a real achievement, because once *you* get interest it is hard to get it away from you." In April, Hilton also had words about his banker's golf game. The last time he and Hilton and the Rev. Paul Poling had played together, Sam's cussing "could have been heard all over the golf course." In a soft spot with no turf, "you attempted to hit one over the trap," but the ball went only six inches: "whereupon you promptly let out a scorcher!" Poling, of course, never said anything "because you are one of his good parishioners, good that is, on Sunday while you are praying, but on other days you do cuss. Regards, C. N. Hilton."[8]

Such moments were wholly forgotten on December 7, 1941 – FDR's "day that shall live in infamy" – when Dorrance Roderick's *Times* put out four extra editions. Their headlines told the dread news. "Japan Attacks U.S.; Army Vessel Sunk: Manila, Honolulu Hit." "Japan Declares War on U.S. and Britain." "Congress to Receive FDR Message on Jap Attacks Against U.S."[19]

The next day, Roosevelt's declaration of war against Japan brought back in Sam's memory the old fears that had clutched him in 1917. "WAR! Nation Rallies to Fight Back Attack," read the *El Paso Times* banner headline.[10] Roderick's editorial the day after that tried to smooth the waters. "Winning of the war will be of paramount importance. But at the same time, we must be calm about it and go about our daily duties as usual," he wrote. "The Southwestern Sun Carnival will be held just the same. The Ysleta Indians will play Wichita Falls in the quarter finals of the state high school football championship next Saturday. All of us must work, eat, and sleep. Our children must attend school."[11]

Within the next few months, 53,000 troops were in training at Fort Bliss, and like every other El Pasoan, Sam was feeling the changes December 7 had brought. "We are all well here," he wrote Fanny and Charlie in February 1942, enjoying life within "the limitations imposed on everyone by wartime conditions." At twenty cents a pound, his 1941 cotton crop had brought him his best profits in at least twelve years. The Bank's rapid growth, however, was a mixed blessing. "The problem of finding efficient help to take over the ever-increasing work and to replace the older employees called to military service is exacting most of my time and attention these days."[12]

Banks in bigger places felt the same shortage. Three different times the First National in Dallas tendered Sam offers. "Be our president, Sam. Start whenever you like." But much as he appreciated their interest, Sam calmly replied that in El Paso, "I don't have any trouble controlling my stockholders." The First National's people, on the other hand, "might not like my attitude. Especially if I tried to run the bank my own way, and I would."[13]

For Betty and Sam the war came especially close when it soon included a female member of "the family." Down in Houston, Governor was holding the fort, but Oveta had just become FDR's Chief of the Women's Section of the U.S. War Department.[14] On that note, Sam read his newspaper each morning now, newly alert to whatever names in whatever big stories might leap to his pained attention.

Out of the blue one morning, a telephone call put Sam in touch again with an old family name he had come to respect. "Mr. Young," said the caller, "I'm Robert O. Anderson. I believe you know my dad, Hugo Anderson, with the First National Bank in Chicago."

"I certainly do," Sam told him. "Together, we tried to avoid some big rancher foreclosures back in 1924 in Carlsbad."

"Well, Mr. Young, my brother Don and I are going into the oil business in Artesia, New Mexico, and my father suggested I call and tell you, in case I should ever need any banking service out your way."

Sam was dismayed to learn that the Anderson brothers had had no experience at all in such a business, "but," he told Robert, "I certainly do congratulate you on your courage."[15]

In happy interludes from the pressures of work, writing personal letters to Woodville, Sam kept the grandparents posted about their El Paso family: "This is Sister's senior year in high school and she feels somewhat of a privileged character." As for Sammy, "Sonny goes fortnightly to dancing school and all the little girls his age wear their evening dresses, so he feels that he is taking his place along with the young men nowadays."[16] Lighthearted reports, however, filled only a small part of his pages. "This war is a terrible thing. I am afraid we will lose all the battles and then spend years in trying to regain the lost territory."

With his salary now $24,000,[17] and with his cotton fields about ready to plant, he wrote home in March that it would probably "take about all I can collect to pay my income tax." But money "should be the least of our troubles until the war is won. If it takes all we have or can get to pay the government's bill, we should be very glad to do it."

Lighter concerns hit Sam on the morning of April 15, when Conrad Hilton phoned him from Santa Fe, New Mexico. "I want to tell you what I've done," said Connie.

Quickly Sam asked, "Well, what? Something terrible?"

"We were out dancing," Connie replied, "and I had a few drinks, so we got married last night."

"What do you mean 'we got married.' Who'd you marry?"

"Zsa Zsa."

It took Sam a long moment to register the news that Connie had married the famous Zsa Zsa Gabor, Hollywood's much-married Hungarian. When he did find his breath, he could only offer a warning. At age fifty-four, Connie had just taken a twenty-five-year-old for his wife. "Connie, you're gonna pay through the nose."[18]

Yet on the swing of another big business deal, Connie soon called from Los Angeles. "The Town House out here on Wilshire Boulevard. Do you want in? Down pay is only $875,000." After putting in a small sum himself, Sam helped swing the C. M. Harveys into buying some stock.[19]

To ease his wartime tensions, Sam resorted more and more often now to the golf course. As the chance opened, so did some of his staff. One morning, an idea hatched in their minds when Jimmy Onick, now a junior officer, spread the word to three others that "Big Storm" was taking the noon train to Dallas. By one o'clock they were driving out Mesa Street for the Country Club when a slow passenger train blocked the traffic.

Onick and his friends were waving goodbye to the faces glued to the train windows when the observation deck came slowly along, with Sam leaning against the railing. Suddenly, all four of his men needed to scramble for something they must have mislaid on the car floor.[20]

Conrad Hilton had another "sure thing" on his mind in November 1942, "if," he wrote Sam, "you can bring your El Paso people along." The bonds Connie owned on the Stevens Hotel in Chicago, the world's largest, were worth big money, provided the U. S. goverment wanted to buy them at $110 per share. Immediately, Sam wrote Connie that he might like to purchase some of those bonds himself.[21] By December, however, after Sam had decided not to take part, Connie wrote him sad news. "The government has bought at $110 – so I made a nice cool quarter-million. Next time, you stay with me on these deals."[22]

Sadder but fully committed to his job in El Paso, Sam presented his current views to his board regarding the Bank's state of affairs so soon after Pearl Harbor: a rise in deposits from $17,000,000 to $28,000,000, more than 3,000 new accounts, and an increase in employees by 30 percent to a total of 88. With a lesser number of active officers, Sam recommended that "certain promotions be made with added responsibilities to all officers to meet the existing circumstances."[23]

The "existing circumstances" improved greatly just then when Gus Bianche joined on as Assistant Trust Officer. Gus's skill in drafting Sam's weightier letters, his stockholder reports, and testimonials for use in the Bank's minutes soon established him as one of Sam's "cadre" men able to do many tasks "yesterday, if not the day before that."

That month, however, a thank-you letter Sam penned himself came straight from the heart. "Dear Mama," he wrote, "Your birthday remembrance came this morning and I loved your thinking of me. I guess you have me just about as much on your mind now as you did forty-six years ago, but I had to become a parent to realize the ties children always have on our heartstrings. Old or young, married or single, I don't suppose it makes a lot of difference."[24]

Though Sam's salary was up now to $25,000, that fact hardly lightened his wartime burdens at work. "We are having a terrible time with employees in the Bank, and it is taxing my nerves to the limit of endurance to look after this job," he wrote Fanny in March. "I sometimes wish I could go to the farm and stay and never sit at another bank desk as long as I live. One of these days I will make up my mind to do that very thing, I hope."[25] Yet the farm situation was hardly better. "Paying twice as much as last year, we can't get enough workers at that. But, thank God, the war looks a little better today. Our boys did a fine job in cleaning out the Jap convoy, and England and America are doing splendidly in bombing the stuffings out of Germany."[26]

Over the long run, however, the farm had prospered so well, its profits had fitted so neatly into Sam's larger plans, that he was ready for action when Martin Lettunich, as an appraiser, testified in a court case involving a neighboring farm. On the stand, Martin was asked the worth of that farm. "About $250 an acre," said Lettunich.

The prosecuting attorney leaped to his feet. "It's not about to be worth that much. Would *you* pay that much for it?"

Lettunich shot back. "Yes, I would. And I will."

Released from the courtroom, Martin rushed to a phone. "Sam, here's what I've done." He spelled out the details. "So, do you want it with me?" Sam's nose for a bargain gave him the lightning quick answer.[27]

With that additional farm space to "play with," Sam sketched out his big plans. To Little Betty, now a freshman at Hollins College in Virginia, he wrote, "You and Sonny have long wanted a farm house where we could all go for weekends and summer vacations, and now Sonny is planning a swimming pool, chicken coops, stables and saddle horses, and what not with a lot of enthusiasm."[28]

But late in August Sam added his profound grief to that of his family when Charles Acton Young, the "Papa" whom he had not understood or ever felt really close to, died at age eighty-two in Woodville. Charlie had never set the woods on fire as a business man – at his death his estate totalled only $4,000 – or stood particulary tall as a church pillar. Yet after the funeral, Sam felt as if he "had been living through events," he wrote Margaret, "that haven't actually happened. Mama is one of the bravest little women I have ever known and it is just marvelous how her great faith supports her."[29]

Soon after the funeral, in an effort to ease Fanny's grief, Sam bought his mother a little house with big trees and a pond about a mile out of Woodville. His brother Cooper agreed to manage it.[30]

Griefs notwithstanding, Sam took time at his desk, piled high though it was now as too much paper work often brought him back to the Bank till midnight, to keep Captain Dorrance Roderick informed with news from home. With Roderick in action in Germany, it was "pretty lonesome" in the neighborhood, he wrote, without the generals and the captains around. "Sorry you can't get home for your usual birthday celebration, but we shall make up for it by using bigger and better jiggers around New Year's." In the meantime, "the old boat is rocking along as usual around the Morning Crimes (Roderick's *El Paso Times*) and KROD, (Roderick's radio station)."[31]

Wartime, however, only improved Conrad Hilton's own circumstances. In March 1943 Hilton and his backers added the Roosevelt Hotel in New York to the chain. By October he and his backers, including Sam's regular group, plus a highly enthusiastic contingent now from around the nation, had bought the fabled Plaza Hotel in New York.[32] To buy that additional hotel, Connie had made a good case with his people. The old dowager's "paint was peeling," her marble was dull, her tapestries faded, but her many permanent residents ("the cream of New York society") paid as much as $27,500 annual rent because they loved her just as she was. The final cost, including renovations: $6 million,[33] a bargain that Sam and his group firmly approved.

By now, Connie's escapades were almost a diversion in Sam's sober bank duties, especially when he reflected about his long-time working

El Paso National's co-founders,
C. M. Harvey (above) and Sam, about 1944.

relationship with C. M. Harvey. Most days Harvey still sat at his desk in the lobby, and Sam was still convinced that Harvey's genial presence there served an advantage. "Everybody knows Mr. Harvey. It helps us all for people to know that a solid citizen like him is with us." By just being there, Harvey was earning his token annual salary, $8,000 now, as a public relations man.[34] By late 1943, however, Sam knew that for all of Harvey's low-keyed worth as "president," Sam's own title, "executive vice president," was misleading to the public and distinctly frustrating to him. Making out-of-town calls, pursuing national accounts, Sam often ran headlong into some doubt on the face of the prospective client.

"Your business card here, Mr. Young, indicates that you are" — there came a slight pause — "the executive vice president of your institution. Unfortunately, we've never met your president himself, Mr. Young. Why is that?"

"Oh, well, C. M. Harvey," Sam had to explain, "has many broad interests, and he's happy enough to leave me in full control at our place."

Again came a pause. "Well, we'll certainly consider you people if we decide to make a change in our situation. Nice talking to you."

Sam understood fully the tone of those hesitations. By late 1943, his title at the Bank was especially irksome when the nation itself tended to think these days of a man's "name, rank, and serial number" as an accurate indication of that man's real identity.

"I know you want to hang on to your title," he explained to Harvey one morning, but after nineteen years, he pointed out, the Bank had outgrown it. "The people I meet don't understand how I can speak for the Bank, when I don't have the appropriate rank. Mr. Harvey, I need a promotion."[35]

For a moment, Harvey looked surprised; then slowly he nodded. At the board meeting on January 12, 1944, he proposed a motion to create himself "chairman of the board of directors." As such, he would preside at all director's meetings: he would advise with the Bank's officers concerning all matters affecting its growth, development and welfare. Harvey paused, then explained his larger intention. "Ever since Mr. Young and I organized the El Paso National Bank together in 1925," it had enjoyed "a healthy and steady growth under the capable and enthusiastic leadership of Sam D. Young."[36] For those reasons, Harvey now wished "to elevate Sam D. Young to the office of president."[37]

The Bank's Statement of Condition on December 31, 1943, when looked at alongside the little Bank's status in the beginning, plainly supported that motion:[38]

Loans and discounts:	$844,822 (up by $369,112)
Capital stock:	300,000 (up by $100,000)
Surplus:	700,000 (up by $680,000)
Undivided profits:	170,977 (up from zero)
Deposits:	$33,749,688 (up by $32,591,160)

When the board – Harvey himself, Paul Harvey, W. M. Banner, John C. Hayes, Thornton Hardie, F. B. Fletcher, and H. A. Jacobs – voted unanimously for that motion, Sam at last held the flag of the bank that, for all practical purposes, had always been "his." His new salary: $26,500.

A day or so later, Sam wrote Little Betty at Hollins. "Now that I'm president of the Bank, Sonny says I'm going to be hard to get along with. Anyway," he added, "I'm proud and that's that."[39]

A V-letter from "somewhere in England" soon brought further appropriate sentiments. Dorrance Roderick had just heard "that you are prexy of the bank. Congratulations! It should have been done long ago."[40]

11

THE MEN WHO BOUGHT THE WALDORF

OFFICIALLY PRESIDENT NOW, Sam reaffirmed his long-standing policy as a bank head. The attitude "largely responsible for our success," read his statement to the whole staff, was "Friendliness." That being the case, all members of the Bank team should look upon their customers "with a smile and a gladness in your eyes." And regardless of how rude a customer might be, "never show your temper (let me do that for us all)." As Harvey and he had said from the start, "The Golden Rule is best. It pays big dividends in happiness and pleasant living."[1] As proof of the continuing worth of that policy, the Bank's year-end report for 1944 noted that assets were up to $43,591,896. Deposits for the year stood at $42,131,623.

Now, though his position had changed, Harvey dedicated himself anew to the role he had always played best: recruiting new accounts for the Bank. One evening in January 1944 Wade Hartrick, a freshly recruited faculty member of the Texas College of Mines, was bedding down in the upper berth of a Pullman when he suddenly needed a safe place to stow his wallet. "There wasn't much money in it," Wade recalled later, "but I couldn't afford to lose what there was. And I certainly didn't want to show up in El Paso, ready for my first real job, empty-handed." Hiding his wallet in his shoe, the young professor slipped it under the blanket and dropped off to sleep.

The next morning, a voice from the lower berth called up. "Say up there, would you be a Wade Hartrick?"

"Why, yes, I am."

"Well," said the voice, "I've got your wallet down here. In the night, I guess it slipped through the crack."

When the voice turned out to be C. M. Harvey's, a little face-to-face conversation ensued. The Harveys were en route home from visiting their son Phil in the Air Force in San Antonio. "And, you sir," Harvey wanted to know, "where are you headed?"

When Wade told them "El Paso," Harvey gripped his hand. "Young man, let me invite you to do your bank business with us." He gave Hartrick his card.

On the basis of that friendly welcome to his new "home town," Hartrick did all his banking at the El Paso National. "Every time I come into the bank, if Mr. Harvey is there at his desk, he hails me. I really enjoy doing business like that," he liked to tell people.[2]

If friendly man-to-man talks had been a bank president's sole role, Sam would have relished it more. Writing Dorrance in Germany, Sam confessed that though he and his family were a thousand steps removed from the war's actual dangers, he had a slight feel of some of the war's tension. "The demands on the few of us business boys who were too old for the war is pretty great," keeping the business community intact, retaining an adequate staff, trying to anticipate each day's needs as a part of some trend.

Yet there was a bright side to the news. Along with Governor down in Houston, Sam and Betty were elated to hear that Oveta had safely landed in Washington after a flying mission through North African and European war zones. "Colonel Hobby is certainly working at her job," Sam wrote Little Betty, "and she seems to be doing it splendidly. She deserves a lot of credit for her initiative and pluck."[3]

And Little Betty herself created happy excitement for the family when she and Ensign Robert T. Hoover, Jr., son of Sam's early friend in El Paso, announced their engagement. Their wedding on July 1, 1944, at the First Presbyterian Church was the grandest pageant Sam himself had ever participated in. He passed Little Betty's hand into Bob's at the altar, then took his seat beside Betty. Twenty-three years before, a similar ceremony had focused on Betty. Since then, the years had been good and fulfilling, but never more so than at this moment.

Within a few days after the wedding reception at the family house, Bob resumed his submarine duty in the Pacific. Three months later, the new couple established a home base in New London, Connecticut.

Later that summer, other emotions weighed heavily on Sam. One related to his concern for Dorrance, now en route to Berlin amidst heavy gunfire. "All the gang in the Bank," including Mr. Harvey, Jake, and Sheley, wished to be remembered to him, he wrote Roderick, but "from me you get my prayers that the Lord will bless you and keep you safe."[4] Perhaps, when "you have grown older, you will find glory in telling the tale to your grandchildren and maybe" – once Roderick was safely back at his *El Paso Times* – also telling the voters what they needed to know.

Saying that, Sam was reflecting on the turn American politics had taken during FDR's eleven years in the White House. As a straight Democrat in the beginning, Sam had voted for Roosevelt, but now his "New Deal" had established too many government "handouts" for entirely too many people. Perhaps Roderick could wake up the voters "if the New Dealers are not entirely overcome by us 'old liners' meantime. You know the real Democrats are speaking up against the New Dealers now and maybe their voices will be heard somewhat, I hope."

Long thoughts were still on his mind in November when Sam wrote his new son-in-law, "If I were just twenty-one," he would try "not to worry" so much. Over the years, he had seen "the disaster" that worry can bring to mankind. Real wisdom had taught him to "do the best possible under the circumstances and let worry go by the wayside." In all things, a person should trust his own integrity and especially "trust to the Lord to guide him safely through those situations beyond his control."[5]

In December, in a similar letter to Fanny, Sam was equally clear about his role as a parent. Sammy and he were going bird hunting the next morning because "he likes to shoot and urges me every bird season to go with him as often as I can. I am not much of a hunter. Would prefer to have my comforts; however, I recall when I was his age that nothing gave me a greater thrill than a hunting or fishing trip" with Buddy Sam, or a young pal or two in Woodville.[6]

Throughout the spring of 1945, Sam kept his letters going to Dorrance in Germany. "We have been expecting momentarily to hear officially that VE day has arrived." But the more likely possibility, he feared, was that some of our boys would "have to detour by way of Japan" on their way home.[7] Yet amidst the good signs of progress in Europe and the Far East, Sam found himself depressed at news of FDR's sudden death. However misguided Roosevelt had been in his domestic policies, Sam noted, undoubtedly President Harry Truman "will make a great president, too. Every move he has made so far seems to have won approval."

At the Bank all signs were bright in June 1945 – the Bank's twentieth anniversary – when Sam and his directors broadened the Bank's lending capacity. By a sale of new shares – as usual Sam bought a sizable block for himself and for Betty – plus a transfer from surplus, the board enlarged its capital to $500,000. A soundly healthy advance, ran the consensus around the table, from the Bank's little $200,000 beginning.[8]

On that note, a called meeting of the board on June 29, 1945, spread on the minutes its pride in the Bank's two decades. On its long ago opening day, total deposits were $1,226,719. Now, on June 19, 1945, its total deposits were $43,712,733.17. "Of the officers, directors and employees who were with this institution at its birth," only C. M. Harvey, Sam D. Young, and John C. Hayes remained. Though "the remarkable success of this bank is due to the energy, intelligence, and characters of many individuals who have served with these three men through the years," the list of their names would be too long to include "within the limits of this resolution." John C. Hayes had been "loyal and cooperative throughout the lean years" and he remained conservative still "during the more prosperous years." While Harvey had furnished the bulk of the capital needed for founding the Bank, "his conservative judgment, his sound financial condition and his integrity of character" had also furnished an especially solid foundation for the institution.

True to Harvey's first suggestion, every meeting of the stockholders, the directors, and the discount committee since 1925 had opened with prayer. As for Sam, the minutes continued, the Bank's success had been largely due to "his vision, energy, honesty and executive ability." At age forty-eight, he was still energetic; and under his guidance "this institution will, beyond question, become the leading bank in the Southwest."[9]

To celebrate its good health, the Bank now bought the entire Two Republics Building in July 1945 for $425,000.[10] Likewise that year, it bought its first company car; no longer were Sam and his officers forced, on purely bank business, to use their personal automobiles.[11]

And further celebration occurred in August 22, 1945, when Betty and Sam's first grandchild, Robert T. Hoover III, was born.

During the Depression, Sam had duly considered Charles N. Bassett's idea that his State and Sam's El Paso National should merge, rather than face disaster apart. While Bassett's notion was clear, no hard feelings had resulted when Sam declined to go along. Since then both banks had waxed strong as healthy competitors, but by now, long after the griefs of the thirties, Sam and the State's highly capable CEO, George C. Matkin, found no common ground for cooperation. The fierce rivalry between the two bankers was no community secret. "If you did business with one," said one observer, "you better not let the other know about it. If you went to a party where both groups were present, 'a Mason-Dixon line' right down the middle set them apart."[12]

Nevertheless, Sam found himself in Matkin's office one morning, discussing a civic matter involving both banks. When the problem at hand created deep disagreement between them, Sam did not budge from his stand: neither did Matkin. Glaring, Matkin rose to his feet. "If you're going to take that attitude, you don't ever need to come back to this office!"

Sam was equally brief. "The hell with you then." He snatched up his papers. "I don't give a damn if I never see you again."[13]

For Sam, it was always more pleasant working with Hilton. After buying the Plaza Hotel in New York, there seemed to be no stopping Connie Hilton's expansion, though when he bought the gigantic Stevens Hotel in Chicago, it had taken all of Connie and Sam's financial acumen. Celebrating the victory, Connie now proposed a big change for Sam. "Come on in with me, Sam. Be my partner. I need your clear judgment. You could make more money with me than you ever can with your bank."

Sam chuckled. "I think I could too" – he paused – "but you might go broke again. *Then* who would you come to?"[14]

Within weeks, Connie was again on the phone to El Paso. "Sam, I can get the Palmer House too, if I get the right people in with me."

"The Palmer House too!" Sam objected. "Connie, with the Stevens Hotel, you've got 2,200 hotel rooms in Chicago already. Why compete with yourself?"

Hilton brushed that detail aside. "I know, I know. But the Palmer House is so well known, and it's a great hotel in a great location. Probably the best hotel location in the world. I really want it."[15]

When Sam still objected, Hilton stood firm. "Now, you look here, Sam. Do I come down there and tell you how to run your bargain counter?" From his many backers now from around the nation, "I've got all the money I need, so I was just letting you in on it. Do you want in, or don't you? I'm not going to beg you."[16]

Facing enthusiasm like that, Sam's Texas people put in $990,000, one third of the Palmer House down payment. Connie's new ally Henry Crown, the Chicago real estate giant, came in for $1 million. Later, when the Palmer House proved to be one of Hilton's best properties, Connie explained his including his friends in his games. "I like to see everybody get a little rich."[17] For Sam, the pleasure was mutual, especially when the El Paso National soon became the Hilton chain's major financial depository.

Like all Americans, Sam had been hoping that with VE Day, the end of the war in Europe in May 1945, Victory Day in Japan would soon follow. Around five o'clock the morning of July 16, that thought was high on his mind when, stepping outside for his newspaper, he saw the dawn's early gray light flash brilliant white. Dismayed by that flash, awed by its silence, Sam stared at the sky, then peered around for someone who might have seen the same thing. Nobody else was stirring.

Back indoors, Sam tried to tell Betty about that strange flash, but he could not guess what had caused it. Nearly three weeks passed before the nation itself knew that that flash had signalled a new kind of warfare; a new kind of bomb had been tested that morning north of Alamogordo, New Mexico, more than a hundred miles north of El Paso.

On August 14, 1945, by the time two of those atomic bombs had caused thousands of deaths in Hiroshima and Nagasaki, Japan laid down its arms. There were cheers and tears and glad cries throughout the Bank that VJ Day had come at last. That night, San Jacinto Plaza was awash with crowds shouting and hugging each other, with children and grownups alike ripping paper to shreds and throwing that "confetti" high overhead. "JAPS QUIT!" shouted the *Times* banner headline the next morning.[18] Sam himself kept his composure, but the end of this war brought memories of the end of "his" war in 1918. Once again, peace had come and once again bloody wounds would in time heal to white scars. At bedtime, Sam remembered Fanny's old admonition and prayed on his knees.

Warfare had left Sam and his family unscathed, but Sammy at age sixteen was ready for action in high school football. Betty was so opposed to Sammy's "having anything to do with a sport so rough and dangerous" that she stayed away from his games most of the season, but when Sam finally persuaded her to attend one game with him, she sat clutching Sam's hand – eyes glued on the field. Each time a pile-up occurred, Betty shot to her feet. "Is it Sammy?" she cried. "Oh, Sam, is it Sammy?"[19]

Later that season, Sam was out of town when Sammy himself persuaded his mother and Grandmother Mimi to attend the final game of the year. All had gone well, they were watching intently when they saw Sammy knocked to the ground. Helpless, they watched him lie writhing, then saw him carried away on a stretcher. "It was only a simple knee injury," Sammy said later, "but it must have been terrible for them."[20]

What neither Sam nor Betty had guessed, Sam and his friend Joe Rector, Jr. were working after school and on Saturdays at the El Paso airport, washing down planes and swabbing out hangars to pay for their flying lessons. Sammy had only recently soloed when his instructor received an order to deliver a new plane to the Y Canyon Ranch in western New Mexico. Bill Mueller would be delivering the plane. Would Sammy like to fly along behind Bill to bring him back home? "You could rack up some good flying time," Mueller suggested. "All you'd have to do is keep me in sight."

When the two planes took off, the weather was clear, but they had hardly rounded west of the Franklins when Sammy saw dark skies ahead. In minutes they were into a snow storm. He had had no navigational training; he had no clue to Bill's course. And now, in the head winds, he had lost all sight of Bill, and his gas was going too quickly.

Through a small hole in the weather below, Sammy did spot a ranch house and a landing strip forking off a dirt road. If this was the Y Canyon Ranch, well and good; if not, he could land and get information. Landing on the strip, he left his engine running (restarting it would have required a helper). He dashed to the ranch house, but nobody was home. To lift off again, he had to taxi all the way down to the road. Gunning the plane, he barely got up in time to clear the ranch house.

Flying through snow, he touched down again when he spotted a truck on the road. "That driver came up to me, looking at me like I'd just lost my mind, especially when I asked which way was the Y Canyon Ranch."

"That way, I think," the driver said vaguely, "about fifty miles."

Aloft again, Sammy could see nothing but snow, though he kept his eyes trained on the ground, hoping to get some kind of sign. At that moment, though the sun had already gone down, he got a clear flash of light. "Nothing could have caused that bright flash," he recalled later, "But I did see it."

Circling down toward the light, he saw it had come from the wing of Bill's plane. He made a pass to find the landing strip and landed. "Just as I made my last turn and started taxiing back, my engine died. Out of gas."

Coffee cup in his hand, Bill Mueller came running. "My god, Sammy, I thought I'd lost you forever."

Sammy only took a quick sip of the coffee. They gassed up and flew home. "I didn't tell my mother and dad, not till years later."[21]

A smoothly experienced team now, Conrad Hilton and his backers and stockholders organized themselves as the "Hilton Hotels Corporation" on May 29, 1946. With stock listed now on the New York Stock Exchange, and with more hotel rooms at his disposal (over 8,000 now) than anyone else in the world, Connie came up with a novel way to thank Sam for his long years of help. When Sam agreed to serve on the new board, Hilton gave him a special gold-colored wallet card. In his own hand, Connie had written on it, "Sam D. Young is to be my personal guest at any Hilton Hotel."[22]

Sam gladly accepted the card, then, shortly thereafter, tried to be sympathetic when Connie called him about Zsa Zsa. Sam did not press him for details that had led them to divorce, but in time Hilton himself made public the gist of their troubles. "When the settlement was made, it seemed ironic that it was the exact amount I had once raised to buy the Sir Francis Drake." But he did not grudge a penny. "A Gabor could bring much laughter and gaiety into any man's life – if he could afford it," said Connie.[23]

Conrad Hilton, Sam's friend who had a kind of a yen for leasing, buying and building hotels.

At the Bank, the same could be said regarding the good of owning its own company car, "if one could depend on it." One morning John Snyder, Harry Truman's secretary of the treasury, was due to arrive at the El Paso airport, then visit the Bank as Sam's guest. For the drive out to meet Snyder, Sam had dispatched Joe Moreno to the Bank parking lot to pick up the Bank's pink Cadillac. With the time already short, Moreno leaped into the seat, turned the key, and pumped the gas pedal. Nothing happened. He tried again, no response. Frantic, he rushed to a phone. "Mr. Young, I can't get it started. I've tried everything." Joe took a deep swallow. "So, Mr. Young, what do I *do?*"

"*Do!* Get it started, that's what!"

Joe tried again, but with minutes ticking away, he flung open the door and leaped out. In despair, he kicked a tire, and the car started immediately. At the airport, as Sam and Snyder shook hands, only Moreno knew his secret skill as a mechanic.[24]

There were times, however, when Sam's temper caused worse reactions. For an hour one afternoon, Sam and Sheley Warnock had butted heads on a matter of policy: they had disagreed point for point. In exasperation, Sam pounded the table. "Dammit, Sheley, who's running this ship?"

Sheley leaped up, then rushed down the hall, and began yanking papers out of his desk. "This ship is leaving!" he shouted at Sam.[25]

Given other stresses not so quickly resolved, the Bank continued its steady growth, but there were frustrating times when Sam had long sober thoughts about the career he had chosen, especially down at the Clint farm. Watching his men planting cotton and chile, he sometimes wanted to go into farming full-time. "We have about 300 yearlings in the feed pens on the two farms and they are looking fine," he wrote Fanny in February, 1947. "Farming and ranching is a much better life than banking, and I hope Sonny will follow that path."[26]

Sonny, however, had other ideas. During his Austin High School commencement on May 22, 1947, Sam and Betty's hearts swelled when the principal introduced Sammy as valedictorian.[27] But when Sammy mentioned in his valedictory speech that he meant to become "a financier," Sam's mouth fell open.[28] That surprise was the first he had heard of any such plan. But writing Fanny after the ceremony, Sam expressed more than mere pride in Sammy's achievement. Better than he himself could have spoken, more calm in front of a crowd than he could ever have been, Sam's letter echoed his old fears about his own graduation. "Sonny's speech before the big crowd was most excellent. I hope he will make further progress in that line."[29]

That fall, progress was uppermost on Sam's mind when he circulated a firm memo expressing his satisfaction in his officers, in "the new ideas developed through the cooperation you are giving one another. This is one of the chief factors, I think, in maintaining the good will our bank has established as the friendliest and most accommodating institution." It behooved all the Bank's officers to "keep up our fences so that this favorable impression may continue to prevail."

Another contributing factor, Sam continued, "comes from the personal calls you are making on customers and prospects." Since calling could do more to create "this good will than all the advertising media we can employ," the chief purpose of Sam's memo was, he explained, "to *urge* you to conscientiously consider 'calling' as one of your *chief duties*." Homer Jacobs and Tom Patterson "may be pressing you for the greatest effort you can put forth."[30]

On the heels of that memo, Sam received a challenge to his own sense of outreach when Katharine (Mrs. Paul) Harvey and a neighborhood Lions Club began urging Sam to organize a new bank at Five Points, a busy crossroads two-and-a-half miles northeast of downtown. Sam had debated taking such a big step. As a separately owned bank with its own board and its own stockholders (Texas law forbade branch banks at that time), such a new institution would undoubtedly benefit its own rapidly growing community, but its first customers would most probably be, he objected to Katharine, "transfers from our parent facility."

Still, with no end in sight to El Paso's expansion in that direction, Sam opened the First State Bank on May 4, 1948, under Hillard Bryan as its managing officer. From the start, the new bank attracted new accounts from the whole neighborhood. In due time, Sam and his partners in the venture took quiet satisfaction in acknowledging Mrs. Harvey and the Lions people as most astute, far-sighted advisors.

For Sam personally, that little bank at Five Points loomed especially interesting its first two summers when, on his own, Sammy got a job there as a trainee. Under Hilliard's firm lead, Sammy learned every function involved in the work day. And incidentally, he found a good place to start learning to be a "financier." In October, leaving for his second year at Stanford University, he already knew he would major in finance economics.

To Grandmother Mimi, college was all well and good, but before Sammy could cut all his home ties, she took him aside. "You're doing just fine and I'm proud of you. But out where you're going, you're bound to be meeting some mighty interesting girls. Quite a few I expect you could live with as your wife." She reached up and patted his cheek. "But I want you to promise me something. Don't ever get married till you meet the one girl you can't live *without*."[31]

Gravely, Sammy nodded down at his grandmother, then grinned. "I expect you'll want a vote about that, when and if the time comes."

As for Sammy's dad, watching his eighteen-year-old son taking his first big step toward maturity, Sam himself knew that the time had come to have faith in the man he was launching.

That same October, as a parent himself, Joe Moreno set off a wave of good feeling throughout the Bank when he proudly announced a happy family event. Nine years before on October 4, 1939, he had handed out cigars when he and his wife Thelma became the parents of twin daughters, Thelma and Velma. Now after nine years to the day, on October 4, 1948, Joe handed out the cigars for twin sons, Robert and Albert.

One morning soon after that, when Sam chided Joe for "never being at your desk when I need you," Joe tossed off a neat little joke. "Mr. Young," Joe grinned, "when I'm at my desk, you want me out in the lobby, helping the customers. When I'm out in the lobby, you want me back at my desk. Mr. Young, I tell you frankly, it's much easier for me to *make* twins than *be* twins myself."[32]

By now, the El Paso business community had heard many big stories about Sam Young's intuitive sense that one man was bankable and another was not. On that score, he exercised once again his old sense when a hesitant young entrepreneur came into his office, hat in hand, to borrow a sum big enough to start a sheet metal business. William Kastrin could pledge collateral worth only $250,000, he told Sam. Expecting a shake of the head and a quick dismissal, "Instead," he remarked with relief after his brief encounter, "that banker Sam Young never even asked to look at my books. He never asked for any evidence at all." In short order, with Sam's $1 million, Kastrin was open for business.[33]

Unlike Bill Kastrin, a group of concerned El Pasoans who visited Sam in 1948 had no wish to start up a business. They were concerned for the community's physical health. Their spokesman, Paul N. Poling, Sam's former pastor, detailed the facts: since the war, El Paso had dangerously outgrown its hospital facilities. Of the five hospitals in town, only Southwestern General, Hotel Dieu Catholic Hospital, and St. Joseph's Tuberculosis Sanitarium were in truly viable condition. The Masonic Hospital at Five Points and the Schuster family's little Providence Hospital at the corner of Santa Fe and Upson Streets were woefully rundown.[34]

For a city the size of El Paso, according to the Texas State Department of Health, 1,500 hospital beds were necessary but, said Poling, the fact was that El Paso had less than half that number. To solve that problem, the group was spearheading a drive to erect a health care center dedicated to excellence in every department. Would Sam serve on its board?[35]

In a few days, when Sam did accept that invitation, he considered the move a token support of a cause worthy like many others. Only later did he find that that project engaged every one of his personal convictions. When his first year of service expired, he agreed to continue, even though by now his commitments both to the Bank, to his Mexico businesses, and to Hilton were expanding daily.

In May, 1948, Sam saw Conrad Hilton's big dreams grow even bigger when Edward Stettinius, Harry Truman's secretary of state, persuaded Hilton and his corporation to extend their management to hotels in several strategic "world" cities. The motive was based on expedience, on post-war America's wish to reestablish international goodwill and promote American business abroad. With "World Peace through International Trade and Travel" as its motto, this Hilton International chain would also accommodate Americans eager to find in foreign hotels all the comforts of home.[36]

Sam registered doubts about the plan's feasibility: too many unknowns, too far from home to keep an eye on. But he tempered his doubts when almost at once Hilton received an invitation from Cuba. With his board's reluctant approval, Hilton bought a palatial hotel in Havana for $2 million. Unfortunately, Connie's pleasure in Cuba was short lived. Revolutionary forces soon confiscated that hotel for their own needs, thus costing the Hilton Corp. its total investment.[37] That expensive experience, however, taught Hilton and his people an important lesson. As the world opened its doors for more Hilton Hotels, the buildings themselves would be locally owned. Hilton would only manage and staff the hotels' operations.[38]

In the meantime, as Hilton rolled ever onward, Sam objected both to Connie and to Connie's treasurer, J. B. Herndon, Jr., when Hilton's expansion costs severely tapped his El Paso National balance. "I wish you would not be so hard on us, we are just country boys trying to get along." It would be too bad for Hilton "to practically close out the account just because you need to meet a few extra payments."[39]

Herndon recognized Sam's concern. "Believe me, I would not draw against the El Paso National unless I had to."[40] But Herndon had his own troubles. "Nothing in the world would please me better than that same old balance at the El Paso National Bank," but Connie had just informed him that if the "W. A. deal" goes through, he would have to dig up, in cash, "$1,125,000!"[41]

To any Hilton insider, "W. A. deal" was the code term for Connie's grandest dream yet, his hope to possess the top hotel in America, New York's Waldorf-Astoria.

At the January 1949 Hilton board meeting in Los Angeles, Sam again mentioned to Herndon Hilton's rather small balance. "I hate to appear in a hurry, but you make your income on daily rental of rooms and we make our income in daily use of other people's money, and I'm sure that's a very logical point in the eyes of a former bank examiner."[42]

Sam's concerns about that were shortly over. When a $500,000 deposit came through in a few days, Sam wrote Connie his thanks. "That gives us nearly a million from the Hilton Hotels Corporation. It swells our pride mightily to see such a good friend and customer as yourself develop into the largest depositor we have on our books. Your accomplishment is indeed phenomenal, and some day someone will probably write your story in book form and most people who read it will likely take it for fiction."[43]

Hilton's "W. A. deal" went through with a flourish on October 12, 1949, though its success came about with Sam's barely lukewarm approval. "It's a great hotel," he had agreed at a recent Hilton board meeting, "but with the Plaza and the New Yorker already, we've got good hotels all over New York. It's the same old problem of self-competition, like the Stevens versus the Palmer House out in Chicago."

Henry Crown, the Chicago financier and now a fellow board member, neatly rebutted Sam's point. "Connie and I will buy the Waldorf and keep it a year. If the Hilton Corporation then wants to buy it from us, we'll sell it to you at our cost."[44]

"In the meantime," Connie added to Sam, "running this Queen of Hotels, I'm going to need your hard-nosed advice. How about joining the Waldorf-Astoria board?"

Still reluctant, Sam nodded. "I'll come along for the ride. But as for buying any stock in this crazy venture, I'll just have to see."

When the "good W. A. deal" did go through, Connie crowed about being "the man who bought the Waldorf." Sam, the conservative, however, felt no elation the evening Betty and he first entered the Waldorf's red and gold lobby. The work to achieve it had been tedious, the risks involved in possessing it now were still great. "Owning this place," he muttered to Betty on the way up to their tower suite, "is going to be no simple thrill."[45]

But the minute he stepped into his marble-lined shower and turned its gold-plated handles, he was as thrilled as any guest could be.[46] When the needle-sharp jet of hot water steamed over him, he knew how far he had come from those Saturday night baths on the porch back in Woodville, standing under his rusty bucket punched full of holes.

Still, as Connie officially opened his new Caribe Hilton Hotel in San Juan, Puerto Rico in 1949, as he displayed his name throughout the world in other "little Americas" bearing his logo, Sam's own sense of adventure took wings.

Much as faraway places, however, appealed to Sam's imagination, he had an even stronger reason now to engage himself with the El Paso group hoping to build a hospital. That committee had just bought the old Providence Hospital from Dr. and Mrs. Michael P. Schuster: it had bought a nine-city-block lot on North Oregon Street for the 185-bed hospital they meant to build as soon as they had the money. On that note, the committee came calling on Sam, but their question came at a very bad time for him. "I've got the Bank, I've got the Zach White estate's tangled affairs to deal with," he explained. "Much as I'd like to, I can't raise the money for the hospital."[47]

Nevertheless, Irene Wulfjen, Paul Poling, L. L. Evans and others insisted. "You're the only right man for the job."

To their pleas, Sam at last gave a shrug. "I'll think about it." That night he fell to his knees and prayed hard.

The next morning he told the group that the answer had come "in a clear certainty, as strong as if a voice in his ear had delivered an order."

He called Poling. "I'll do it," he said.

At the hospital's ground breaking ceremony on Sunday, March 6, 1949, Sam mounted the speaker's podium, a position he still shied away from, and told the large crowd the specifics involved in the project:[48] the $1 million the campaign needed to achieve the quality of care this new Providence Hospital would offer El Paso.

The May 1949 issue of *Southwestern Medicine* magazine fully outlined the details: a surgical suite containing four major operating rooms, a patient-nurse intercommunication system installed at the patient's bedside, an obstetrical floor with nurseries, an isolation wing for contagious disease, a special pediatric wing, a Masonic Memorial Wing, a crippled children's ward, a laboratory and research department, and many other units "essential to the operation of the most modern hospitals."

"From the moment he enters the modern and handsome lobby until discharged, the patient's surroundings would instill confidence." A barber shop and a flower shop, as well as a modern chapel designed to suit "the religious tastes of all, whether Catholic, Protestant or Jew," would be part of the hospital's main floor.

"Incorporated as a non-profit, non-sectarian educational hospital," the magazine story continued, Providence Memorial "is managed by leading business men who serve on its Board of Directors without pay. Because it will also serve in the training of young physicians and medical students, the hospital was granted $500,000 by the Federal government.... Physicians, who will serve on the staff, will donate their services; neither board members nor physicians will receive special privileges of hospital service."[49]

During the financial campaign, Sam put into practice a theory of fund raising he had long ago come to trust: "You have to state loud and clear at the start exactly how much you yourself are giving."[50] Unless prospective donors could see that the leader was sold on the project, they would not contribute a dime. Sam himself took on the major merchants and business heads, as well as the doctors. "You people that I'm talking to first, I regard as our pace-setting group. What you folks do will set the tone for everyone else. On this card here, I've got you down in the $2,500 class. That is for three years in a row."

"Three years?" they groaned. "Seventy-five hundred dollars?"

"For the good of this community, we've got to." Sam uncapped his pen. "That's all we're asking. Sign here."[51]

While the campaign was in full swing, Connie Hilton was in El Paso and Sam invited him to come along to a luncheon. "Most of the guests, you've known a long time." En route, Sam explained that the point of the lunch was a drive for a new hospital. "Frankly, Connie, I think you ought to contribute $25,000 to it yourself."

"Twenty-five thousand dollars!"

"Sure. Over the years, El Paso has done a lot of good things for you."

"That's too much, Sam, I can't do it," Connie said firmly.

At the luncheon, Sam explained that if the total goal of $1 million[52] was to be met, each person there would have to contribute at least $25,000. "So," he announced, "my good friend here, Connie Hilton, has already pledged that figure, all on his own."[53]

Connie choked, then he shot a hot glance at Sam. But in a moment, he grinned and lowered his head.[54]

Sometimes the gifts came from people who had not been asked. After a golf game one afternoon, Sam was dressing for home when the locker man, Richard Harris, said to him, "Mr. Sam, nobody asked me for the hospital, but my wife and I want to give too. These $150 in greenbacks is all I've saved up, but I want you to use it."[55]

The leg work and repeated telephone calls fully paid off with a total of $1,800,000 pledged in the El Paso area, plus $1,500,000 from a federal grant. The new building itself was well underway on January 5, 1950, when the Providence Hospital board unanimously elected Sam Young their president.[56]

Accepting that office, Sam explained that during the past recent months, he had got so imbued with the hospital's needs that he wanted to continue. "You know," he said, "it's good to put something back into the lifestream."[57]

12

BE MY GUEST

SAM'S INVOLVEMENTS in other men's businesses, not just his own at the Bank, took on a new dimension in March 1950 when John Payne, vice president of the Texas and Pacific Railroad, commented to Sam at a party, "I've just realized that in spite of all the good business El Paso does with our system we don't have a single one of you folks on our board. Will you join us?"[1] Though Sam's time had to stretch once again to accept Payne's invitation, the community's good was involved; in his new role, he could "represent the transportation interest of the people and industries of El Paso."[2] In a small sense, at his first T&P board meeting in Dallas, he participated in a major change in the line's operations: its thunderous old locomotives puffing black smoke became things of the past. Henceforth, streamlined diesel-electric engines would power its trains.

With more and more of his own business involved now in travel, Sam and Betty were in Mexico City for three weeks during March 1950 as guests of the Eloy Vallinas and the Carlos Trouyets,[3] when they renewed a friendship from back in the 1920s with Anna and Floyd Ransom, an American who owned an office machines business, Proveedor de Oficinas. From that visit, Sam brought home Ransom's very solid dollar account for the Bank. That account typified, as his board had learned long ago, the worth of Sam's sizable travel expenses. Sam was often "away from his office," one director commented, but "he's never away from his work for the bank." Once again, Sam had "come home with the bacon."[4]

As usual, Sam dashed to check up on things down the valley. "The farms are in excellent shape now and I think this is the very prettiest season, when the ground is ready for planting," he wrote Fanny.[5]

Likewise, business itself paid off in sheer pleasure in May 1950 when twenty-three-year-old Conrad "Nicky" Hilton, Jr., married the eighteen-year-old movie princess Elizabeth Taylor in Los Angeles. Betty and Sam and Sam Jr. attended the wedding along with Fred Astaire, Ginger Rogers, Spencer Tracy and Debbie Reynolds, then helped see the newlyweds off for their honeymoon in Europe. Later that summer, Sam got a phone call from Nicky. "We're stopping in El Paso for a visit with my mother. Then I'm bringing Elizabeth over to see you at the Bank."[6]

When that news swept through the building, Sam was besieged with pleas from every department. "Please, Mr. Young, bring her our way. We just have to see her."[7] The dark-haired beauty responded gallantly with quick little chats as Sam escorted her and Nicky through all the work areas, then upstairs to meet the directors. For the rest of the day, the starry-eyed people who had seen "Elizabeth Taylor in person" had trouble settling back down to business. Little Betty spoke for all the folks who had seen her. "She was so gorgeous it was startling, those purple eyes."[8]

Like everyone else that evening at a dinner dance in Juarez, Leo Schuster, Jr. was all eyes for "that gorgeous creature" when his turn came to dance with her. Until then the music had been easy standards like "Moonlight in Vermont," but as Leo led her onto the floor, the band struck up "Put Your Little Foot," the one dance "I can't do," he laughed sheepishly. Elizabeth laughed too and she was still laughing when he delivered her back to Nicky.

The next afternoon Elizabeth created another stir when she accompanied Nicky to the El Paso Country Club for his golf game with Connie, Sam, and Sam Jr. While they were out on the course, Elizabeth amused herself at the slot machines in the game room, but later when the men were slow getting showered and changed, Elizabeth charged down to speed things up in the locker room. Sam Jr. was about half dressed when he heard a girl's voice coming down the stairs calling,

"*Nick*-ee! *Nick*-ee-ee!" "Boy, in a second," he said later, "everybody was flying every which way, grabbing for towels." Laughing, Nicky blocked his bride from entering the room, whisked her upstairs, then rejoined the foursome, still laughing.[9]

Glamour aside, a birthday ranked uppermost on Sam's mind on June 29, 1950. For twenty-five years, the Bank had weathered many an onslaught, and Sam and his team found ample reason to celebrate. "The accounts on our books as of December 30, 1950," Sam told his stockholders, "totaled 37,764, an increase of 4,403 during the year. Our three loan departments made a total of 19,418 loans. Our tellers handled 8,076,197 items. The Trust Department ended 1950 with a net gain of twelve new estates and personal trusts, adding $878,377.15 to the department's assets."

The January before, Sam had closed his report, "As we enter together our Silver Anniversary year, let us resolve to make 1950 a memorable one in every respect, growth, earnings, and goodwill." Now at year's end, he felt sure that the statistics fully demonstrated "that our achievement has been satisfactory."[10]

To spread that good news, Sam had his publicity people mail out an elaborate announcement bearing inside it a small facsimile of the Bank's first statement, the little two-page folder dated June 30, 1925. From that publicity around the nation, Sam received a flood of congratulations. "It was a lucky day for El Paso when you decided to move West.[11] You have made a remarkable record in a very short space of time and I hope that the fiftieth anniversary will find you still in control and the bank one of the largest institutions in the country," wrote Joseph Moss, Jr. of the Irving Trust Co., New York. O. B. Wallace of Continental Illinois National in Chicago noted the little facsimile. "It is hard to believe the two statements were made on the same day only twenty-five years apart."[12]

Walter Wightman at Chase National, New York, also liked the little "statement-within-a-statement." "Of course, the enviable record is a direct result of the very able management you and Mr. Harvey have given to your fine bank."[13]

In great style, Connie Hilton also brought it about that word of Sam's bank should be heard nationwide. A half-hour ABC radio show featured a spoken testimony by Connie and the music of Frankie Masters from the Boulevard Room at the Stevens, Bob Grant from the Persian Room at the Plaza, Guy Lombardo at the Roosevelt (his Royal

Canadians played 'Anniversary Waltz'), Sammy Kaye from the Waldorf-Astoria, Harry Brandon at the Mayflower, and Pete Rivera at the Caribe Hotel in Puerto Rico.

"I particularly appreciate your remarks," Sam wrote to Connie. "Just put me down as a mighty grateful guy!"[14]

The next day Sam wrote his grateful feelings to Fanny. The Bank had had "the blessings of the Lord" along with "remarkable luck" and the hard work of loyal officers and staff members. All these people understood, he said, that service to the Bank and the Bank's customers was not merely the Bank's prime rule but also its major claim to success, as the comparative statements clearly made plain. Assets on June 30, 1925: $1,446,719. Assets these twenty-five years later: $70,514,287.

Regarding that rise, Monday morning Loan Committee meetings were a case in point. Long ago Sam had made it his practice to look around the table and ask each officer how many calls on loan customers he had made over the weekend. When Sam questioned Bill Foreman one morning, Bill answered candidly, "I didn't make any, Mr. Young. I had to stay home and supervise my yard man."[15]

"Your yard man?" Sam glared. "Next time, get somebody else to do that."

The Bank's good showing also involved other behind-the-scenes expectations. When Sam observed Joe Nelan's disarranged desk, he commented, "Why can't you keep your desk neat, like mine?"

Knowing the upward flow of the Bank's paperwork, Nelan grinned wryly, "You desk up there is neat, Mr. Young, because my desk down here is messy."[16]

Through its civic outreach, the Bank had also reaped gains. Its elaborate float was always featured each New Year's Day in the Sun Carnival Parade along Montana Avenue. Now Sam and his officers began hosting a "porch party" to watch the mile-long procession of Fort Bliss troops, sheriffs' posses on horseback, scores of beautiful girls in open-top cars and floats passing by. Though the food and the drinks made a lavish spread, it was work day for a regular committee of officers. James Onick, Joe Moreno, and others aided Sam in entertaining the Bank's major customers and out-of-town correspondents, making certain they never grew hungry or thirsty.

One year, Sam was shaking hands right and left when he glanced at a platter mounded high with tamales. "Dammit," he roared at the officers manning the table, "who already shucked all those things? Don't you know everybody's supposed to do that themselves. Quick! Get rid of that mess!"

Since to get rid of the mess, Onick later recalled, would have left the party with no tamales, two of the officers carried the platter inside and reshucked the entire supply.[17]

Back to business soon after, along with raising Sam's salary to $37,500 and promoting Gus Bianche from assistant vice president to vice president, the January 1951 board meeting welcomed Conrad Hilton as a new director. For that, Connie expressed his loyalty. "This will mean that I am to go to El Paso more often which suits me fine, and this will give me an opportunity to be with my many friends."[18] Though he had already been asked to join the board of the First National Bank in Chicago, "I told them I wouldn't be on anybody's bank board but Sam Young's."[19] Hilton made his goodwill even more clear when he deposited a nice fat check to his Hilton Hotels account. "Even in these days of astronomical figures," Sam wrote him, "$319,760 is a lot of lettuce. If you have any friends who can make deposits like that, I'll devote my entire day to acknowledging them."[20]

From out of the blue one morning, ten years since their first telephone visit, Robert O. Anderson phoned Sam from Artesia. "Don and I bought the refinery up here and we've been doing well with it. We've got a lot of good leases and oil production. But" – Sam listened carefully – "our cash flow right now doesn't take care of our payroll. This is Wednesday, and I've got to meet that payroll next Saturday."

"I see. Now tell me, Bob, how much would you need?"

"Mr. Young," Bob answered slowly, "I hope you won't ask for my figures, but I need $60,000."

"I won't ask, but I do need to know if you can meet this loan when it's due."

"Yes, yes, I can, Mr. Young."

For Sam, the time clearly had come again to show his confidence in a man. "Then go ahead, draw your draft. I'll forward your money today."[21]

It was "faith" time again in February 1951 soon after Fred Hervey became mayor of El Paso. Sam complained to Hervey about serious inefficiencies he had observed in the Water Department's structure.

"Well then," said Hervey, "give me an outline of the reorganization you'd favor, but I don't want any politics in it. To help you, I want people that will work hard and well together."

Supporting Hervey's dedication to good government, Sam sent the mayor his list of public-spirited citizens. "Fine," Hervey replied, "now get your plans going.[22] I'm calling this group the Public Service Board."

With Harlan Hugg, a civil engineer, in charge of the Water Department, the city bought thousands of acres of land in northeast El Paso to assure the city's access to the area's underground water. Working with Fort Bliss and Biggs Field, the department soon discovered vast new subterranean aquifers. In time, the water resources northwest of town were also found to include three separate levels of potable water. Using only the top level, El Paso immediately doubled its resources.[23]

For years, both as banker and citizen, Sam had found another factor in the life of El Paso frustrating. Under Fred Hervey, it seemed apropos now to raise questions about South El Paso, the area between the business center and the bridges to Juarez. For more than a century, that land had caused dissension between Mexico and the United States because the Treaty of Guadalupe Hildago, signed by the governments of both nations in 1848, and subsequent treaties had designated the middle of the river as the official international boundary. That wording was clear, but because the river often meandered at will in its sandy bed, the boundary could change overnight. Thus the national sovereignty of properties in this Chamizal area of some six hundred acres was always uncertain. For this reason, "Chamizal" remained a troublesome orphan as El Paso and Juarez grew up around it. As a safe place to live, as a practical place to do business, that neighborhood in El Paso was a festering slum, yet its potential for good challenged every concerned citizen. Sam called in the Bank's lawyer, Thornton Hardie.

"Research the whole problem," he told Hardie. "Find out, if you can, why it isn't already resolved."

Hardie's detailed report clarified the issues, but he had found no easy hope for a solution. Sam laid the matter aside for more thinking, though as more and more problems came to his desk regarding cloudy deeds to Chamizal properties and loans to Chamizal businesses, he firmly declared that, one fine day, he would help cure that intercity distemper.

On June 17, 1951, when Sam Jr. graduated cum laude from Stanford, he had studied every course having to do with theories of economics. "The fact was, however" – he smiled – "that's not quite the same thing as being a banker."[24]

To celebrate after commencement, Sam and Betty hosted a party at Trader Vic's restaurant in San Francisco. When Sam Jr. ordered a "Suffering Bastard," Betty pretended amazement. "A *what?*" she asked pleasantly.

"You heard it right," Sam Jr. assured her. "It's great. You ought to order one too."

Betty looked helpless, then shyly smiled up at the waiter. "Well then, could you just bring me one of those Suffering" – she paused – "Suffering Gentlemen drinks?"[25]

His schooling completed, Sam Jr. joined the Air Force. "Although the Korean War outlook is brighter now," Sam wrote Fanny, "we do not believe that will alter his plans to serve for at least a couple of years. We do wish we had him at home."[26] In September Sam was more frank. "We want him to do his full duty, but we are praying that this war will come to an end before his training is over."[27]

Those fears aside, on January 10, 1952, Sam realized the hospital board's grand dream when he officially declared the shiny new Providence Hospital open for business. At a big ceremony, he stated the hospital's central policy: "All who will may enter here," then thanked the hundreds of people who had contributed time, money and energy toward the building's completion: architects Carroll and Daeuble; builder Robert E. McKee; Dr. Leigh Wilcox, president of the El Paso County Medical Society; and especially the fund raisers who had collected the cash "without which all our other efforts would have gone for naught."

Sam paused to nod at Fred Hervey. "I'm especially glad to see our mayor with us today," he grinned. "A few days ago I caught him checking all over this building for some reason, but I just want to say to you now, Mr. Mayor, that you can forget about us ever being on your tax rolls. We are, thank the good Lord, strictly non-profit, tax-exempt."

The First State Bank at Five Points had flourished for four years when Sam and its stockholders formed a corporation on January 12, 1952, to acquire control of it as an affiliate of the El Paso National. With a fifty-year charter and capital stock of $200,000, the corporation would be called the El Paso National Company. Homer Jacobs explained the specifics. "Each owner of bank stock received a proportionate amount of stock in the new company. The company will be counted as an asset of the Bank and will come under the same federal inspection that the Bank and its other assets come under."[28]

That was good news to all the Bank's friends, but sad word fell upon them on February 15, 1952, when C. M. Harvey, at age eighty-three, became gravely ill. Sam rushed to his bedside. "You shouldn't be here at home, Mr. Harvey. Providence Hospital is all ready now, and they can make you feel better."

Harvey grumbled about leaving home, but when he finally agreed, the hospital put him under an oxygen tent. Sam took a chair by his bed and they were having a chat when Sam excused himself for a minute. "I need to go down the hall."

"Go ahead," Harvey replied feebly, "but I'll be dead in ten minutes."

"No, you won't, Mr. Harvey. I'm coming right back."

When Sam returned, Harvey had fulfilled his prediction.[29]

The next day, Sam's words about Harvey were publicized fully, but Harvey's special meaning to him and the Bank were detailed in the Bank's private minutes. "A sincerely religious man," a man whose deep-rooted Christian principles "were as much a part of the man as his keen mind and kindly heart." Harvey would sorely be missed, "particularly by those founding directors who well remember the influence of his warm personality and kindly human qualities in molding the spirit and policies of the new little banking institution" that in twenty-seven years had risen to a place among the nation's strongest.[30]

In respect to Harvey's memory, all four El Paso banks – the State National, the El Paso National, First State, and the new Southwest National Bank – closed at noon the day of the funeral. To Fanny, Sam expressed his great personal loss. "Ever since our acquaintance began back in 1919, I don't think I've ever had a better friend in the world."[31]

Business, however, had to go on. On a nomination by Conrad Hilton, the next meeting of the board elected Sam to replace Harvey as chairman of the board; they elected twenty-seven-year-old Eldon Phillips (Phil) Harvey to replace his father as director.

And still the good word kept coming from Hilton. In December, Connie had just become the first individual depositor in the Bank's history to show a balance over $1 million. "Did you ever dream this would happen," Sam wrote him, "and if you did, how long ago?"[32]

Connie's reply suggested a smile. "No, I did not dream about this." Twelve years ago he had felt comfortable with only $10,000. "I don't

Fred Florence and Eloy Vallina at far left with Sam (hat in hand) on a fact-finding tour through the Chihuahua tall-timber country, 1952.

know how much more comfortable I am now, but at least more comfortable than the time when I didn't have even $1,000 on deposit at your bank."[33]

With prospects in Mexico ever more interesting, Sam, Eloy Vallina, Carlos Trouyet, Sam Rosoff, and Martin Lettunich purchased the Mexico Northwestern Railroad. In addition to its tracks and its rolling stock, the company owned vast timber lands and timber rights. After only a few months, the Mexican government paid them $3 million for the railroad, but the partners retained their timber acreage. On the strength of that handsome sale, Eloy Vallina now approached Sam with plans for even more attractive investments, first in Bosques de Chihuahua, a new logging enterprise, and in Celulosa de Chihuahua, a company that converted much of the Bosque's wood pulp into high grade paper, rayon, and Kleenex.[34]

To examine their new operations, several other Bosques de Chihuahua stockholders, plus Fred Florence from Dallas and J. C. Peyton, an El Paso meatpacker, accompanied Sam and Eloy on a train ride through Casas Grandes and villages high in the mountains through Cumbres Pass, and down to Chihuahua. The elaborate train featured Pullman cars, a posh dining car, and an observation deck for anyone interested in watching the scenery. Though most of the group favored a hot poker game, that little diversion soon developed into a problem for Sam. "How high are the stakes?" he asked Eloy.

Eloy glanced overhead. "I'd say about as high as that sky."

Too careful a banker to risk buying the heavens, Sam turned in his cards. "You boys are too rich for me."

By dinner time in El Largo, the company's major sawmill, one player had already lost $30,000.

As Sam's grasp of solid business in Mexico grew, as he felt increasingly easy about his personal investments there, he became more and more willing to involve the Bank itself in loans south of the border. When an outbreak of aftosa (hoof-and-mouth disease) brought serious inconvenience to El Paso cattle importers and threatened ruin for Mexican ranchers, Sam, lending Bank funds, enabled Juarez investors to set up meat canneries. In canned form, the Mexican beef posed American importers no problem.[35] As those industries flourished, Sam approved further loans for Mexican flour mills, soap factories, distilleries, molding and door factories, and soft drink bottling works. As their profits soared, Mexican business was soon contributing 25 percent of El Paso National's own volume.[36]

In August 1953 First Lieutenant Sam D. Young, Jr. completed his two-year stint with the Air Force. Soon afterwards, he followed Sam's footsteps into banking. After more work with Hilliard Bryan at First State, serving as paying teller, savings teller, note teller, collection and exchange teller, Sam Jr. transferred downtown for further training in loans and discounts with Jack Ryan.[37] After that he too turned to bank examining, though his level was national, and his boss was the U. S. Treasury Department, Office of the Comptroller.

That same year, when M. R. "Bill" Prestridge, a lumberman from Alamogordo and Cloudcroft, opened an office in the Bank building, he soon became another one of Sam's colleagues-in-spirit for whom the game of investing wisely brought almost as much pleasure as the profits they made. The same was true now for Dorrance Roderick, who joined the Bank board in January 1954. For Sam, that addition was cause for special delight since Dorrance had long declined Sam's invitation lest his newspaper seem to favor Sam's bank over the State National.

In May, a Hilton board meeting at the new Castellana Hilton Hotel in Madrid, Spain, gave Betty and Sam a pleasure they had been anticipating ever since the *El Paso Herald* in 1930 had noted Sam's hopes someday for a chance to travel. "Betty, Sammy and I are building air castles," Sam wrote his sister Phebe, "about a possible trip to Europe in May. We have wanted to go, of course, all our lives."[38] Once again mixing business with pleasure, he paid business calls in several European bank centers, shoring up correspondent accounts, picking up leads on international trends that might affect economic factors at home. To cover his costs, the board authorized him a $3,000 expense account. Back in harness that fall, he cheerfully reported many new prospective correspondents, many new insights gained from those visits.[39] The year-end report for 1953 held its own proof of the Bank's vigorous health: total deposits, $94,587,083 as compared with the State National's $101,196,664.

On the heels of that trip to Europe, Sam now participated in another Conrad Hilton coup, buying the Statler Hotel chain. Though Sam and Hilton's other directors expressed mixed emotions about that $110 million investment, the biggest in hotel history,[40] Connie cajoled them,

Sam (at left) with Carlos Trouyet, Manny Escajeda and Eloy Vallina at a Bosques de Chihuahua board meeting, Mexico City, about 1957.

"Look at it this way. There'll never be another opportunity like this. We have a chance to buy eight fine hotels, proven hotels, in top cities." Sam and another director, Frank Freeman, agreed very reluctantly. "I move that we let Connie go ahead and try to make the deal," said Frank, "and pray that he doesn't."[41]

On October 27, 1954, when Hilton bought those Statler properties, it was the "largest real estate transaction the world has ever known,"[42] Connie crowed. The number of Hilton hotels in the U. S. and abroad rose to twenty-eight, with more a'building.

As for "coups," Sam relished his own kind of victory when the 1954 year-end report brought him high cause to celebrate. His deposits were still not ahead of the State National's, but . . . well, let him share the good news with his officers. At a banquet at the Paso del Norte, Sam was all smiles when he greeted each guest.

"None of us knew at all why we had been summoned to dinner," Bill Foreman reported later, "but it was obvious Mr. Young had something spectacular on his mind when, after dinner, he stood up, smiled around at all our tables, then boomed out the reason. 'Gentlemen and ladies, for the first time in our history, during the year just ended our deposits totalled over $100 million. Better than that, $104,420,093, and it's all because of your good work. All your combined efforts helped us bring this about.'"

At that, "Everybody in the room leaped to their feet, applauding each other."[43]

The *American Banker* itself noted the Bank's rapid rise. In the past four years, the El Paso National Bank had come up forty places in its national ranking in size: as of January 31, 1955, it stood 225th in the country.[44]

Yet size and rank still gave nobody the right to ignore the basic dictates of good service. Sam was passing through the lobby one morning when he spied an elderly lady waiting in a long line. Immediately he grabbed a desk chair, settled her in it, then took her place in the line. When her turn came at the window, she thanked him, and in turn he thanked her for her business. "Good people like you are mighty important to us."[45]

Oftentimes now, Sam could credit good luck, or other people's goodwill, for several good turns in his own fortunes. Such was the case when Bill Prestridge came to Sam regarding a gypsum deposit he owned near Phoenix. "If it turns out to be as rich as it seems, I want to organize a company to mine it. Care to participate with me? I'm driving over there next week to look over the property." On the promise Sam clearly saw on that trip, he invested $50,000 in Bill's new Union Gypsum Company.[46]

Fully convinced of Bill's special business talents, Sam remembered his early confidence in Conrad Hilton. Yet, when Hilton Hotels went international, the move brought an undreamed-of special perk that Sam and Betty clearly affirmed in June 1956 when they attended the opening of Hilton's elaborate hotel in Istanbul, Turkey.

That gala featured dignitaries from Turkey and Greece and, as an added glamorous note, Hollywood's Irene Dunne, Ann Miller, Merle Oberon, Sonja Henie, Jeanne Crain, Louella Parsons, and Hedda Hopper. Sam and Betty sat with the Premier of Turkey and his wife at the banquet's head table, and Sam had the added pleasure of dancing with the first wife of the Greek shipping magnate, Aristotle Onassis. About that trip, Hilton commented later, "I don't want to sound like a missionary, but what's wrong with showing the world the fruits of American freedom?" By making jobs for people, by promoting travel, local construction, a better understanding among people, "I honestly believe that Hilton International is contributing something to the cause of world peace. Before I die, I'd like to see at least one of our hotels in every leading city of the world."[47]

In 1956, a drastic change in the Bank's business hours caused some long faces at first. Indeed, "Saturday closing" threatened to create many hardships, but with many stores now willing to cash their customers' personal checks, no Bank client necessarily had to find himself "caught short" on the weekends. To counteract any difficulties for farmers and ranchers who had always done their "in town" business on Saturday, Sam opened a walk-up window outside. At year's end, the Bank had clearly suffered no serious loss from its shortened work week: it had grown in deposits to $107,015, 840 as compared to the State National's $110,503,713.

After nearly nine years now, the guest card that Connie Hilton had so happily given Sam was proving very expensive for Connie. Hither and yon, Sam had used it on his personal travels, and Connie had never questioned the bills that that card had smoothly charged off. Now in 1956, Sam had particular reasons to treasure that privilege

Sam with Eloy Vallina (presiding) at a Telefonos de Mexico board meeting, Mexico City, about 1959.

after Hilton bought the Statler chain. Since that deal had not included the Statler Hotel in Dallas, Hilton contracted Sam to negotiate its purchase and the interest involved. Standing his ground with the sellers, Sam parlayed that interest rate downward from 4 percent to 2 percent. But when Hilton gratefully offered Sam a $25,000 commission, Sam shook his head. "I'd rather just make the usual use of my old Hilton card." Then he thought a minute. "Oh, but you *can* put my name on the door of the Petroleum Suite in the Statler Hilton in Dallas, and the same goes for the El Paso Suite at the Beverly Hilton in Beverly Hills." Wincing a bit, Connie accepted Sam's terms.[48]

Family matters, however, were just as high on Sam's mind at the time. "We celebrated our thirty-fifth wedding anniversary last Friday," he wrote Fanny.[49] "Can you imagine that – thirty-five years! We were treated to a surprise dinner party arranged by my secretary and my assistant, Mrs. Gill and Mr. Bianche. I can't recall an evening we have enjoyed more."

Within a few months, Connie remembered Sam's gold wallet card while preparing his autobiography. "Sam, send me that card. I want to put it into my book." Sam played cagey. "Ah, Connie, I don't want to send it to you. You might not send it back."

"Oh, now, nothing like that," Connie assured him. "I just want to put it into the book, that's all."

"Naw," Sam drawled, "keep it out of the book."

Sam had good reason to prize it, he explained later. "It's the only card Connie ever issued like this."

Sentiment justified part of Sam's tight grip on that card, but with Hilton's constant opening of new hotels, the card only got better each time. The next year, when Connie's book did appear bearing the friendly title, *Be My Guest,* Sam grinned. "Well, all right, I'm willing." Then he leafed through it to see what Connie had said about him. Connie had spelled out their early transactions together, but reading page 212, Sam came stiffly alert.

"Now Sam and I had never minced words," Connie had written. "As a matter of fact, once, not too many years before (buying the Palmer House), we stripped off our coats in front of his bank and prepared to settle an issue with bare fists until a friend intervened."

Reading that, Sam swept the book off his desk. "That's bullshit," he muttered.[50]

Once again the willing fund raiser, in June 1956 Sam agreed to head a campaign to enlarge El Paso's Loretto Academy. Before long, he was offering Conrad Hilton another good way to prove his gratitude to El Paso. Due partly to Sam's leadership, partly to Hilton's interest in the work of the Loretto Sisters, the success of the drive was due to the shrewd psychology and prayers also of the school's superior, Sister Francetta.

Only later did Sister Francetta divulge the core of her own wily scheme. The night of the kick-off dinner at the school, "I made sure I danced Mr. Hilton's favorite dance, 'Put Your Little Foot,' with him. Then, during many long nights after that, "with the palms of my hands clamped together and my fingers straight up, I prayed for both Mr. Young and Mr. Hilton. With one hand I prayed for their souls; with the other I prayed for their wads."[51]

During the dedication ceremony on April 28, 1957, of Loretto Academy's new $250,000 gymnasium/auditorium complex, Sister Francetta explained why she had named it Hilton-Young Hall. "Without Mr. Hilton's contribution and Mr. Young's tireless efforts and financial aid it would not have been possible."

As to his own part in the campaign, Sam himself spoke about his discussions with Connie. Hilton had proposed that "if I would undertake to raise $75,000, he would agree to contribute $50,000." Sam thanked the other benefactors, then introduced Hilton.

Acknowledging the crowd's applause, Connie told them, "You never regret contributions to buildings of this type. The spiritual and educational benefits to these young women and those of tomorrow will go on and on and cannot be counted."

Sister Francetta's "thank-you" letter a few days later neatly wrapped up Sam's part in the campaign. "It all seems like a dream until I look out my window at beautiful Hilton-Young Hall. It was such a joy," she noted, "for us to see the pleasure you took in the dedication ceremonies and the reception."

Answering that letter, Sam felt a little abashed. It was good that Sister Francetta had detected his pleasure, for "usually when I am scheduled to speak to so large an audience, the apprehension I feel just before getting to my feet is, I am afraid, evident to everyone." He suspected that Sister had "graciously overlooked the quiver in my voice as I began to speak."[52]

Nerves aside, by the spring of 1957 Sam was ready again when George W. Burroughs, his minister at First Presbyterian, asked him to help establish a United Fund in El Paso. Until now, local charity agencies had always operated on their own individual pleas to the public. Sam questioned one detail in Burroughs's request. To head the campaign, Sam required one condition. "You hope to have the fund in full operation by fall of next year, but I can't have that sort of thing on me that long." The drive would have to be over by the upcoming fall.

Burroughs looked stunned. "In only six months? Is that possible, Sam?"

"It *is* possible. But I won't head it if nobody thinks so but me." He and Burroughs shook hands, and Sam picked up his phone. With sturdy help from Gus Bianche as campaign coordinator, Sam focused his sights on $1 million. When the drive ended, its coffers held the largest take any El Paso drive had ever achieved, $980,000. With such community support behind him, Sam agreed now to serve as the United Fund's first president.[53]

Achieving his goals as a fund raiser, winning his struggles in many other public campaigns, Sam often missed out on the easier moments at home where there was nothing urgent to strive for, nothing financial or civic to gain. One evening, he mentioned his regret that so many projects he had tackled in recent years had been made, he fully realized, at drastic cost to his home life.

Smiling, Betty reached for his hand. "I know the good you're doing. I've always known you could do whatever you set out to do."[54]

13

A DREAM IN CONCRETE AND STEEL

WITH TWO YEARS EXPERIENCE BEHIND HIM as a national bank examiner, Sam Jr. was ready by early 1957 to settle down at his own permanent desk. He was considering offers from Fred Florence in Dallas and James A. Elkins at the First City National Bank in Houston when Homer Jacobs phoned him. "We need you back here, Sam. With your good grounding at Stanford; with the field work you've been doing since then, you're not a beginner. There's plenty of room for you here. Certainly, there's plenty of challenge."[1]

For Sam Jr., the El Paso National would indeed offer a challenge: ever since high school he had studied in that direction. What was more, he liked the idea of moving back home to his roots. Though the *Herald* at the time of his birth had stretched the point, had there not always been the assumption in the Bank family that when he grew up Sam Jr. would occupy "his" own desk at the Bank? One additional challenge, working full time for a dymanic leader like Sam, was a matter for calm reflection.

In the end, Sam Jr. at age twenty-seven returned to the Bank, not "just as the boss's son."[2] An experienced professional now, he came equipped with all he had learned on his own. In April on a motion by Jacobs, the board unanimously elected Sam Jr. a vice president at a salary of $8,400.

Sam Sr. kept his own counsel about this latest recruit to his team, but he felt a quiet pride in watching Sam Jr. quickly assume his responsibilities. Now Sam himself proceeded – as firmly as ever – playing the banker role he liked best: funding a client's big dreams. Since his four years as mayor, Fred Hervey had seen his local chain of drive-in Circle K groceries expand to thirteen stores. Envisioning Phoenix, Arizona as the most promising place to try next, he paid Sam a call.

"I've struck a brick wall with the State National, even though they've got all my accounts. I've tried every banker in Phoenix, but they think I'm nuts. 'Every corner in town's got a Chinese mom-and-pop grocery on it already,' they keep telling me. So –"

"How much do you need?" asked Sam, calmly.

Hervey stifled a gulp at the figure. "The fact is," he blurted, "a million dollars."

Telling about it later, Hervey still felt his thrill of surprise. "Sam didn't even insist that I move my accounts to his bank. He just reached in his drawer, pulled out his pad of note forms, and wrote out my note for the million."[3]

Backing people like Hervey, Sam had always enjoyed. But in the spring of 1957 when he looked at his own operation – the Bank now had 280 employees – and at its growth potential, he took a long step in backing himself. The Bank needed much larger quarters. The present building could not be remodeled again nor enlarged any further. And – well, his Bank deserved a new building, a tall one and proud.

At the July 9, 1957, meeting, when the board authorized a feasibility study for such a big step, Sam came alive with ideas of what he really wanted. Nonetheless, amidst the elated prospects, he felt the sudden misgiving the typical loan applicant always felt in Sam's own office. "Can we afford it? Is this the right time?"

Homer Jacobs had not been feeling well for some time and had gone, at Sam's urging, to California to rest. Sam put through a call to him. "How sound would it look to you, Jake? Would it be wise? Can we do it?"[4]

Jacobs answered him straight. "It's sound. Don't let anybody talk you out of doing that. Sam, we can do it, and we should."

With backing like that from a team member who knew the Bank almost as well as he did, Sam rested easier. But profound shock hit him and the Bank on July 23. Homer Jacobs – the man who, Sam often said, "could read my mind at long distance" – died in surgery in La Jolla.

Incredibly, one week later, Manny Escajeda also was gone. In soliciting new business accounts for the Bank that Saturday morning, he had dropped dead on an apartment building stairway.[5]

Amid the shock for Sam and the Bank, the best Sam could do was offer his help to both families. "First Homer Jacobs, then Manny Escajeda," he wrote a friend in Dallas, "both of these gentlemen were the best teammates that a man could have in the business world. I know I am going to miss them sorely."[6]

Within a few days, the directors expressed their own loss. "Homer Jacobs was a man who, quietly, almost shyly, made a place for himself in the hearts of his associates. His unfailing interest in others endeared him to all – directors, officers, clerks and customers alike. He enjoyed the friendship of bankers everywhere who recognized in him the qualities that made everyone feel at ease in his company."[7]

About Manny, the directors spread their full respect on the minutes. "Manny's banking career was distinguished by his devotion to the cause of developing and expanding the relationship between Mexican and American businessmen in the Southwest.... His work was largely responsible for the growth of the Bank's Mexican business and for the recognition of the important role played by our bank in the economy of our border area. A gentleman in the fullest meaning of the word, Manny Escajeda had a deep-rooted sense of personal responsibility to uphold the dignity, traditions, and culture of the people of Mexico from among whom his forefathers had sprung. He succeeded admirably and held the respect and deep affection of friends and associates everywhere."[8]

Still, the loss of Manny and Jake had to be faced and Sam, as usual, had to be busy out on the road. With his ever-increasing travels, a banker friend, H. W. Bell in Tyler, gave him a good luck token. "Take it, you need it." The St. Christopher medal fitted comfortably in Sam's pocket alongside his silver dollar, but a small event soon featured that medal. Columnist Paul Crume first broke the story in the *Dallas Morning News* on July 26, 1957. "After a recent business trip to Dallas," Crume wrote, "the El Paso banker Sam Young started home but he had hardly settled down on the T&P Eagle when he discovered that his prized St. Christopher medal was not in his pocket."

When the porter suggested, "Maybe you gave it to the redcap in the Dallas terminal," Sam replied, "Maybe I did." The problem ought to be easy, said the porter, the baggage tags carried the redcap's number.

When Sam phoned the redcap from El Paso, the redcap remembered the medal, but when he tried to exchange his tips for folding money—"they wouldn't take it."

"Well, where is it now?" Sam wanted to know.

"Home in my dresser drawer."

That night, the redcap's wife told him she had given it to the milkman. It soon developed that the milkman had turned it in to his dairy office. That office was sorry: that day's cash had already gone to the bank. At the bank, the searchers hit a brick wall. "How are you going to find a St. Christopher medal that looks like a half dollar?" asked several tellers. After three days, a teller did find it and he started it back through channels.

"And thus," so wrote the *El Paso Times* on July 29, "St. Christopher, as befits a patron saint of travelers, finally found his way safely home."

At its meeting in August, the board elected Sam Jr. to fill Homer Jacob's place,[9] and in November 1957, Sam himself took on a new role when he attended the inauguration of the Celulosa plant in Anahuac, Mexico, sixty miles west of Chihuahua. Sam and Eloy Vallina's associate in that venture was Carlos Trouyet, a Mexico City tycoon who had risen from scratch to financial eminence. Born in a Mexico City slum of a Mexican mother and a French father,[10] Trouyet was now one of Mexico's richest men, the chairman of many boards, and the friend of presidents. "It is the lower middle class that is building Mexico," Trouyet said of himself, "and I am proud to be of that class."

About Anahuac, Sam gave a full report to the board. "This program should bear fruit in the years to come as it will provide means of producing articles for national consumption which heretofore have been imported from foreign countries." Backed by a group of financiers, including such "close friends of our Bank as Eloy Vallina and Carlos Trouyet," Anahuac was but one of Mexico's progressive programs close to El Paso, Sam continued, "which will tend more and more to strengthen their economy. As El Paso's neighbors become more prosperous, their prosperity will be reflected in additional purchasing power and increased trade, both beneficial to our border territory."[11]

Bearing that prospect in mind, in December the board authorized an architect firm to draw plans for a new Bank building, a structure to rise—in fact and in symbol—from solid bed rock.[12]

With the Bank running smoothly, Betty persuaded Sam in May 1958 to take a long leave and get some much needed rest, "which I can't seem to get in the United States because I won't stay away from home longer than two weeks," he wrote Cullee Mann, his old Woodville friend. "Betty says if I get over across the pond that I will stay away at least six weeks, and I think she is right."[13]

On the trip over, Betty put her foot down to make certain Sam got the rest she had ordered. On the *Nieuw Amsterdam's* outward voyage, the passengers were asked to group themselves by the states they came from, then elect one of their people to tell about it. Quickly, the Texans chose Sam, but at the thought of making that speech, Sam felt an old tension taking control. When he told Betty what the Texas people had done, she gave him an order. "Making a speech makes you too nervous. Say 'No.' You don't have to specify why."[14]

The fact that his St. Christopher medal had come home gave him some hope in July when Sam wrote Betty's sister Martha and her husband Dean Herman a worried letter. "Somehow I lost my old silver dollar between the time I showed it to some of the guests at the party in your home (in California) and the hour we arrived at Glasgow." For more than forty years, the value of that old dollar had been "more sentimental than anything, and while I hate to trouble you, I will be thankful for your efforts in trying to find it."[15] Much to Sam's relief, some months later when he was packing for another big trip, the beloved old coin showed up in a crease in his suitcase.

True to his convictions about Mexico's potential, Sam entertained now a suggestion from Eloy Vallina. After spending a year in research, Eloy was convinced that buying Mexico's telephone system, Telefonos de Mexico, would yield almost immediate profits. Indeed, the investment should prove self-liquidating in about eight years. The current owners, Erikson Telephone Company of Sweden and International Telephone and Telegraph Company of New York, were willing to sell for $26 million. With Carlos Trouyet already a partner, there was a full partnership waiting for Sam, if he could finance the deal through American banks. For that service, Sam would receive 10 percent of the stock.[16]

Immediately, Sam put through a phone call for Fred Florence. When Sam had outlined the telephone company's prospects, Florence quickly assented. "I'm ready. Go ahead, Sam."[17]

At the closing with Erikson and ITT in New Jersey, those groups were represented by their own staff attorneys, and both were surprised that Eloy and Sam had brought along no attorneys at all. Sam easily explained that matter once he was back in El Paso. "Eloy's attorneys in Mexico, my people here, and Florence's staff in Dallas had picked at the transaction from every possible angle. They knew we had a good thing, and we knew it too. It was no trouble at all for us just to sign our names on the papers and walk away happy."

With that deal accomplished, Sam's "new building venture" occupied his thoughts even more, for despite Homer Jacob's firm assurance, sober study soon proved that the Bank would need a healthy brigade of renters above its own floors to help pay its costs. The downtown area badly needed new office space, but to be sure of his plans, Sam went to Paul Kayser.

Though Kayser's gas company had its own eighteen-story office building now, it rented overflow space in several neighboring buildings. When Sam tried to convince Kayser to join him with a substantial long-term lease; Kayser backed away from such a commitment. Sam went to him again, but again Kayser declined. On the third try, Sam played his last trump. "Paul, you've got to approve this for the benefit of El Paso as a whole."

"Well," Kayser slowly agreed, "maybe you have got a point there."[18]

Within a few days, when Kayser leased most of the building's fourth floor and all of the fifth and sixth floors on the Franklin Avenue side, the deal paved the way for Sam to proceed with his plans.[19]

Apropos of those plans, Sam persuaded Harlan Hugg, who had worked with him on Hervey's Public Service Board, to join the Bank in October 1958 as its head engineer. Hugg would maintain the current physical plant and, most importantly now, advise Sam in shaping the Bank's new quarters.

In February 1959, Sam and Betty were traveling again with Conrad Hilton attending the opening of his new Hilton Hotel in Cairo and the groundbreaking ceremony for a new Hilton in Athens. In a board meeting, Sam had already cast the deciding vote that that building should face "directly toward the Acropolis. From the roof garden, that would be a spectacular sight."[20] Together, that night they looked south toward the Parthenon bathed in floodlights on its high hill. "Spectacular," Sam said again.

In March 1959, Sam and the Bank faced another significant question regarding equipment. With the Bank's ever expanding out-of-town business (its correspondent accounts now numbered nearly one hundred), Sam proposed that the Bank should have its own airplane. Though the board listened as always to Sam's presentation, practical factors raised serious doubts. At the next meeting, directors Bob Price and Phil Harvey stood firmly "Opposed."

"Commercial airlines are safer," Price argued.

"And considerably cheaper," Harvey insisted, "given the plane's cost of at least $100,000, plus the expense of a full-time pilot."

"That's true," Sam added. "But our own plane would speed up my trips to board meetings, and please bear in mind too how vital it is that I keep soliciting new accounts all over this country and Mexico." Seeing that light, Bob and Phil raised no further objections.[21]

The five-passenger Beechcraft Twin Bonanza – top speed 200 mph – was put to work immediately after Sam chose the new pilot, Connie Strickland, a former Air Force instructor. Sam was direct in outlining his duties. "I want you to be in complete charge of the plane and all the trip details. I want your judgment to make the decision. I don't want you to turn a wheel on that airplane unless you think it is safe for us to go. In fact, I'd like you to sign a statement to that effect."[22]

As the plane became more and more strategic in Sam's operations, as Sam Jr. often flew it on his own professional missions, the new facility quickly proved its worth to the Bank.

In 1959 Dorrance Roderick and Sam were thinking ever bigger about the city's potential when, at Roderick's urging, the El Paso National Corporation opened another neighborhood bank, this one at Northgate Shopping Center. Now headquarters downtown had two satellites convenient to the major areas of El Paso's expansion. In line with that step, *The American Banker* in June 1959 ran a story under Sam's picture and byline detailing the big bank's own status. El Paso, the fifth largest city of Texas, had led the nation the previous year in increased building permits; it rated 24th in dollar volume of permits issued. Since 1900, "the sleepy town on the Rio Grande with 15,906 people has grown to a city of 280,000. El Paso is a vast business and cultural center of a vast area of the Southwest."[23]

Industrially, its economy was highly diversified. Several plants were rated among the largest of their kind, with products ranging from telescopic gunsights to concrete blocks. In its giant clothing industry, over

4,000 employees were engaged in making blue jeans and work clothes. All told, Sam declared, seven principal factors were contributing to El Paso's spectacular growth: military expenditures at Fort Bliss and Biggs Field, agricultural output and income, economic conditions in northern Mexico and its import and export business through El Paso – the largest port-of-entry on the Mexican border – the tourist business, mineral output and ore processing and ever-expanding manufacturing.

In the past ten years, Sam's report continued, bank deposits had nearly doubled. A recently chartered state bank was about to open to serve "the mushrooming eastern portion of El Paso," and charters for two other state banks were in process.

One detail in particular, Sam proudly noted. His eighteen-story bank and office building would cover a block which was once a part of the Spanish land grant deed in 1827 to El Paso's first settler, Juan Maria Ponce de Leon. One additional detail spoke straight from Sam's enthusiasm for the town he had been helping wax strong for thirty-four years. "The apparent graceful charm of El Paso's Spanish heritage, though still apparent, is successfully merged with the dynamics of industrial and business development. The brightest aspects of the city's awakening from the Land of Mañana to the City of Today is the great interest of its citizens in planning for the future."[24]

Several trips over the years to La Jolla, California crystallized in a long-range plan in November 1959 when Sam had a serious talk with his friend, John Murphey, a real estate developer in Tucson. Murphey owned several beach lots between the La Jolla Beach and Tennis Club and the pier just north of the Scripps School of Oceanography. Visiting those lots with Murphey one afternoon, Sam remarked, "You know, I might be interested in acquiring either a home or a site on this beach, if one were available."

"Why, you're just in time," Murphey said. "Near our own house, a widow from Tulsa wants to sell hers."[25]

Betty was cool to the notion while Murphey was driving them up to the house. "Really now, Sam, can we afford it?" Besides, with the place on Cumberland Circle and the fully livable quarters at the farm, "we have enough homes to manage already." But after inspecting the house's three bedrooms, three baths, its flower-filled patio, and its wide verandah overlooking the ocean, and meeting the friendly neighbors, Betty had warmed to the idea. "Well, I've changed my mind. If you want to buy it, Sam, it's all right."

Within a few weeks, Betty and Sam were fully involved in La Jolla's social routine. For Sam especially, those attractions quickly included a daily bet on the ponies at Del Mar race track.[26]

One of the Bank's major fundings a few years before had been the Border Steel Company, a plant which recycled scrap iron into rebars. Of late, however, that company's heavy reversals had so troubled Sam and the directors that to help right it, Sam urged Bill Prestridge to take over. "Basically, about all that company needs is tighter control in its management. How about it, Bill?"

"It's a personal challenge," Prestridge agreed, "but my doctor has warned me not to undertake any more responsibilities." Shortly however, Bill offered to change his mind "if you, Sam, can talk its stockholders into selling me a big block of their stock at a bargain."[27] Partly on the strength of Bill's resounding success with that company, the Bank board elected Bill a director in January 1960.

While Connie Strickland, the Bank pilot, had signed on fully aware of his responsibilities, there were times, especially on the five-hour flights down to Telefonos meetings in Mexico City when the weather turned "hairy." With air pockets often a problem, the only radio contacts en route were Chihuahua and Torreon. Beyond Torreon, Connie was pretty much on his own. Headwinds slowed the flight so severely one afternoon that Sam came to the cockpit. "Connie," he asked tensely, "how can we keep flying when we're so long overdue?"

"It is long," Connie replied, "but we've got enough gas to alternate to San Luis Potosi. I'll get us there." Safe into San Luis Potosi, Connie found the available gasoline so high in water content that he was obliged to strain 200 gallons of it through a chamois cloth, one bucketful at a time, before they could finish the flight to Mexico City.[28]

In much more style and safety, at Easter in 1960 Sam and Betty and Henry Crown flew with Conrad Hilton to Brazil to estimate the potential for a Hilton Hotel in its new capital city, Brasilia. On its own, the Brazilian government had broached the highly attractive matter to Hilton but, Conrad told Sam, "I need my old banker's clear eye." While they were in Rio de Janeiro, President Juscelino Kubitschek de Oliveira entertained the Hilton group at a lavish lunch in the Presidential Palace. But in Brasilia they found the new hotel far from ready for their inspection. To register, the Americans had to tiptoe along a boardwalk through water flooding the lobby. Next day, while they were being escorted around the new town through the heavy construction, the wind was so strong that no one could gain any real sense of the young city. "The red dust was terrific," Sam told his friends when he safely reached home. "My hair was actually pink."[29] The upshot of his report to Hilton: "Building not ready. Too early to make any commitment."

Sam and Betty were scarcely home from Brazil when appalling news reached them from Chihuahua City. On May 16, 1960, Eloy Vallina had been murdered. Speculations ran rampant at once. Had politics motivated the murderer? Was it some personal vendetta primed by Eloy's spectacular financial rise? Had his bank's expansion into Multibanco Comermex—now Mexico's fourth largest bank holding company[30]—given him too much power? Had the motive in fact been something more intimate? Though the facts were slow to come clear, rumor held it that as Eloy had opposed his son's infatuation with a girl from another city, the girl's father had become bitterly resentful. In anger, the shooting occurred.

That family's grief plunged Sam into deep sadness. In Eloy he had found a heart-to-heart kindred spirit. After attending the funeral in Chihuahua, Sam wrote Eloy's widow Maria. "I had implicit faith in him and complete confidence in his capacity to do successfully anything he set out to do. I have never known a man of higher principles, integrity and honor," or a man with a loftier "sense of patriotism and obligation to his nation, his state and his home community." The enterprises he established to provide jobs and homes for the people, his charitable contributions, his establishment of schools and orphanages symbolized his wish to show his "gratitude and appreciation for the good things that had come to him."

Other than words, the best Sam could offer Maria was his help in the crisis that Eloy's departure had created. In Eloy Jr., Sam pointed out, Maria could rest assured that the affairs of the Vallina family and Comermex lay in good hands.[31]

The next month, when Sam Jr. finished "with distinction" a seminar program at the Southwestern Graduate School of Banking in Dallas, he dedicated his thesis to Vallina, "a shining example of a self-made man, who inspired every young banker who knew him. Above all, however, to me, he was a dear friend."[32] A bit later Sam Jr. spoke of Eloy in more personal terms. "Eloy Vallina was the only Mexican I ever

El Paso National's third home, its own building, on the corner of Mesa and Main, May 1963.

knew who could think exactly like an American." A perfect bridge between the two cultures, totally fluent in English, he knew "all the weaknesses, all the characteristics of both the Mexican and the American, and he could smooth the differences so there were no misunderstandings between the two parties. Eloy was a master."[33]

In 1960, if anyone had asked Sam about the need of a college education, he would have replied, "That depends on the work a fellow wants to get into." But he often felt a wordless regret that he never had had the chance to attend Texas A&M. Indeed, there were times when it pained him to listen to other men smoothly refer to recent literature they had read or neatly quote some famous author. Work had left him too little time for reading a book for its art and its wisdom.

On that note, however, Sam clearly knew with other people in town that El Paso's ambitious little Texas Western College, a branch of the University of Texas, was hardly more than a stepchild in the eyes of the State Legislature. The point came to a head in 1960 when faculty salaries at TWC fell so low that civic leaders, under Sam's eager command, raised $60,000, free and clear of legislative control, to supplement their salaries. TWC President Joseph R. Smiley would distribute the money as he saw fit.

At the shareholders meeting on January 10, 1961, Sam looked back at the preceding year's effects on the Bank and its effects on the city of El Paso, now forty-sixth in size in the nation. Ever since June 29, 1925, the Bank's conservative policy had been designed "to serve every credit-worthy customer according to his capacity and his needs." That policy had paid off in profits as well. Of the nearly one billion credit dollars the Bank had put into circulation by now — Sam paused to savor that figure — the Bank's unrecovered losses had amounted to only $343,414.20. "In other words, losses as a result of the extension of credit have averaged only $9,800 a year."[34]

Sam might have boasted as much about his personal investments. Bill Prestridge's Union Gypsum Company in Arizona had prospered so well that in 1960, when he sold it to the National Gypsum Company, Sam's $50,000 seed money paid off in a bumper harvest: $450,000.[35]

Late in 1961, a call report caused Sam to peer at the figures closely. After thirty-six years, the year-end totals said what he and the whole Bank had been striving to read ever since 1925. Against the State National's deposits of $136,435,526, the El Paso National's totalled $141,422,342.

Throughout the Bank, Sam spread the glad word. "For the first time ever, we beat them! And not just by a nose. We're ahead by nearly $5 million!"[36]

All over the Bank faces lit up. That victory meant more than just dollars: it translated into good work and team spirit. Alongside of Sam, everybody aboard knew they could crow. "The biggest event in the Bank's history," Bill Foreman called it.[37]

For Sam, that praise came at a dramatic moment. At sixty-five, he had reached the Bank's stated age to retire. When he offered to do so, however, the board immediately declared him a firm exception: no question about it, don't quit.[38] Nevertheless, the annual meeting in January 1962 did recognize the fact that the time might be approaching when Sam would wish to slow down. All on it own, the board elected Sam Jr. executive vice president, at a salary of $14,400.[39]

Now Sam could turn his attention to urgent concerns in that other place he cared most about, his local, international community. Ever since 1951, he had pondered the old Chamizal dispute, the difficulties it always presented when long-range, expensive improvements were considered within that blighted, borderland six hundred acres. Now in 1962, the question of a right course of action came to a head when President John F. Kennedy and his ambassador to Mexico Thomas Mann, Sam's old friend from Woodville, urged him to assemble a group of prominent El Paso citizens to discuss the whole matter. The President had stated his own views clearly in Mexico City some months before. "The U.S. position is indefensible," he had told Mann. "Back in 1910, when the boundary issue arose once again, we agreed to abide by the decision of an arbitration board composed of a U.S. commissioner, a Mexican commissioner, and a disinterested third party, Eugene Lafleur of Canada. That board granted two-thirds of the land in dispute to Mexico. Their decision was clear, and we abide by it still."

After several meetings in Sam's office, U.S. Boundary Commissioner Joseph F. Friedkin, Thornton Hardie, Dorrance Roderick, Francis Morgan and others drew up a set of suggestions. When Sam presented that list to a large community group, the El Paso International City Association, many favored their proposal, many opposed. At last, "I just had one or two bucking the settlement," Sam later reported, "among them Thornton Hardie, who strongly questioned the honesty of the Canadian member of the 1910 arbitration board."

Sam drew Hardie aside. "Well now, whether he was honest or not, that's past history. Let's forget it."

When Hardie still opposed the proposition – so many acres to Mexico, so many acres to the United States, with a concreted river flume as the permanent boundary between them – Sam told him firmly, "We've got to get on to business."[40] With that, the ICA dispatched its views to Washington.

Sam's letter to Commissioner Friedkin on December 20, 1962, summed up the importance of the local group's suggestions. "There is no doubt that our relations with Mexico are productive of great support to our economy." Though "we on the border have been long aware of this, most Americans seem to have the idea that the roads to Mexico are one-way streets with American dollars flowing to the south and very few pesos returning." Now, he told Friedkin, he profoundly hoped that El Paso's new congressman, Ed Foreman, would work closely with the State Department "in getting this Chamizal problem resolved."[41]

With those recommendations en route to President Kennedy, Sam's daily hard-hat inspections around the new Bank building kept him informed. Working his way through the scaffolding with building engineer Harlan Hugg, he learned how to question the builders and how to get the results he wanted. When he looked skyward, there, rising slowly above him, was his dream becoming concrete and steel.

As Texans especially concerned with a satisfactory Chamizal settlement, Sam and Betty were guests of Vice President Lyndon B. Johnson at a Washington party in 1962. Lady Bird greeted them at the door, but Lyndon quickly came forward. "Lady Bird," he declared, "I want you to take Sam and Betty around and introduce them to all these people." Then he paused. "No, wait, I want to do it myself." With that, LBJ escorted them out onto the terrace to meet a circle of high dignitaries, among them the secretary of the treasury and the comptroller of the currency.[42]

Partly in response to hospitality like that, Sam played host several times to LBJ in El Paso when Johnson's assistant, Walter Jenkins, called him from Washington. "Sam, Lyndon is coming down to Fort Bliss, and he wants to use that bank suite you've got over there at the Paso Del Norte. He wants three bottles of Cutty Sark ready and waiting."

It was an easy request; Sam obliged.[43]

Weeks later, Jenkins called Sam again. "Now he wants you—as chairman of the El Paso Chamber of Commerce Armed Services Committee—to go with him by helicopter up to White Sands Missile Range."[44]

That afternoon, Sam was too committed to make any such trip, but when Johnson insisted he wanted to visit with him out at Biggs Field, Sam answered the summons. Unfortunately, other planes coming and going made so much noise that nothing important came of their shouted conversation.

On the home front, however, Sam did feel a deep sense of accomplishment when, once again, one of his fund drives paid off. Being photographed with his friend Federal Judge R. Ewing Thomason during the dedication of the First Presbyterian Church's new sanctuary brought home a truth he had learned long ago. A little friendly persuasion on the telephone could achieve money miracles when funds were needed and houses of God to be built.[45]

With the new Bank building nearly complete, Sam wrote Paul Kayser a grateful letter in January, 1963. "Sure, I'll join your Gas Company board." From the start of their friendship in 1928, he and Paul had looked at El Paso with the same creative ambitions. While it "seemed needless" for him to tell Paul of "my admiration for you as a man and my high appraisal of your character, integrity, and capacity," it was those qualities, he told Paul, that had placed his gas company among the foremost energy enterprises in the nation. "Your efforts alone have done more than any other combination of forces to develop the resources and commerce of the southwestern economy."[46]

Writing those words, Sam had to smile. Some years before when the Kaysers and Betty and he had shared the presidential suite at the Waldorf, Sam had commented about his old friend's limitless energy. "How do you manage to never slow down?"

"It's no trouble," Paul grinned. "Fifteen years after I die, I'm still gonna be living on momentum."[47]

Now scarcely three years after Eloy Vallina's death, Sam was amazed anew at the continuing results of Eloy's intuitive financial acumen. In February 1963 Carlos Trouyet notified Sam that Telefonos de Mexico had paid off all its American dollar notes. Furthermore, that its board, in line with a new government policy regarding foreign investors, had elected a Mexican to replace the American Sam Young on its board. While that move severed Sam's active connection with Telefonos, his shares – the compensation Eloy and Carlos had given him for his services – were now worth $900,000.

Shortly after that big announcement, Sam celebrated a personal victory much closer home. During his new building's tall rise, Sam's pleasure had grown along with it, watching it soar higher and higher, watching it become solid proof of his best aspirations. There was not quite such a moment, however, as the morning he stood in San Jacinto Plaza on the Mesa and Main Street corner and watched the sign company install, letter by letter, the proud name EL PASO NATIONAL BANK high on its tower. Assets and deposit totals, statement of condition reports in the newpapers' fine print were the standard ways any bank demonstrated its status. But up there, writ large in the blue sky, stood ineluctable proof to the public that his dreams in 1925 had come true. The biggest bank in El Paso was also the tallest.

By February 25, 1963, the Bank was fully moved into its handsome new quarters, and its 349 people were ready to welcome its first depositor when Kenneth Simmons, construction supervisor for builder R. E. McKee, captured that distinction.[48]

Like all its meetings over the years, the board's first meeting in its new board room on March 12 opened with a grateful prayer. Likewise, at the meeting in April, Paul Harvey spoke for the board to express "our deep appreciation and heartfelt thanks to Sam D. Young – man of broad vision, great courage, unexcelled ability, unfailing perseverance, abiding faith, dominant energy, unimpeachable integrity." Lacking C. M. Harvey's own presence today, "the pleasure he so would have enjoyed" devolved upon his two sons, Paul and Phil, "who, in his memory, offer this resolution."[49]

For celebrating such moments, the new building included a members-only retreat on its top floor. Like the Petroleum Club in Dallas and the Houston Club in Houston, the El Paso Club quickly became the city's most elegant social facility for cocktail parties, receptions, and banquets. Seated at his own special lunch table overlooking the city, Sam, as the Club's "Number One" member relished his daily chats with customers and friends, out-of-town guests, and the Bank family coming and going.

After Sam and Betty attended the formal opening of the new Hilton Hotel on April 21, 1963 in Athens,[50] Sam was back in his office when a

Betty Young, Rabbi Floyd Fierman, and Maude Harvey, at the Bank's ceremonial opening, May 19, 1963.

phone call came from Robert O. Anderson in Roswell, New Mexico. In the years since his first call to Sam for help with a payroll problem, Anderson had risen to the top in the oil industry. His Atlantic-Richfield Co. (ARCO) had placed his name among America's major petroleum tycoons. Now Robert O. was calling mainly to tell Sam he had just sold all of his oil properties. "I hope you got the full price you wanted," Sam told him.

Anderson sounded happy enough. "I got a bushel of Gulf Oil stock." From there he could shoot for the moon. Chatting about his coup, Anderson recalled a small moment far back in his association with Sam. "That payroll you covered me for, that just about saved my life."[51]

Much as Sam regretted Conrad Hilton's resigning from the Bank board in March 1963 – too busy now "travelling all over the world, opening about ten new hotels, breaking ground on four or five others"[52] – Sam was proud that Connie's name was carved on the new building's granite cornerstone along with his fellow directors. "I know it will be a source of pride to them and to the public generally to look upon the name Conrad N. Hilton in the years ahead with pride in the man's accomplishments."[53]

For flowers and music, ceremony and speeches, however, the truly big day for the Bank was Sunday, the nineteenth of May. Facing the uncertain future thirty-eight years before, Sam had felt no elation: the record of banks in El Paso could not have been worse. Yet those 456 prayers at the monthly board meetings had borne fruit in the skyscraper (wits below stairs had already dubbed it "Fort Sam") that he dedicated that day.

After El Paso's Roman Catholic Bishop Sidney M. Metzger's invocation, after Sam's minister George W. Burrough's prayer of dedication, Sam mounted the platform and acknowledged the guests and the many hands that had planned and constructed the building. "Without Mr. Harvey's helping and guiding hand, the roads to the Bank's success might never have opened." Sam specified his gratitude to Maude Harvey, "whose persuasive influence" was responsible for Harvey's "entry into the bank organization." He thanked Betty, his "particular overseer and superintendent," his "steady helpmate" for forty-two years.

Sam at a meeting of his El Paso National Bank board of directors, about 1960. From left to right (seated), Elward Kelly, M. R. "Bill" Prestridge, Phil Harvey, Dorrance Roderick, Sam, F. B. Fletcher, Paul Harvey, Thornton Hardie, Francis Morgan, and R. B. Price. From left to right (standing), Sam Jr., Sheley Warnock, Joe Nelan.

To the audience itself, Sam spoke directly. "This building, ladies and gentlemen, we hereby dedicate to the use, convenience, and, yes we say pride of an understanding people. You have helped us to build it, and certainly you shall share in the benefits through the years to come."

After Sam's graceful comments, after Rabbi Floyd Fierman's benediction, Maude Harvey and Betty, using a great pair of scissors, cut the chain of red roses spanning the entrance. Officially, they rode the escalators up to the main banking floor.

Chatting with the large crowd, Sam spied an old colleague. "B Bull," he called, "get yourself over here. Bring your husband." Sam grabbed their hands. "Mr. Knight, when your pretty wife worked for me, we were doing business down there in that little three-story building" – he nodded through the big picture window – "where Sheldon Jewelry is now. And we thought we were" – he and Bertha both chuckled – "so big."[54]

14

HANDS ACROSS THE BORDER

ONCE THE FESTIVITIES surrounding the new Bank's opening were over, Sam and Betty sat back and flew with Connie Hilton, Sam Jr., the Dorrance Rodericks and their daughter, Mrs. Frances Barnard, to open new hotels in Tokyo and Hong Kong. Lavish parties entertained the hundreds of special guests including Hollywood stars Irene Dunne, Ann Miller, and Bob Cummings, but A. P. di Tullio, Hilton's manager in Hong Kong, noted especially Sam Jr. "Your very fine son," he wrote Sam, "was the hit of the party and my eighteen-year-old daughter does not stop talking about him."[1]

Home again, Sam addressed the consequences of MacIntosh Murchison's recent death. With no son to succeed him in his Mortgage Investment Co., Mac's widow Louise and their daughter Patricia were faced with choosing a head for the firm. Since Patricia's husband Jonathan Rogers had only a B.A. from Yale and only limited business experience, Louise brought her concern to Sam. After several meetings together, Sam sensed in young Rogers real promise. With offers to help in any way possible, he recommended Rogers to the position. "At age thirty-five, of course, it's up to you, Jon, to make good."[2]

Similarly, a new appointment just now manifested how well a long-ago story of trouble had ended. Throughout the Depression, Sam had cheerfully reassured Mrs. Frank Feuille, Jr. "Things will get better. You and I both know they will." The times had indeed got better. On January 2, 1964, one of that lady's six children, Richard H. Feuille, joined Sam's board of directors.

The fact that Sam himself had also made good was applauded on January 30, 1964, at a dinner of the National Conference of Christians and Jews. Herbert Schwartz, Adolph's grandnephew, read the testimonial to Sam. "His distinguished and understanding leadership in civic, business and philanthropic affairs" had advanced the common welfare of his fellow citizens of "all religious beliefs and racial, economic and cultural backgrounds." In his contributions to El Paso, his state, and his nation, Sam had spurred the growth of good human relations "by his recognition of – and dedicated adherence to – the highest principles which motivate men in their relationsip to each other as children of God."[3]

Now at the January 14, 1964, board meeting, a dramatic change took place for Sam, for Sam Jr., and for the Bank. On Paul Harvey's motion, Sam at age sixty-eight retained his CEO status. At age thirty-four, on Sheley Warnock's motion, Sam Jr. was elected president and chief administrative officer at a salary of $22,500.

Equipped now to shoulder his new duties, when anyone asked Sam Jr. which of his many teachers had proved the most valuable, he firmly replied, "After seven years of on-the-job training? Sam D. Young!" Though he had come out of Stanford an "egghead" economist, he had learned through the school of hard knocks the whole process of negotiation and lending. From school and his summer sweat work on the farm, he was also fluent in Spanish.[4]

Now, as his own man, Sam Jr. assembled his own team of "right hands:" Jim Turnage, Jerry Roberts, John Thompson, John Dorris, and General Ernie Roberts, fresh from a distinguished career in the Korean War and at Fort Bliss as assistant commandant of the Army Air Defense School.

About his own feelings, Sam Sr. wrote William Bateman, vice president at Chase Manhattan, "My experience proves that it is most satisfying to a father to see a son succeed him in his endeavors and to feel secure in his faith that the son will not only carry on very successfully, but do a far better job."

In that direction Sam Jr. was by now well underway in his own board memberships and civic commitments. A trustee of the Texas

Teacher Retirement System, a member of the regional Export Expansion Council, he was also director of the El Paso International City Association and chairman of the Advisory Board of the El Paso YWCA.[5]

Seldom if ever since they were babies had Fanny had all her nine children under one roof, certainly not since they were grown. But on March 23, 1964, Sam laid business aside when the whole crowd – from Teah age seventy to Jack age fifty – went home to celebrate Fanny's ninetieth birthday. At the table that groaned under heaping platters and a cake ablaze with so many candles, Fanny in a navy blue dress sat smiling as people passed by to give her a kiss. There was much laughter; there were perhaps a few tears. But there was no speech except one when Fanny glanced slowly around and softly remarked to her family, "I have had every one of you children close to my heart for at least fifty years."[6]

During that happy occasion, Sam stood a little aside and let himself feel a deep satisfaction as he looked at the brothers and sisters who had always concerned him. All of them now were mature individuals fully into their own lives. Teah was Mrs. Fletcher Ryan living in Houston. Cooper was well again after his recent stroke and able to function again as Mama's companion. Thomas had his own hotel in Longview, a profitable establishment he had bought from Conrad Hilton. Brother Pete was, well, Pete's drinking made him still "just our Pete, our problem." Mike owned two grocery stores in El Paso, and for some years now he had been connected with one of the city's major real estate firms. Margaret, now Mrs. William G. Parker, lived in Houston. Phebe was married to Houston architect Dan Armstrong. Jack was president of the State National Bank in Corsicana.[7]

Soon after that happy event, Sam himself had occasion to credit the good help he had received from certain Bank people. Over the years his various secretaries had worked diplomatically and energetically in his high-test office, and it came as a serious loss when Christine Gill, his sweet-tempered head secretary for fourteen years, died in 1964. Suddenly, Sam was aware in ways he had not wholly perceived until then, of the vital assistance a loyal aide-de-camp in his outer office supplied. To replace Chris, nobody seemed qualified.

When Faye Hartman, however, took her turn as Sam's administrative assistant, she had already been on his team for ten years. Rising through many departments, she had learned how all the parts in the Bank's "jigsaw puzzle" fitted together. In college, she had made the dean's list. More importantly now, she could take orders, but she could also maintain her poise.

To play his own new role effectively, President Sam Jr. instituted a training program for the officers and the employees. He established an improved performance evaluation system covering all the Bank's employees; he restructured the planning and budgeting systems; and, to improve management control, he enhanced the data processing system.[8] As the old guard was changing, he instituted operational changes no less dramatic. His report to the shareholders in January 1965 described the new Burroughs B-270 Electronic Data Processing equipment.[9]

Yet in his general statement of policy, Sam Jr. articulated anew the policy set down in the beginning. "We have always held that there are no 'little' customers, only 'little' bankers whose vision is clouded by dollar signs on the lenses of their eyes. It is our hope and belief that El Paso National Bank will always recognize the importance of each individual, without prejudice because of his financial stature, or lack of it."[10]

Hearing that reaffirmation, Sam himself settled back in his chair, still content with that stand. The guiding principle of all the Bank's endeavors still rested on fairness, integrity, conservative respect for the customer, and also – let it be added – a bit of down-home regard for other people's good fortune. By now, in addition to his friendly handshakes around town, Sam had adopted a special method to encourage new savings accounts.

Whenever a "new baby" announcement came in the mail, he summoned Faye Hartman. "Send out our baby letter. To – let's see here – to Juan D. Ochoa, born May 23. Enclose a deposit slip for $25. And tell the proud parents he owns our newest savings account. Wish them well. Tell them to come in and see me." When the baby belonged to one of his Bank family, he paid the deposit himself. When it belonged to a client, he used his Bank discretionary fund.[11]

People reading their *Times* of April 1, 1964, were astonished by a photograph on page 1. According to the accompanying story, most of the huge sign atop the El Paso National Bank Building on the Stanton

Street side was missing. Since "the letters are some 18 stories above street level," whatever culprits had stolen them had "risked their lives." The FBI expected to handle the investigation. Since the building "was erected over the Bataan Trainway on air rights," no other agency "had any legal jurisdiction."[12] The chatter in the carpools coming to work ran high until they sighted the actual building. The sign stood unharmed. Only then did the date on the paper dawn clear. "April Fool!"

Death brought heartache to Sam and his family in June, when they attended Governor's funeral in Houston. LBJ's message to Oveta's family fully matched Sam's own feelings. "He viewed the world with tolerant eyes and his wit and humor always salvaged a time of crisis and made it endurable."[13]

Soon after, a friend asked Sam what Governor had meant to him over the years. Slowly, Sam put his long thoughts into words. "Nobody could ever say enough about that good friend. What did he ever see in a man like me?"[14]

Indeed, heavy concerns were on Sam's mind, when he wrote Teah in February 1965. Though Betty was "slowly improving from diverticulitis, we face the ordeal of an operation to remove part of the colon as soon as she is strong enough." After that surgery, Betty's convalescence was long, and her spirits flagged often. Slowly, she was back on her feet, though eager for bed long before her normal routine.

Along with his worry for Betty, the fighting in Vietnam in May 1965 weighed so heavily on Sam that he delivered his thoughts to Lyndon Johnson. "In Vietnam your acceleration of our retaliatory blows should prove far more effective in bringing about lasting peace than any attempts at the conference table. We know that you were most reluctant to jeopardize the lives of more American boys, but indecision and delay in these troubled areas could, and most likely would have resulted in far greater casualties."[15]

"Dear Sam:" Lyndon Johnson wrote back, "I'm hopeful that our decision to save lives and freedom in our hemisphere will be judged right by the final arbiter – the objective light of history. In the meantime, I'm deeply grateful that you approve."[16]

Then it was June 29 once again, forty years since that date became special to Sam and the Bank. To recognize its specialness now, the Bank's Statement of Condition as of June 30, 1965, referred to the Bank's first statement. Their comparative figures told a big story.

	1925	*1965*
Loans and discounts:	$ 476,744.29	$ 73,612,036.60
Furniture and fixtures:	10,000.00	896,114.50
Capital stock:	200,000.00	5,500,000.00
Deposits:	1,226,719.16	146,275,685.65

Sam's response to a flood of congratulations was typified by his thank-you letter to Eugene Tamillo, vice president of Continental Illinois National, Chicago. "You, Jim Johnson, and your 108-year-old banking giant were mighty nice to remember us at El Paso National." Though for the Bank's 36 officers and 363 employees, June 29, 1965, had begun much the same as any other bank day, "we took the time to look back over the past, not without some nostalgic twinges by those of us whose bones are beginning to feel the ravages of time!"[17]

The ravages of time and the job were also uppermost on Gus Bianche's mind in late 1965 when he told Sam he had had enough of the tensions at work and the long hours his right hand position required. Writing press releases, drafting letters for Sam's signature, indeed preparing annual reports to the stockholders had taken their toll. Their goodbye was cordial, but Gus used that occasion to speak his thoughts straight to the good friend who had been at times his task master.[18]

To others, Gus was equally frank about "Mr. Sam." "He was really a man who was shy and who had a feeling that he was not as competent as people thought he was. To make up for that, he would bang his desk and yell at you." Still, all in all, Gus continued, "he was the most generous man I ever met. I said to him once, 'Under that hard veneer, you're as soft as putty.'"[19]

That October, twenty-year-old Rob Hoover III wrote his grandparents that he meant to become a banker. Answering Rob, Sam was pleased "that you think you will be happy in banking," but Rob must never feel that his granddad would be disappointed if he changed his mind. "The greatest ingredient of success is to be situated happily, to actually enjoy work," and see one's efforts "bring smiles and happy situations to the people you have served." Service, even at some personal sacrifice, "brings greater satisfaction to the soul than any other compensation one might expect or receive."[20]

"Personal sacrifice" was the last thing on their minds while Sam and Betty were staying at the Waldorf-Astoria in December. After dinner, they returned to their room in the Waldorf Towers only to find that

Betty's locked suitcase had been broken open: jewelry worth $15,000 was missing. The room showed no sign of forcible entry, but the New York detectives later surmised that a stiff plastic strip had been used to force the lock on the door.[21]

Stripped of her favorite bracelets and earrings, most of them Mimi's family heirlooms, Betty fought back the tears. She had often asked Sam when he was contemplating some expensive purchase, "But, Sam, can we afford it?" Now she knew she certainly could not afford the heartache involved in losing those family treasures.

Sam and Sam Jr.'s adopting new methods, streamlining procedures wherever appropriate, increasing use of the Bank's data processing facilities under John Dorris had clearly paid off by April 5, 1966, when the Federal and State call report was published. In deposits, El Paso National outranked the 10 other banks in the county, it ranked 12th in Texas. In the United States, the Bank ranked 228th. And "in the entire free world," so read the report, it measured 477th.[22]

As CEO, Sam maintained his strong profile throughout the Bank's operation, though nowhere more prominently so than in a case where forty years of experience overrode younger opinions. A loan application had come from a local church. For its new building, it needed $800,000. The loan committee had done its full homework; each member had studied the packet. Consequently, when the time came to discuss that application, Sam's call for opinions made the rounds of the table. In every case, the reply was, "No collateral, not a bankable loan," till the question came back to Sam. "It's sound," he declared firmly. "Anything is all right if it's covered by pledges for the work of the Lord."[23] With the Bank's $800,000, the congregation did erect their building. They did pay off their note on time.

Sam had long enjoyed his La Jolla neighbor, Frank Freeman, a Hilton director and head of Paramount Publix Theatres, but never more so than when they agreed on politics and the state of the nation. In 1965, Freeman mentioned a conversation he had recently had with actor Ronald Reagan. "This country needs straightening out," Reagan had said to Frank many times, "and to do that we need to cut out all the monkey business Roosevelt started up there in Washington."

"Just how would one plan to do that?" Freeman wanted to know.

Reagan's answer was quick. "To do my part in that effort, I want to run for governor of California."

"But, Ronnie," Frank laughed, "you couldn't get elected. You're just an actor."

Reagan did not laugh back. "Maybe I am just an actor. But there's nothing like trying."

Freeman studied Reagan a moment. "Well, if you run, I'll support you."

Shortly after those talks, as Freeman commented to Sam, Reagan got in touch with Freeman again. "I'm going to run," he told Frank.

"And you know," Freeman related later, "I still didn't think he meant it, not till he did run and got himself firmly elected. Nationally, he'll be a figure to watch from now on."[24]

Throughout the winter of 1966-67, Sam and Betty busied themselves with the new house they were building on the western slope of the Franklins. Though the site overlooked green valley land and the tawny dunes of the New Mexico desert, they filled their new home with reminders of their East Texas past and their foreign travels. The white French chateau at 841 Cherry Hill "reflects the elegant good taste and meticulous planning of the gracious chatelaine who designed the home herself," reported the *Times*. In the family room, near the game table was a painting of an old East Texas sawmill." In its own wing, Sam Young, Jr.'s quarters were "masculine and practical." Large cabinets contained "his guns, his skis, and his golf and tennis gear."[25] For Sam personally, though the new house was a thing of peace to come home to, its backyard was uniquely convenient because it abutted the Coronado Country Club golf course.

On the home front, there was another cause of rich satisfaction for Sam now as he watched his own brother's career. In July 1967, after a stiff workout as a state bank examiner and a distinguished career in commercial banking, including the presidencies of two East Texas banks, Jack Young became president of El Paso National's Northgate National Bank.[26]

For more than five years now, Sam had prodded and buttonholed on behalf of his firm conviction that the Chamizal international land question must be laid to rest once and for all. Though he was out of town at the time, he took a parent's own pride in the headline proceedings that took place on October 28, 1967, in El Paso. At the center of the new Bridge of the Americas spanning the Rio Grande, Presidents Lyndon Baines Johnson and Gustavo Díaz Ordaz formally celebrated the settlement of the Chamizal Dispute between their two nations.

Together, they dedicated a stainless steel monument on the international border, now forever demarked by a concreted river channel.

Díaz Ordaz declared, "What we are doing here today is an example of what can be achieved when reason, good will, and sincere desire to maintain friendship between peoples prevail." Lyndon Johnson affirmed, "Let this monument and this place stand as testimony to the world of what two nations, working together, can accomplish."[27]

The commemorative bronze plaque that Sam received shortly thereafter bore presidential words that precisely echoed his own convictions, "We approached the council table with respect for each other's rights and determined to achieve a good and lasting settlement," from Johnson. "Friendship will not flourish unless it is between men who know how to respect one another," from Díaz Ordaz. A gift from Lyndon Johnson, the plaque featured a bas relief view of the two friendly cities together.[28]

Díaz Ordaz and Johnson themselves had recognized the end of the Chamizal dispute back in October, but on June 21, 1968, a black-tie ceremony at the Mexican Embassy in Washington recognized Sam's own special role in that settlement. Months before, Ambassador Thomas Mann and Carlos Trouyet had suggested to Díaz Ordaz that Sam deserved special gratitude, and Leo Schuster had written a strongly supportive letter.

Now, Hugo Margain, Mexico's ambassador to the United States, assembled his aides around Sam and spoke of Mexico's deep affections for Sam, especially for his abiding economic confidence in that nation and particularly for his efforts to solve "Chamizal." He then presented to Sam, on El Presidente's behalf, the Aztec Eagle Award, the highest honor Mexico bestows on a foreigner.

Gripping his script, Sam cleared his throat, took a deep breath to shore up his nerves before the audience of two hundred dignitaries, relatives, and friends, then moved to the podium. "Mr. Ambassador" – he again cleared his throat – "distinguished guests, and friends: The people and the government of the Republic of Mexico have done me great honor today. Your gracious reception, your kind words and, above all, the presentation of this most coveted distinction have touched me deeply." He paused to glance at his audience. "From the teachings of my childhood, and through the lessons I have learned in my adult years, I have come to believe profoundly that the greatest single formula for a happy and productive life is exemplified in the

Sam's Aztec Eagle Medal, the highest award Mexico ever bestows on a foreigner, June 1968.

Sam and Betty, with Olga and Dorrance Roderick, about 1965.

words passed down to us over the centuries, those which admonish us to love our neighbors as ourselves."

"In 1924," he and his wife – he glanced at Betty – had sensed that "the people of two nations, with completely different cultures, had settled down to live side by side, in dignity, mutual respect, and relative harmony." After a short time, their friends included many Mexicans. With them, over the years, they had shared some of "the most meaningful and satisfying moments in our lives." Nodding toward the Vallina family, Sam remembered especially Eloy Vallina, Sr., who had shown him "that difference in language, heritage, and culture" posed no actual barriers, that "the *will to understand* was the mortar that joined us inseparably together."

Nodding toward Carlos Trouyet and Floyd Ransom, Sam referred to their part in "the joint ventures and willing cooperation between Mexican and El Paso capital which had been notably successful for both parties."

Sam referred then to the larger world. With "nations and ideologies seemingly in constant contention," the "only real hope for survival," he said, was for "neighbors to be good neighbors, and for friends to be truly good friends, in every hamlet, village, city and country – wherever people live in the world." With the Chamizal settlement, "the keystone has now been set in place. It is for us – all of us – to build upon and around it, for all the world to see that brotherhood knows no border."[29]

When he reached home, a letter from Washington confirmed the same sentiments. "Dear Sam: I share the pride that must have been yours as you received the Order of the Aztec Eagle from the Mexican Government. Our neighbor and Sister Republic could not have chosen better. And this President could not be happier for their choice. Your long and tireless work for Mexican-American relations has enriched the lives of both our peoples and has strengthened a friendship that knows no boundary. Please accept all our congratulations, my friend, and our best wishes always. Sincerely, Lyndon B. Johnson."[30]

Then the floodgates were open. An *El Paso Times* editorial declared Sam Young's Aztec Eagle award a "compliment to the good feeling that exists between El Paso and Mexico. All of us like that."[31] At the behest of State Senator Joe Christie, the Texas Legislature passed a resolution[32] commending "Sam D. Young for his diligence in fostering friendly relations between the Republic of Mexico and the United States."

And Ambassador Mann wrote him similar high praise in August. "I am certain that it would not have been possible to have a suggested negotiation without the skillful and helping hand which you extended early in the game when very, very few people thought it would be possible to succeed when so many others had failed."[33]

But for Sam, Rob Hoover's letter from his naval training base in San Diego was especially welcome. "Perhaps it might seem presumptive," Rob supposed, "for a grandson to tell his grandfather that he is proud of him, but I am proud of you, Pappy."[34]

The festivities climaxed on June 26 at the El Paso Country Club when the Trouyets and the Vallinas hosted eight hundred guests at a dinner. After cocktails around the swimming pool blanketed with gardenias flown up from Mexico, Sam gave a short form of his remarks in Washington. The dancing lasted till six the next morning.

At nine A.M., Conrad Hilton charged into Sam's outer office. "Where is everybody?" he asked Faye Hartman.

"Well, I'm the only one here, so far. You know the party did go on pretty late."

"Oh, you bet I know," Connie grinned, "But when is Sam coming in?"

"I don't really know, Mr. Hilton. Would you just like to come on into his office. He should be here shortly."[35]

Connie cooled his heels for more than an hour. When Sam finally showed up, Faye could hear their laughter recounting the whole celebration.

15

HAVE A GOOD DAY AND PASS IT ON

FOR SAM, THE SUMMER OF 1968 was almost continuous high ceremony. On June 12, nine days before the Aztec Eagle festivities in Washington, the Providence Hospital Board took matters into their own hands when Sam refused to recognize a "new business" motion. "I move we call the hospital's new wing the Sam D. Young Tower," Dorrance Roderick called out.

Shaking his head, Sam thumped the table. "The meeting will come to order."

"But I still move we – " Dorrance insisted.

Grinning, Sam thumped it again. "And I still refuse to accept that motion."

Dorrance, however, refused to back down. "Well then, Mr. Chairman, with all due respects I'll take that motion myself." In spite of Sam's protest, the motion carried unanimously.[1]

Apropos of those words, Jack Curlin, a former El Paso National Bank officer and a hospital board member now, spoke straight from watching President Sam in action at Providence. "It's clear to me that his motives are truly religious. He really is dedicated to the good of the community. His time at the hospital gets him nothing at all except the satisfaction, he says, 'in trying to do what needs doing.'" At the Providence board meetings, "Sam always runs a tight ship," Curlin continued, "always expects up-to-date reports from his chief of staff, his director of nursing, and the hospital administrator himself. And interestingly enough, he won't have any doctors on the Providence board. 'They'd be too jealous of each other – professionally, financially, temperamentally.' he says. But he is strongly convinced that people like Dorrance Roderick, Francis Morgan, Ruth O'Hara, Bob Price, and Irene Wulfjen – community leaders not medically oriented – can best see the big picture. Interesting too, he always begins his board meetings with prayer."[2]

On December 13, Sam and Betty were on hand to witness the final ceremony regarding the Chamizal settlement. Afterwards, Betty and Sam were guests at the luncheon at the Paso del Norte that President Johnson and Lady Bird hosted for Mexican President Díaz Ordaz and his wife. The large crowd of other dignitaries included many people who had contributed in one way or another to that long-awaited happy outcome.[3]

Friendly relations, internationally speaking, were no more important to Sam even now than the congeniality he still expected every day at the Bank. One morning John Dorris's secretary of only three days answered her telephone. "Mr. Dorris's office."

The caller's voice was quick and direct. "Let me speak to him."

"All right, sir," June Fore replied. "May I say who's calling?"

Suddenly, the phone at her ear erupted. "Of course not. I'll be damned if I'll have a secretary around here asking 'Who's calling.' Put Dorris on."

By now, June was too upset to know what to do. All of her secretarial training "had instructed me to ask just what I had asked that angry man on the phone."

As soon as the call was over, however, John Dorris came out and told her the caller was CEO Sam Young himself. "I should have explained that it isn't Bank policy to ask who's calling."

The next day, the voice called again. "This is Sam Young, calling to apologize for the way I talked yesterday. I should have explained that this Bank is open to everybody that wants to talk to any of us, no matter who or what time. When we say we want to be El Paso's friendliest bank, we mean it. I'm sorry nobody told you."[4]

After that, June came to like and respect her new boss, especially one morning "when I got to the building a few minutes early and I saw him out on the sidewalk all by himself picking up the stray trash."

Sam with the Providence Hospital board of directors and administrators, March, 1968. From left to right (seated), Bob Byrne, C. G. Whyburn, Irene Wulfjen, Sam, Louise Murchison, W. V. Holik, Allen Grambling. From left to right (standing), Jack Curlin, Rev. Paul Poling, Paul Harvey, Dorrance Roderick, H. D. Fulwiler, Edward Schwartz, A. R. Arnold, Gordon Foster.

"Why, Mr. Young," she hailed him, "why are *you* doing that?"

Sam looked up and smiled. "Well, I kind of think of this building as mine and I like keeping it neat. I want it nice for everybody that comes along here today." With that, June helped Sam finish his chore.[5]

Within the family, Sam Jr.'s personal life underwent a distinct change late in 1968. At a party in California, he met Mrs. Marilyn Mays Beard. Though Betty and Sam, and indeed Grandmother Mimi, had often chided him "for not, well, bringing home a nice girl and sharing your plans with us," the many dates Sam Jr. had brought home had never been serious. And to the time of her death in 1955 Mimi had clearly understood why. True to his long ago promise to her, he had never met quite the one girl "you can't live without."[6]

From the start of their friendship, Sam Jr. had known that Marilyn was exactly that girl, but Marilyn herself had several factors to weigh. By her former marriage, she had three young children – Elizabeth, Emily, and Allison – and any change she made now must bear them in mind.

For the next several months, flying back and forth every weekend or so to La Jolla, Sam found the visits were always pleasant, and each time, he came home more certain than ever how he felt about Marilyn. But each time, he came home "empty handed." In late June 1969, he called La Jolla. "Marilyn, I'm coming out there next weekend and you're either coming home with me, or you're not. And that will be that."

Marilyn replied that she would think about "that" until she got back from a sailing trip, then let him know. A week later, Sam Jr. was playing in a golf tournament at Fort Bliss when a sergeant came running. "Urgent phone call from La Jolla. You're to call them right back."

On the phone, Marilyn told him straight. "You don't have to come get me. I'll be there tonight." That night, a Monday, he gave her a ring. When they told the family that they were planning to marry the following Thursday, Betty wailed, "But you can't have the wedding that soon. I left all my hats on an airplane last week. I don't have a hat."

Sam Jr. grinned, "Well, get you another hat."

The wedding took place at the First Presbyterian Church on July 16, 1969, before a large crowd of family and friends. Later, Sam Jr. commented, "It was the most exciting time of my life."[7]

A few months before that happy event, a big change had come to the Bank's credit system. In Master Charge, El Paso quickly perceived the advantages in using "plastic money." Now, a three-party transaction could occur in the one place most convenient for all, the counter next to the merchant's cash register.[8] All over town, the red and gold circles of the Master Charge logo vastly extended the Bank's credit facilities and in due time, its profits.

To house that new operation, 3,000 square feet of basement floor space were remodeled into offices. Like a path, two bright green stripes in the hall flooring guided the customer straight from the elevator to the Master Charge Department. Soon, the Bank adopted a distinctive new logo, a golden sun surrounded by eight bright swirls of light. Though each swirl represented a "C" characteristic of the Bank's trade area (climate, cotton, cattle, commerce, clothing, culture, and "the confluence of two great nations"), somebody commented that the logo should now include two additional swirls, one for "credit," the other for "card."

Freer now to circulate over the country, flying to board meetings in New York and Chicago and Mexico City, Sam often made simpler trips back home to Woodville to see about Fanny. Now in September 1969, Fanny's death at age ninety-five grieved him profoundly.

It had been years since he had tried to explain to his mother the dramatic leaps his life had taken "out there, so far west from home." Discussing his busy routines, he had concentrated mostly on family, his farms – of late he had taken a special delight in planting pecan trees – and the doings of Little Betty and Sam Jr. When he mentioned the current prices for cotton and chile, Fanny nodded. She smiled when he noted Connie Hilton's latest forays. But the most she usually said was couched in a few words. "You are still my hard-working big son, and I'm proud of you."

For Sam, as he hugged her, that was enough.

Within a few days, Oveta wrote him from Houston. "Dear Sam, I was deeply distressed to learn of your mother's death," but she did hope that he could find consolation in knowing "that no mother ever had a more devoted son."[9]

The next fall, Sam was no less concerned for his own offspring. At the University of Colorado, eighteen-year-old Doak Hoover was asserting himself in a manner Sam found "difficult." During his first visit home, Doak's full beard had caused such a strong reaction in Sam that he wrote Doak a troubled letter. Doak was "a very fine looking young man," but why was he choosing to look like a hippie?[10]

Doak's lengthy reply covered the hair and a few other subjects. "I was very sad to hear that my appearance is so very important to my family's opinion of me. I've always hoped that some day people would not judge others by appearance, but I'm learning that some things as trivial as 'looks' make so much difference. As to the reference 'hippie', I didn't realize that I was entering the anti-establishment class. I still believe in capitalism and I don't think people should 'be given something for nothing.'" Emphatically, he said, "My moral and philosophical outlook hasn't changed since I've been here," even though a girl no older than he had asked him recently, "When are you going to shave that shit off your face?"[11]

That weighty matter accepted, Sam had reasons aplenty to reaffirm his own capitalist views in December 1970 in Mexico City. Among the Mexican government's special guests, Sam and Betty attended the inauguration of new president, Luis Echeverria. They welcomed the invitation, but the inaugural speech Sam found "deeply troubling." Though it contained many references to the distribution of private lands into vast government-controlled *ejidos* and to the dire needs of the poor, it gave no clear details regarding solutions. To the man seated next to him, London banker Leopold de Rothschild, Sam whispered his fears. "Communism." Nodding his head, Rothschild agreed.[12]

A personal matter that proved even more troubling occurred on May 7, 1971, when seventy-four-year-old Sam suffered frustration at the El Paso airport. His long-time driver, Ruben Green, had attempted to pick up Sam's luggage in the baggage claim area, but since his ticket pack lacked a claim check, the attendant Billy Holt refused to release the bag. Apparently, Sam tried to tell Holt, the check-in official in Houston had failed to give him a claim check. Lacking that, he showed Holt his I. D. card; he showed him his driver's license. He even offered to describe the bag's contents, but the attendant stood firm: no claim check, no luggage. In frustration, Sam grabbed up his bag; an angry scuffle ensued; and Sam struck Holt in the chest.[13]

A long-distance phone call the next day explained the missing claim check, but it came too late to erase the problem. The man who had checked in just behind Sam had reached home in California, only to discover that his ticket packet contained an extra claim check. The harm already done, on July 26, 1971, Billy Holt filed a $20,000 personal injury suit against Sam.[14] The case would take months to receive a verdict.

In May 1971 at the urging of clothing manufacturer William F. Farah and other eastside business people, Sam and Sam Jr. opened a third satellite bank. With Travis Johnson as board chairman, this new Border City Bank at 7738 Gateway East quickly became another star producer among their trio of neighborhood banks. As a result, the corporate owners of the three independent affiliates and the venerable parent now needed to form themselves into one holding company, the better to manage them all.

Sam Jr. explained the new step to his people. In addition to the major shareholders, many smaller owners were not fully benefiting from the close relationship now between the three little banks and the big bank downtown. To give these individuals "a little bigger cut of the pie," Sam and Sam Jr. had decided to combine all the shareholders into one company. "All we are doing is putting into actual form what we already have in substance."[15]

While such a step was declared "outside the intent of the law" in 1948 when the First State Bank was formed, now in 1971 a new Texas banking commissioner sat in the judgment seat, and the Federal Reserve Board itself, under the Bank Holding Company Act, had long ago approved "affiliate" banks in other states. With those factors in mind, the new Trans Texas Bancorporation, Inc. ought to have "smooth sailing ahead."

On the home front, fifty years had now passed since Betty and Sam's wedding, and the time had come to celebrate at a cocktail buffet hosted by Little Betty, her new husband Martin Bauman, and Marilyn and Sam Jr. at the El Paso Club.[16]

Likewise, another family event so pleased the Bank board on December 14, 1971, that it recorded its happy good will in its minutes. "Eleven hours before this meeting," Marilyn and Sam Jr.'s daughter Whitney Blair Young was born, a fact which made her "the youngest stockholder in our history."[17]

Helping Little Betty and Martin Bauman celebrate their first wedding anniversary soon after, Sam and Betty were on a cruise with them in the Black Sea when a young woman came up to Sam at a hotel in Odessa, Russia. "I am graduate engineer," she whispered. "If I get $600 to buy ticket, I can leave Russia." In dismay, Sam stared at the girl. "Only $600," the girl whispered again.

Slowly, he studied her meaning, then shook his head. "There is nothing I'd rather give you," he said. "I'm afraid, however, that that would violate the laws of your country."

"Little money," she pleaded, "for ticket?"

Disturbed for the girl, yet ill at ease in the whispered exchange, Sam saw no possible way to help her. Sam was still pondering the matter back aboard ship.[18] The other Americans all shook their heads, but they stood firm with Sam. "There was nothing you *could* do. Or be sure she could have bought the ticket. If that was, in fact, why she wanted your $600."

From his deck chair, watching Odessa's palm-fringed coast line fading away in the distance, Sam was still disturbed by the challenge the woman had posed him. "For the first time in my life," he said later, "I had to realize that no amount of American dollars could help a human being in trouble." Shaking his head, he reiterated, "Frustrating and bad."[19]

Back in harness at home, Sam soon learned that his hopes for "smooth sailing ahead" for his Trans Texas Bancorporation promised to be very short lived. On March 29, 1972, the Anti-Trust Division of the U. S. Department of Justice filed suit against it, charging that "consummation of the proposed acquisition by Trans Texas of the four El Paso banks would have a significant adverse effect on competition in the El Paso banking market."[20]

Glumly, Sam shook his head. Back in 1971, when he and his colleagues had launched that new venture, of the thirteen banks in El Paso County Sam's market share had been over 41 percent. Irked now at the Justice Department's objections, Sam could perceive, nonetheless, how clearly that percentage figure indicated his own bank's solid progress. Back in 1925, little El Paso National had enjoyed a market share of only 6 percent.[21] Another factor in the Justice Department's charge was even more annoying. The four Trans Texas Banks, so it held, were in "actual competition with themselves." Indeed, it affirmed, there was some degree of "impermanence in the informal common control relationship" which existed among them.[22]

About the whole matter, Bill Deffebach, the Bank's legal counsel, detailed for Sam the corporation's position. In this area of cases, "We are pioneering the law. There is not one single precedent for evaluating our chances. The effect of 'common ownership' on mergers or acquisitions subject to Section 7 of the Clayton Anti-Trust Act has not been determined by the courts. Furthermore, on more than one occasion, the Supreme Court has decided that 'common ownership' of the participants does not excuse their anti-competitive conduct under the Sherman Act." Worse still, warned Deffebach, "the Department of Justice has not lost a Section 7 case in the Supreme Court during the past twenty years."[23]

Sam pondered Deffebach's candid opinion, then shook his head. "The die is already cast," he insisted firmly. "We won't buckle under." Deffebach should push now for the earliest possible trial date. Until the court verdict, Trans Texas was floating in limbo.

Meanwhile, minding the store, in April 1972 President Sam Jr. reaffirmed his long-standing appreciation for the Bank's customers when he congratulated nine staff members who had just completed the Bank's Customer Service Training School. "Without the customer walking into the Bank and walking out happy and satisfied, we are lost." Distributing completion certificates to Jack Battaglia, Jim Classen, Candy Cline, Winfried Dorn, Leo Kramer, Jesus Mena, Ellen Miller, Paul Montez, and Joe Teitsworth, Sam Jr. added, "The reports are terrific on the success of this class. I'm delighted you've done such a good job."[24]

Keeping customers happy, especially out in the motor bank, could involve some drama. Over the years Ray Pierce, the Bank's head security guard, had been honked at, bumped, and backed into. "It's a three-ring circus,"[25] Ray often commented. "Sometimes stalled cars had to be pushed out of the line. Once the car of two University of Texas at El Paso students had to be pushed up to a window so they could cash a check for some gas. On windless days in the summer, carbon monoxide fumes could build up to 'eye burning' levels. But windy March days could be worse."

One spring, Ray heard somebody yell, "Stop that woman!" Across Mesa Street, a little old lady was being hurled around by the wind. When Ray reached her, she was prone on the pavement, her glasses gone, her lip bleeding. But, as he grabbed her, she bristled up at him, "Leave me alone," she cried, staggering onto her feet. "I'm no sissy!"

Since 1925, El Paso's cultural life had grown to include a symphony, several live theatres, an art museum, a history museum, and several permanent concert and lecture series. Now, in line with the Bank's long support of the community's good, Sam Jr. co-chaired a campaign to establish public television. Once the campaign succeeded, the city became so quickly enamored of this latest improvement that it could hardly imagine itself without it.

That fall, Sam himself was back in action again as a fund raiser when he agreed to serve on the Republican National Finance Committee to re-elect Richard M. Nixon. When he decided also to chair the local campaign to re-elect Senator John Tower, it was time again to pick up the phone. To Tom Gunning, a First State director and owner of a chain of drug stores, Sam came straight to the point. "Tom, can I put you down for a contribution?"

"Gee, I don't know, Mr. Young, I –"

Gunning was about to say $100 when Sam volunteered, "Perhaps $1,000?"

Tom gulped. "Well, uh, uh, maybe $500?"

"Fine. Fine," Sam replied brightly, "Thank you very much, Tom."

Telling his wife Emily about it later, Tom still was not sure what Sam had done to him. "Mr. Young was so slick, I don't know if I lost $400 or saved $500."[26]

For almost fifty years now, Sam and Dorrance Roderick had relished the ways each could work for the good of the El Paso community. By 1972, however, Roderick had reasons to simplify his routine. "My only son died in 1970," he explained, "and it's a question of carrying on something."[27] When the Gannett newspaper chain offered him $26 million for his *El Paso Times*, Roderick's big sale involved Sam in the profits. For his own stock in the *Times*, Sam reaped a harvest of $480,000.[28]

Like Roderick, Sam might have receded into retirement. With Sam Jr. as president and Sam as CEO, the fact was that with the Bank's ever-increasing endeavors, two heads at times were distinctly better than one. Especially, when the loan committee needed Sam's sharp, practiced eye.

"It never fails," John Garrett, one of those loan officers, explained to a newcomer, "that no matter how well they all prepare their cases, Sam immediately fingers their weak points. As one of us falls before the boss's attack, the rest of us – one by one – silently slide our papers under the desk." When Sam asked if anyone else had a recommendation, "we all shake our heads. Later, we laugh, but at the time it isn't so funny."

Garrett grinned wryly. "Oh, he can be tough, but he never is mean. Young is always tightly conservative, and for that reason his officers are irate, many times. But a banker has got to be careful. To most of us, Mr. Young is kind of like your daddy. He can give you a licking, but then everything is all right again. It all stems from whether or not you respect and admire the man, and we certainly do. You take your medicine and then you get on with your job."[29]

Bill Stevens reported the same impression. "He can grind you down if you let him. But when I stand up to him and say exactly why I do what I do, he cools off. He may comment, 'I still think it's a risky loan, but I trust your judgment.'"[30]

The case against the Trans Texas Bancorporation took a new turn on September 25, 1972 when it came to trial in Federal Court in El Paso, with Judge Ernest Guinn presiding.[31] Six weeks later, on November 13, Guinn ruled in favor of Trans Texas, but the Department of Justice appealed to the Supreme Court. Again, the future of Trans Texas looked highly uncertain.

Meanwhile, when Sheley Warnock retired on December 29, 1972, after forty-four years as one of Sam's "steady right hands," Sam could look back at those years with Sheley as total profit. Matching Sam temper for temper, Sheley had worn more administrative titles than any other employee. From assistant cashier, he had risen to vice president, first vice president, senior vice president, executive vice president, and vice chairman of the board.[32] Acknowledging that rise, Sam spread on the board's minutes his thoughts about Sheley's retirement. "He came to us at a time when the Bank needed him very much, and he leaves us at a time when the Bank needs him very much."[33]

Five months later, an event sobered the Bank and the El Paso community when Richard S. "Cinco" Rogers, president of the Border City Bank, was killed in the bank on May 1, 1973, in an apparent extortion attempt. The murder had come with no warning: no principle was clearly proved in the death. But the next week, Sam Jr. used that event to illustrate a serious point in his welcoming speech to the Texas Bankers Association's state convention in El Paso. To those five hundred bankers, Sam pled for the association's aggressive support for new laws to prevent other such crimes. "Tuesday was a dark day in El Paso. And there will be more dark days like that one unless overtures are made to the legislature to increase the penalties for such crimes so that no one will ever think of attacking a bank."[34]

A much brighter day for the family – Sam's and Sam Jr.'s – came on the first of April when Samuel Doak Young III arrived, healthy and squawling – at Providence. Again, Sam himself relived his old pleasure in welcoming another new member into his clan, this one made just a bit special by the name his folks had chosen to give him.

At long last, through laborious due process, in June 1973 the U.S. Supreme Court upheld Judge Ernest Guinn's verdict that Trans Texas Bancorporation as a bank holding company could own its four member banks in El Paso. By a vote of six to three, the government – i.e., the Anti-Trust Division of the Department of Justice – suffered defeat. Immediately, bankers and anti-trust lawyers from around the country, "shocked by the importance" of the Bank's victory, besieged Sam and Sam Jr. and Bill Deffebach with questions.[35]

In answer, Sam Jr. hailed that decision as a "great thing for the banking business. It finally means the start of some guidance for multi-bank holding companies. Now we can get back to business."[36] Confirming that point a few months later, the case of *United States of America v. Trans Texas Bancorporation, Inc. 412 U. S. 946 (Sup. Ct. 1973)* became a precedent for the Supreme Court's favoring a bank holding company in Georgia. Throughout Texas, newly formed similar companies began rising up tall on the horizon.

An old friend, in his own realm, had risen up tall long ago. Back in 1938 Sam had cheerfully accommodated H. B. "Pat" Zachry, the San Antonio builder, when he encountered a payroll problem. Since then, as Zachry's business had grown nationwide and worldwide, Pat had become one of his state's largest civic supporters. Of late, he had helped fund the San Antonio Hemisfair with a sizable donation out of his own pocket. Now, Sam was visiting in San Antonio when Pat phoned him at the new Hilton Hotel. "Let me give you a lunch, Sam. I've got a few people I'd like you to meet."

At that lunch, Sam was not prepared for Pat's little speech to his guests. "This man is exceptional," Zachry told them, "If it hadn't been for him, there wouldn't have been a Zachry Contracting Company.[37] He saved my life. Without his timely aid, my career would have become a disaster."[38]

While such praise was gratifying, a family matter just now pleased Sam much more. In April 1974 Rob Hoover III, now a national bank examiner in Oklahoma, asked Sam a serious favor.[39] "Since you aren't, as far as I know, planning on writing your memoirs, would you please write me a letter giving me your thoughts on — " Sam glanced through Rob's list. Among the other topics, he wanted to know about banking as a career, the banker's right role in his community. Filled with good cheer, Sam picked up his pen to give guidance to a banker.[40]

1. Beware of the stranger. Never deal with him until positive identifications and reputation are definitely established.

2. Beware of close personal friendships. Impositions are most likely to arise from this source.

3. Insist upon certified audits. Both borrower and lender are frequently misled by inaccurate information.

4. Establish the proposed borrower's character, capacity, and capital requirements as a primary requisite to consideration of a credit advance.

5. Determine if the loan itself is large enough for the job. Too often, bankers move in prematurely with a "temporary" loan, then, finding themselves in too deep, must consider sending good money after bad, a step that rarely works well for the customer or for the bank.

6. Be sure that every loan is made with a satisfactory liquidating program that the borrower can reasonably meet.

7. Establish diligent loan review procedures. Then follow through with corrective measures in the weak cases. As with a doctor, "an ounce of prevention is worth a pound of cure."

8. Establish a hard-nosed collector squad, as many as needed, to push the indifferent or recalcitrant debtors.

9. At the outset of a transaction, plan with complete understanding between lender and borrower. In that manner, most troubles with loans will be avoided or eliminated.

As for banking as a career, Sam ranked it squarely among the professions "pursuing the welfare and improvement of humanity.... A banker gains wide knowledge of the economic circumstances of the people of his community; he comes to know about the character, capabilities, and habits of many of them. He keeps abreast of all important developments and happenings that affect their lives and is generally equipped to apply practical solutions to their problems. As a practical thinker, apart from theory, he possesses the qualities for community leadership perhaps better than his contemporaries."

As for Sam's own respect for religion, there could be "no satisfaction in life" without it — in business, in banking, and in all walks of life. "I think the soul derives greater peace and tranquility when all members of the family are of the same religious faith," but the important thing was religion itself. No man should ever forget that.

Sam ended his letter with a bit of a smile. "In re-reading what I have said," it was obvious that he had been redundant, "but when you believe in something and get all fired up, that's likely to happen."[41]

If Sam had other sobering thoughts on his mind as he was writing that treatise, he did not mention the fact. But in June 1974, when he took Betty in the Bank plane out to a hospital in La Jolla, he tried to trust his deepest religious convictions during her surgery. Though the doctors found a suspicious polyp, the future, they told Sam was hopeful. No worse prediction came out during Betty's convalescence, but fear rode the minds of them both when her normal "bounce back" came only slowly.

That mood was still heavy upon him when the Bank plane figured in his deep personal loss in August. Again and again, the plane had proved convenient not only for business, but at times on missions of mercy when friends of the Bank needed emergency trips, when death itself changed major plans. In August 1974, when Sam's special good friend and former neighbor, Leo Schuster, died in California, the Bank plane brought the body back home.[42] At home, Sam tried to express the extent of his grief. "I don't have a friend that I can talk to now. Everybody needs a friend like Leo," he told Little Betty.[43] "He was one of my best friends and the longest, right to the end."[44]

Despite the Bank's conservative style, its poise was profoundly shaken in September 1974 when Renato Ruiz of the El Paso Coin Co. took a trip into bankruptcy court. As Ruiz's landlord (his company occupied the building's ground floor corner on Stanton and Main) the Bank was forced to endure, Sam said bluntly, "a great fiasco."

Though the Coin Company had been buying and selling gold coins throughout the United States for as much as $8 million a month, Ruiz's chaotic mismanagement had caused its collapse. By the time that occurred, the El Paso National had suffered a charge-off of loans totalling $1 million, his checking account was overdrawn by that much and more. Where the Bank had been careless or unduly accommodating to its harried client – Sam's hot temper addressed both opinions when he got word of the Ruiz problem – the Bank had done so in honoring the Coin Company's checks even when its balance was "temporarily insufficient." At long last, on Ruiz's own instructions, the Bank had stopped payment on several big checks written close to the time of the bankruptcy.

According to the angry crowd of Ruiz's other creditors left stranded now by that development, the Bank had violated several bank laws. On these grounds the Bank found itself summoned to court.

Through a complicated court process, the Bank was absolved of all charges, but facing expensive appeals, it petitioned to settle the matter outside of court. After several hundred thousand dollars' loss to the Bank, the fiasco was over.

In the meantime, reported the *Herald-Post* in August 1977, Renato Ruiz, though charged with mail fraud, bankruptcy fraud, and making false statements to a bank in a twelve-count federal criminal indictment, had jumped bail and headed for Mexico.[45]

And now, after four years, the case against Sam for assaulting Billy Holt, the baggage handler at the El Paso airport, reached a court verdict on January 15, 1975. To Sam's annoyance, the court awarded the plaintiff $13,000 in "actual and exemplary damages." Though the amount was later adjusted downward to $9,000 in an out-of-court settlement,[46] the case had proved mostly embarrassing that the seventy-nine-year-old defendant had so forcefully lost his temper, not that he had inflicted much bodily harm on the young baggage man. Sam swallowed his pride and paid up.

And, let it be said, Sam returned to arenas where he knew how to play by the rules. On May 15, 1975, when Providence Hospital celebrated its twenty-fifth anniversary with a banquet at the El Paso Club, Vice President of the Board Gordon Foster explained how Providence felt about its president. "Mr. Young's prudent fiscal policies have enabled Providence to reinvest $11 million into the hospital for expansion and purchase of equipment" without going to the citizens of El Paso for additional contributions. "To talk about the history of and contributions of Providence Hospital is to talk about the work of Sam D. Young."[47]

Equipment that Sam had authorized for purchase within recent years was almost an index of the technological advances made in the nation's health industry: an EMI brain scanner, a new cardiac catheterization room, a computerized Gemsaec machine for blood analysis, Zeroradiography devices, a telemetry unit for heart monitor-

Sam with Sam Jr., 1975.

ing, multiplanegraphy x-ray equipment, an intensive care nursery for critical infants, a Linear Accelerator for cobalt cancer therapy, and a landing port to accommodate helicopters.[48]

Apropos of that Providence honor, Sam faced a sobering fact. The time had come for him to lead an easier pace. On May 8, 1975, he resigned from the board of the Hilton Corporation. After Connie announced that Sam Jr. had been elected to replace him, a little ceremony took place in Beverly Hills. Eighty-eight-year-old Connie presented his old friend and supporter a gold plaque. Signed Conrad N. Hilton, Chairman, and Barron Hilton, President, the plaque read: "On your retirement from the Board of Directors, and in recognition of your unstinting dedication to the interests of the Hilton Hotels Corporation, the members of the Board in unanimous vote, extend this expression of their deep gratitude."[49]

Throughout 1975 the Bank's ads reminded its trade territory that for the past half century it had been serving them well. But late in June, the Bank celebrated that fact with three full days of refreshments, souvenir key chains, guided tours through the building – and a black-tie dinner dance for the stockholders.[50] On the big day itself, June 29, the board sent out to 91,000 El Paso homes an eight-page tabloid, "50th Anniversary," relating its growth since 1925. Its personnel now numbered 524; El Paso itself had grown to 415,000 people. "As we celebrate our 50th anniversary," read the tabloid, "we reflect on the past with pride and look into the future with great expectations."[51]

Shortly after, Sam himself created another big moment in the Bank's history on August 12. "My fifty years' tenure at the helm of El Paso National Bank," so read his letter to the board, "seems to have gone by with amazing rapidity. Every day for years I have thanked our Lord and Creator for His guidance" and for the loyalty and help of the stockholders and directors he had had "in this long and happy career." But the fact was, he explained, that effective on August 15, he wanted to relinquish the title of chief executive officer to Sam Jr., who was fully prepared "to assume the great responsibilities of the office." He was confident that Sam Jr. "will receive the same assistance, support, and cooperation" that the directors had always "so generously extended to me."

But, Sam pointed out, this was not a total swan song. He wanted to continue as chairman of the board, still available for consultation with "those who seek it." From now, he would concentrate his own efforts on the development of the Trans Texas Bancorporation.[52]

Folding his paper, Sam knew that fifty years of his life and that of the Bank were too much to attempt to express in a short letter. The Bank's minutes told the much fuller story and, incidentally, attested to the fact that in that long span of time he had never missed a board meeting. As of now, the Bank's current motto spoke his thoughts well enough. "Have a good day and pass it on."

As for the rest of his sentiments, Sam left that for the Bank's September 30, 1975, Statement of Condition to make. Assets now stood at $376,711,845.

16

OLD HEADS AND YOUNG

DURING THE MONTHS IMMEDIATELY FOLLOWING his change in position, Sam found no reason to question his big decision. Sam Jr. had brought to the Bank a "modern day outlook." He had made the transition "from the old days to the new much easier" than the staff and the organization might have expected. "Old heads," Sam insisted, "are not as adaptable to change as the young ones."[1]

At least, so ran the gist of Sam's views. Other experienced men on the team early sensed, however, a friction in the Bank's traditionally smooth operation. Under Sam as CEO and board chairman, Sam Jr. as president had understood clearly his responsibilities. No disruptive confrontations had ever occurred between them: their distinct operational guidelines were clear and explicit.

On that basis now, Sam Jr. began his regime as CEO trained in the concept that Sam Sr. had always embodied. Subject always of course to board policies, the CEO ran the show. Unfortunately now, though Sam did not articulate the matter for anyone, he found it impossible as chairman of the board to entrust "his" bank to a new head, a new team, and a management style that, to his taste, delegated too much authority to too many subordinate ranks.

Forced into that position, Sam Jr. found himself increasingly frustrated, and his own cadre – Jerry Roberts, John Thompson, John Dorris, Ernie Roberts, James Onick, and James Turnage – soon realized that if their new CEO's orders could, at any moment, be rescinded by Sam, Sam Jr. was their "real boss" only in name. Within weeks, the tensions increased to such heat that more than one officer counseled Sam Sr. accordingly. "You've got to trust your own son. You've got to let him take charge. We want to trust him and we do trust him. You've got to trust him yourself. Hell, yes, he may make some mistakes. But how will he ever learn to be boss if you don't give him the chance? To begin with, in board meetings, you've got to stop contradicting his judgment."[2]

As more and more often now tempers flared in both father and son, Sam Jr. did at times achieve a certain composure, knowing Sam's background. The tight money scene in his childhood; his always heavy concern for Charlie and Fanny's finances (too often, the whole family came straight to him when they were in trouble); Sam's early grounding in the "good banker's duty" to his customers and to his stockholders during the rough times in Eastland, in Carlsbad, and throughout the Depression. Sam Jr. understood all this clearly. Sam Sr. would forever honor the interests of those with whom he did business. He would do whatever necessary to see that no mistakes – either in deed or in judgment – would ever occur.

Yet for Sam, there were now even more important concerns than the Bank on his mind. In 1976, after Betty underwent more surgery at La Jolla's Scripps Hospital, the family shared the doctor's dread news: "Anderocarcinoma of the liver, life expectancy, eighteen months."

Knowing the medical facts, knowing as well his other life-long resource in times of trouble, Sam went home and prayed fervently. As the malady spread, as Betty steadily weakened, he tried to believe that even that change in Betty was a kind of answer. It was not, however, an answer he easily came to accept.[3] The most he could do was spend more and more days at home with her, talking when she wanted to talk, holding her hand when that seemed the best use of their limited time.

Still, to keep up Betty's spirits as well as his own, Sam tried to maintain his regular office routine. Now, he had time to recall the favors many men had done him in his youth. Courtney Marshall, and George Briggs, and Governor came quickly to mind. After *Financial Trends* magazine featured "Banker Sam Young" in its June 7, 1976 issue – detailing his rise with Conrad Hilton – Sam welcomed a note from Oveta. "You and Sam Jr. looked very handsome and distinguished, as always, 'in the illustration,' and it was a wonderfully interesting article. I couldn't help thinking, though, that I could have written an even better story about Sam Young, banker; Sam Young, humanitarian; and above all, Sam Young, dear and true friend."[4]

On that score, he himself took a renewed, friendly interest in the young men coming on. In El Paso, William D. Sanders had already distinguished himself with IDC, Inc. (which later became La Salle Partners, Inc.) a "full service" real estate firm. Now when Sam learned that Sanders hoped to carve out a career for himself in Chicago, he phoned Henry Crown, his Hilton Board colleague. "Henry, Bill Sanders is a good man. You might want to talk to him. If you found a place for him, you wouldn't need to entertain any doubts about him at all."

On that recommendation, Crown answered immediately, "Sure, send him up here. I'll be happy to see him." The result of that chat was exactly what Sam had expected. His friend Crown put Sanders to work managing two of his major office buildings down in the Loop.[5]

At home the time for true friends was more and more urgent now as Sam and the whole family gathered at Christmas, 1976. Their smiles were cheerful, but as Betty took her seat at the table, she observed almost matter-of-factly, "Maybe I myself had better return thanks today. I may not be here when you all meet again for Christmas."[6]

Their responses were lighthearted. "Of course, you'll be with us," cried the whole table. "Whatever made you say that?" Smiling calmly around at her family, Betty's quiet look seemed to suggest that she knew the truth, even if her loved ones pretended they didn't.

Sam's years with Providence Hospital had brought him the satisfaction time and again of seeing miraculous cures come about. As the staff doctors needed more sophisticated equipment, he had made certain that the hospital bent every effort to buy it. When the community's needs dictated new medical specialists in town, he convinced a Houston heart surgery team to establish a practice in El Paso.[7] He had seen thousands of rosy-cheeked patients stand up and walk out of the hospital unassisted. In his own family, he had hoped for that kind of miracle for so long that on October 15, 1977, when Betty's condition only grew worse, he and Little Betty flew her to a cancer clinic in Freeport, in the Bahamas.

Sam with President Jimmy Carter, the White House, 1978.

During the next few weeks, under the care of a "scientist-doctor" who had met with some success in eradicating certain localized cancers there seemed to be new cause for hope. Lamentably, his skill did not cover cancer in the liver. On November 16 Betty died.

For her final days, she had had with her Little Betty and Martin Bauman, the Bauman girls, nurse Lynn Bacon, David Hoover – and Sam. Sam Jr. was attending a Hilton meeting in Hawaii, but he came immediately on the Bank's new Lear jet, and together Betty's family sadly brought their accompaniment home. On November 19, with her grandsons and nephews as pallbearers, the funeral took place at the First Presbyterian Church. Paul Poling officiated, with Rev. Ron Thompson of St. Clement's Episcopal Church assisting. Later, that afternoon a friend commented to the newspaper that Betty Young would always be remembered for her beauty, "inside and outside. She was a very beautiful woman, a kind woman who was known for her great beauty and generosity."[8] In 1964, the paper noted, she had been named to "Who's Who of American Women." She had been a long-time member of the Pan American Round Table; she had served in the auxiliaries of Providence Memorial Hospital and the University of Texas at El Paso. For fifty years, she had been a member of Zeta Tau Alpha sorority.

In gratitude for her life, Sam and his family gave their church four hundred copies of the Bible for use during Sunday services. It was Sam's heavy task now to reorder his personal priorities. Lacking now any real voice and affections to come home to, he busied himself at the Bank, at the social occasions his friends made him attend, but the emptiness was always dogging his footsteps.

Later that fall Trans Texas opened its fourth satellite, the Chamizal Bank at 5230 East Paisano. With Jack Young, Sam's brother, as CB and president,[9] the new bank was close to the border, close to the acreage that had once been an international sore spot: "Chamizal."

Given their knowledge of the frictions still rife at times between their CB and their chief executive officer, the Bank board on January 10, 1978, confirmed their satisfaction with Sam Jr.: a salary raise to $100,000. In turn, Sam Jr. recognized the good work of the people who served on his team. As in Sam's day, retirements continued to receive solid appreciation. When Mary Cleveland retired as assistant cashier and officer in charge of Proof-Transit, ending twenty-eight years, Sam Jr. gave her a goodbye hug and an 8-track stereo.[10] "I know I'll miss my job," she said, accepting the gift. "Every day was a different challenge. I'll even miss all the noise!"

Likewise, when Bill Foreman rounded out his thirty years with the Bank, Sam himself presented Bill with thirty red roses. Bill placed the bouquet on a side table "so that he could get on with his work." But in a few minutes Sam looked in on him. "Why did you put them back there out of sight? Put them up here on your desk, so everybody will ask, 'What's the occasion?' I want everybody to know that we really appreciate good people like you."[11]

That spirit of friendly professionals working together prompted a piece in the Bank Newsletter for December 1978. For catching forgeries and counterfeit greenbacks – tens, twenties, fifties, and up – a crowd of sharp-eyed, responsible people deserved special thanks: Rosa Campos, Carol Gravis, Leslie Heinsch, Bob Bailey, Debbie Jessup, Rosa Picazo, Gus Placencia, Nancy Brubaker, Debra Bean, Edna Bannister, Tina Garrick, Isabel Champion, Kim Pries, Manuel Chavez, Mary Ann Drake, and Greg Jones.

Good service to customers also rated applause, especially when a big new account like Northrup Worldwide Aircraft Services involved a good story that had been begun years before. At the Bank's William Beaumont Hospital Unit, teller Frank Carrasco had helped a young service man named Holland. Now Mr. Holland, a top offical with Northrup, remembered Frank's friendly assistance. When Northrup landed a major contract at Biggs Field and needed a bank, Holland brought the El Paso National his company's business.[12]

In turn, recognizing good service wherever performed, the Lions Clubs of El Paso in May 1978 gave Sam its Outstanding Senior Citizen award for his many contributions to the community.[13]

For more than fifty-three years now, Sam had maintained his practice of always contributing to both political parties: "Face facts," he said, "Democrat or Republican, government always costs money." And for most of those years, his defection from FDR's liberal camp had been known and discussed in local political circles. For that reason, Travis C. Johnson, a major Texas Democrat and former El Paso county judge, was prepared for Sam's hesitation when he delivered, by hand, an invitation from President Jimmy Carter. In a few days, Travis explained, the President wanted "to chat about things in general" with some thirty Texas business and industrial leaders. The name "Sam Young" was high on Carter's guest list.

El Paso Natural Gas Company's board of directors in 1974. From left to right (seated), Franz Schneider, Paul Kayser and Howard Boyd. From left to right (standing), Travis Petty, Alfred Glassell, Jr., Willard Rockwell, Richard Williams, Hugh Steen, Sam Young, C. L. Perkins, George Carameros, Arthur Dean, W. Burney Warren, Frank L. King, Scott Cumming.

"I'm flattered to hear that," Sam commented to Travis, "but in this election year, it would only be a big mob scene with a lot of talk going on and nothing accomplished."[14]

"The President really does want to hear from people like you," Travis insisted. "You could give him some helpful straight talk."

As the day for the trip drew near, Sam set down a three-page memorandum of subjects he wanted Carter to know. "Mr. President, most business people with whom I am in touch realize you have a tough job, that every change you wish to make in government is met with much resistance," but in his honest opinion, he wrote, "our people are becoming tired and sore backed about inflation, government regulations and red tape." All recent American presidents had tried to check inflation, "but the very root of inflation is excess government expenditures, of deficit spending," and no check of it could be made until the government started "living within its means." As for government regulations, they should be "minimized immediately" as "too irksome, too burdensome, too expensive, and too wasteful in time." Though there was an upcoming election, politics must be thrown out the window. "Right now, Mr. President, we believe it takes much intestinal fortitude to lead this country down the right path. If a valiant effort in the directions I have pointed out is successful, even in some small measure, you could go down in history with an image that will glorify your memory, and that alone should be more appealing than a second term."

At the White House visit, when President Carter entered the conference room, the visitors, including Morris Jaffee of San Antonio and John Mecom, Jr. of Houston, fell silent. The President smiled a few pleasantries, then said he sincerely wanted their views on his economic program and anything else they had on their minds. He paused. There was silence. Again, Carter said, "I really do welcome your comments."

After another long silence, Carter said lamely, "Well, I thank you for coming. Now I need to get back to work."

With that, Carter moved through the group, shaking hands. When he approached the four El Pasoans – C. F. "Paco" Jordan, County Attorney George Rodriguez, Jr. and me (as Travis commented later) "Sam was just like the rest of us, apparently so 'awed by the office' that he couldn't get out a word."

Travis nudged Sam. "Your memo," he whispered.

With that, Sam jerked out his paper and outlined his thoughts for the President. Carter and he chatted just long enough for Carter to say, "Fine, now let me keep your paper to study," then posed for a picture with Sam.[15]

From the White House, the El Paso people moved on to the Washington Hilton, where Sam used his "Be my guest" card to get them their rooms. Leaving for home the next morning, they found it amusing that Sam packed up the hotel manager's gift of fruit and fine wine and brought it along.

Back in El Paso, Sam received a White House packet a few days later. Carter had highlighted and underlined several points in Sam's memo. The first page was inscribed, "Thank you, Sam, Jimmy C."[16]

Matters between Sam and the State National were still far from friendly, but Bill Kastrin, now one of Sam's Bank directors, suspected that rivals could swallow their differences when a customer needed more time to settle his debts with them both. On behalf of the friend, Bill "engineered" a lunch visit between Sam and the State National's Hal Daugherty, Jr. at the El Paso Club.

Sam approached that meeting reluctantly, but during the lunch, he gave a chuckle. "Hal, while you're over here, how about opening a nice checking account with us?"

Daugherty looked taken aback, then threw back his head laughing. "Why, that's very kind of you, Mr. Young. May I think about that?"

Sam chuckled again. "Take your time."

Later, when somebody asked Daugherty if anything had come of Sam's invitation, Hal laughed again. "I haven't acquiesced yet."[17]

For nearly a year since Betty's death, Sam's time at home and La Jolla had grown heavy and grim, with nobody to ask him "How was your day?" when he trudged in the front door. The social round at La Jolla, its golf games and horse races, the work and play scene in El Paso lacked another person to give him some sense of a future that mattered. Dining alone in the big house, or at Sam Jr.'s, or at Little Betty's was not the same thing as having a life of his own.

What he needed, it slowly came clear to him, was a new wife. A suitable marriage at age eighty-two, however, would not be easy to plan: the right woman for him would be a widow perhaps, age sixty or so and wise enough to ponder the age factor carefully. For more than a month now, Sam had been harboring such an idea when on a Saturday night in August 1978 he attended Georgia and Al Baltz's dinner party in La Jolla with Sam Jr. and Marilyn. Invited as an escort for Georgia's mother, Sam was enjoying that role over cocktails when Sam Jr. and Marilyn introduced him to "Our friend, Mrs. Mary Lou Daves, of Bel Air and La Jolla."[18]

During the conversation, Sam asked Mrs. Daves if she liked horse racing. When Mrs. Daves nodded "Yes," Sam chuckled. "Well, so do I, though half the time I'm better at 'supporting' the ponies than winning anything on them." Mary Lou's sympathetic laugh led him to ask, "Would you like to go to the races with me tomorrow?"

Mrs. Daves was sorry, but she already had an engagement that day.

He phoned her the next day. "How about tomorrow?" Again, Mrs. Daves had plans. Two days later he called her again.

"Oh, dear, I am so sorry," she replied.

"Well, then," said Sam, "I guess I might as well write you off."

"No, no," she said, "I'll cancel my date and we'll go to the races next Saturday."

"Fine," said Sam, "I'll pick you up at a quarter after twelve, and we'll have lunch at the track."

At a quarter till twelve, Mary Lou was driving up home from the post office when she spied Sam driving down hill from her house. Rolling down her window, she called, "I thought you said a quarter after twelve. What are you doing here a half hour early?"

"I did say a quarter after twelve. I was just making a trial run to see if I could find your house."

About that, Mary Lou told a friend later, "I thought that was terribly endearing. We had a wonderful day; Sam had a lot to say; and he was fun to be with."

Whether Sam won or lost at Del Mar, that afternoon visit with Mary Lou was clear gain. Like Sam, she had recently suffered the loss of a spouse. With Delmer Daves, her husband for thirty-nine years, she and their three children had toured the world while he directed films on location, or enjoyed their vacation house in La Jolla, entertaining many of their Hollywood friends. Delmer's major films had included *Task Force* with Gary Cooper; *Never Let Me Go* with Clark Gable; *Dark Passage* with Humphrey Bogart, Lauren Bacall, and Agnes Moorhead; and *Broken Arrow* with James Stewart and Jeff Chandler.

As for herself, Mary Lou explained to Sam, she was the former Mary Lou Lender of Columbus, Ohio. As Mary Lawrence, she had had her own fruitful career in films and in television, particularly in the Bob Cummings comedy series, playing Bob's sister. Now retired from that strenuous life, she was happy watching her children (Michael, Donna, and Debbie) living lives of their own. "And that," she said proudly, "is just as it should be."

Hearing Mary Lou voicing her thoughts so openly, Sam was reliving his similar loss, but he was also sensing a new chapter in his life beginning. Next evening at dinner, Sam had a plan ready: he would not pretend otherwise. But Mary Lou was equally candid. "You are coming on too strong. Please, Sam, don't get any ideas. I intend to go to my grave as Mrs. Delmer Daves."

"Oh, you should never say that!" Sam objected, "You don't know what's going to happen. You're going to meet somebody who's going to change your mind, and you know something? That somebody is me."[19]

At that, Mary Lou lightly turned the conversation to politics, especially to her enthusiasm for Ronald Reagan's conviction that incentives have to be put back into American life. "That's just basic, isn't it, Sam?" In her Hollywood days, she went on to tell him, she and Delmer had been close friends of Reagan and his wife, Jane Wyman. Since Reagan's divorce and remarriage, the Daveses had continued to know Ronald and Nancy; indeed they had hosted a fund-raising garden reception for the Reagans in 1966 when Ronald was campaigning for governor of California.[20]

Since then, Mary Lou had turned her hand to writing. Her full-color art book, *Mother and Child* (New York: Crowell, 1975) had featured the favorite mother and child paintings chosen by the friends she had made in the course of her work and her travels. Each person had written a brief essay explaining his choice. Grace Kelly's tribute to de Vasselot's marble statue, *Madonna and Child* in the Palace Chapel in Monaco, Mary Lou found particularly touching. "This *Madonna and Child* has a very special meaning for me. I saw it on the day I arrived in Monaco, shortly before my marriage in April 1956. Upon entering the palace, which is located in the old unfortified city, my parents and I were first taken to the chapel, where we knelt in prayer. There, towering above us, was this strong yet lovely work of art. The Blessed Virgin had such a soft and sweet expression and gentle regard toward the round infant Jesus on her arm that I felt warmed and welcomed to my new life."[21]

The next time Mary Lou was traveling in Europe, she had stopped first in Monaco to present Princess Grace a copy of the new book. Then in Rome she enjoyed the special pleasure of being received by the Pope[22] and his accepting his own copy too of *Mother and Child.*

Mary Lou had a full social season ahead, a trip to Europe with the Friends of Venice, an art patrons' group, but she promised to think about Sam's idea. Once Mary Lou was home from Europe, Sam proceeded with his plans for her part in his life. Together, they considered their special circumstances: two adults with families from former marriages, but more importantly, two individuals who deeply enjoyed each other's company.

After their engagement was sealed, Mary Lou invited Sam in October to go with her to her home town, Columbus, to celebrate the golden anniversary of its Ohio Theatre, the venerable institution that had helped inspire Mary Lou to become a theatre person herself. At Thanksgiving, Sam took her to Yucatan, Mexico where she met his friends the Anibal Iturbides and the Floyd Ransoms. Immediately afterwards, he introduced her to his El Paso friends at an El Paso Club dinner, then within a few days, he escorted her out to Bel Air to meet an old colleague and friend.

Conrad Hilton had suffered a decline in health since Sam had been with him at a Hilton meeting, but Connie was his jovial self as he and Frances, his wife of two years, entertained them in their sixty-room mansion in Bel Air. Connie was reminiscing over old times when, suddenly, he leaned toward Mary Lou. "You know, there's a fact about this fellow Sam here that you may not realize. Looking back over my hotel career, I want to tell you there never could have been a Hilton Hotel chain without his aid in the very first several years. His confidence in my honor" – Connie shot a friendly grin at Sam – "and my integrity, plus his close friendship, were the main source of my confidence in forging ahead."

Sam motioned his gratitude. "Connie, you've always been the right man at the right place at the right time. Your success was founded on that firm a base. And your personal life has been capped with" – he nodded at Frances – "this lovely lady as your wife."

At that moment, Connie's mind seemed to go blank. "Wife? I'm not married," he said. "I have the same arrangement you do."

"Arrangement!" Sam and both ladies exploded. "What arrangement?"[23]

Looking tired and confused, his hands trembling, Connie set down his glass.

Within a month, on January 3, 1979, Sam received word that Connie had died of congestive heart failure in Santa Monica. At that time, 185 hotels and inns in the United States and 75 hotels in foreign countries carried his name.[24] Two weeks later, when Connie's will was probated in Los Angeles, his personal worth totalled $100 million.[25]

Reminiscing, Sam tallied up the many ways his faith in the man Hilton had repaid him. In friendship: much laughter and many tough games on the fairway. In business: many good trips and interesting meetings, helping Hilton create his empire. In dollars: three or four million, at least.[26]

And each time he made a visit back home to Woodville now, it amused him to hear his old boyhood chum Mayo McBride explain his own progress into the big time. Back in 1908, Mayo and he had sworn that farming would never be the life for them. Instead, in his own relaxed way, Mayo had amassed a sizable fortune in Wall Street. "Lounging around here in the bank every morning, drinking their free coffee, I pick up some mighty hot market tips. It beats working," he grinned.

In December of 1978, the *El Paso Times* addressed a rather formidable question under the headline, "The Influentials." Was it "powerful men or events themselves," the *Times* asked, that shaped history? If the answer was "men," which of those men in El Paso was top dog? The nine-part series began with a close look at the heads of the city's two biggest banks, Sam and George Matkin.

Whenever Matkin, now eighty and "thin beneath the suit that hangs on his frame, his slate-blue eyes still alert and wary," said the *Times*, looked from his seventh-floor window, he could see the fruits of his own decisions, comfortable neighborhoods and new shopping centers which had led to "the boom that caused the city to grow east instead of west."[27]

When Sam Young, now eighty-two, looked from his window, continued the *Times*, he could see "the monuments" of the major institutions he had been closely aligned with over the years: hotels, Schwartz's Popular department store, Kayser's gas company, Tony

Sam with his widely traveled St. Christopher Medal, safely returned, July 1957.

Sam with El Paso's other top "influentials." Left to right, George C. Matkin, Judson Williams, Sam, Charles Leavell, Fred Hervey. 1978. (Cartoon by Lamberto Alvarez, El Paso Times)

Lama's boot plants, Willie Farah's pants factories, and the mushrooming new growth in the Chamizal. "Despite the home he keeps by the California seashore, his frequent trips to Paris, Algeria, Houston, the East Coast, this is a view dear to him. Sam Young can call men in the offices of all the tall buildings he sees around him, and they will listen."

But the central question remained? Which of those names on the wide horizon was the most influential? Using a point system, the *Times* people picked Sam.

When individual community leaders spoke up, their opinions varied, but all spoke of Sam's long involvements in civic affairs. "I'd tie Sam Young and Charles Leavell (one of the major building contractors in the Southwest)," said former mayor Judson Williams. "They've made their fortunes in El Paso, built institutions. Their names have been synonymous with progress. If either of them came out for something, it would have great influence. A lot of people still know them, their names. In the financial community outside of El Paso they are significant."

Leavell himself disagreed. "I think Sam Young is the most powerful man in El Paso. I think you'll have 100 percent on that."

"I think I'd put Young Sr. as number one," said W. J. McDuffee. "And George Matkin number two." These dynamic people "would have made their mark anywhere; Minneapolis, Miami, or in the little crossroads town up the highway, Anthony."

"Your number one man is number one," from Maury Page Kemp. "Look at all the boards (Sam Young has) been on. Church work, civic. The El Paso National Bank Building, the commitment of building it. The good it did for downtown. The jobs."

Sam Jr. himself sidestepped the question. "I don't want to pick a number one," he said. "It's a team concept."[28]

"Me?" asked Sam himself when the *Times* reporter shot him the same question. "No, I don't think so. No thanks."

A significant portion of the views that placed Sam Young as Number One "was a product," said the *Times*, "not only of the depth of his influence, but of its breadth." In an interview soon after the polling, Sam explained his long interest in politics. Because "it was hard to get a good man to run for public office," in the 1940s and 1950s, "we had a Committee of Fifty for a long time that would urge people to run and finance their campaigns. So you'd get good government. If you didn't do that, you could get just anybody and have chaos."

His point was, "We were trying to do it for the benefit of the community; we were interested in the city administration and the school board. We were concerned with statewide senatorial races. The congressional seat had a strong interest. There was never a candidate for mayor we didn't have an interest in."[29]

But, the reporter asked Sam, with all the power that El Paso's "Influentials" had had to make the city a better place, could they have achieved even more?

"Yes," Sam answered. "Our leadership has been sort of mediocre. We didn't have the influx of well-educated people in the industrial and commercial world. Phoenix did." Sam thought a minute. "Personally, I think our slow growth has been much better for us."[30]

Regarding the city's future, the reporter opened his pages to Sam. "El Paso has lots of new manufacturing enterprises, and the Twin Plants concept" (American factories sending their manufactured component parts to Juarez to be assembled by cheap labor, then brought back as completed products into the United States) "is helping a lot. There will be a continued growth over a period of years. I think El Paso will outpace other southwestern cities."

Cities like Houston and Phoenix? Even at eighty-two, said the reporter, Sam Young showed "the perspective he's acquired from decades of running his empire on the El Paso/Juarez border." Sam did not face that question head on, but "his eyes took on a shrewdness. They are looking into the future."[31]

Earlier in the *Times* series, Sam Jr. had avoided the question about Sam's "influential" position. However, he did express himself on a personal matter. "At best it's a very difficult thing to be involved (in business) with your family; father/son combinations are difficult. Emotions always come into it. You're so much closer to your family than anyone else. Sometimes things get distorted. That's nothing new, it's historic; it's just hard for a father and son."[32]

Back in August that year, when Chairman Howard Boyd of the El Paso Company (the holding company of which El Paso Natural Gas was now a part) and Bob Hibbert of Houston's Texas Commerce Bank were visiting in La Jolla, Sam had given them a dinner with Mary Lou's help. She was confused, however, by a dramatic turn during the dinner.

"Sam"—Hibbert had leaned toward his host—"we want you to

merge your bank with us, Texas Commerce Bancshares. You can write your own ticket. Come on down to Houston. You can have an office, an apartment. We want you to help us, be our leader."[33]

"Me?" Sam replied. "Why me?"

"Because you've had more experience than anyone else in Texas banking. You have a better record. Besides that, you're"—Hibbert poked a finger at him and grinned—"you're tough and you're mean."

Mary Lou stared at him. "What do you mean, that he's *mean?*"

"Oh"—Sam and Hibbert both laughed—"that's just banker talk," Hibbert explained.

When Mary Lou asked Sam later about Hibbert's Houston idea, he dismissed it. "I'd never consider leaving El Paso."

Nevertheless, with the rapid development now of big Texas bank holding companies, there was a background for Hibbert's straight offer. Whereas El Paso's major concerns had once been home-owned, operated and patronized by folks who knew each other as neighbors, more and more steadily now their corporate reins were passing to outside hands. Roderick's *Times* to the Gannett newspaper chain in 1972. Gunning-Casteel's twenty-four drugstores to Zale Corp. of Dallas in 1978. Bob Price's dairies to Creamland of Albuquerque just recently.

Now, at the end of the *Times'* "Influentials" series, Sam was asked a firm question. "Any chance that the El Paso National might go the same way?"

Sam considered the question, then he nodded. Big as the Bank's holding company was now—with assets of $532,494,000—"we have thought that we'd like to develop a very large regional bank," Sam replied, "rather than join with Houston and Dallas. But we're determined to stay with home ownership."

"But"—now the reporter was addressing Sam Jr.—"might a change come in due time?"

"Eventually I think there will be five or six major systems in this state," Sam Jr. replied. "Like Bank of America and Wells Fargo in California." Ben Love, chairman of the Texas Commerce Bank's holding company in Houston, had already made overtures, but those gestures were too premature to warrant serious thought. "Whether it would be good for El Paso National Bank to join one of the systems, I can't say. I'm not advocating it, neither do I say it would be a disaster."[34]

At the January 9, 1979, board meeting, salaries for its top officers reflected the board's understanding of the relationship that prevailed now between the two Youngs in authority. As chief executive officer, Sam Jr.'s salary rose to $110,000. As chairman of the board, Sam Sr.'s to $50,000.[35] To Sam, the board awarded a three-months leave with full pay, ample time for the cruise he had been planning with Mary Lou and the Jimmy Dicks.[36]

After that cruise, Mary Lou and Sam journeyed to an El Paso Natural Gas Company board meeting in Paris. Before inspecting the company's giant LNG plant in Algeria, the board, including director Ben Love, were quartered at the Ritz Hotel. During dinner the first evening, Love commented, "Sam, while we're here, let's talk again about the El Paso National Bank's merging with Texas Commerce. It makes financial sense for you and your stockholders, and the similarity of our banking philosophies makes sense for your customers and employees."

"Well, then" – Sam cocked an eyebrow – "come on up to my room and let's visit."

Upstairs, Sam remarked, "To keep myself fit, I've always maintained a stiff exercise program. And every day without fail, I eat five pecans from my orchard. Pecans, you know, are good for your cholesterol. So, Ben," he grinned, "before I'd sell my bank to anybody, I'd have to know that he could stand the hard work. I'd need to be sure he could do right by my bank, by my town and my stockholders. Love, I need to know if you can do twenty full push-ups."

"Twenty full push-ups!" Ben exploded in laughter. "Sam, I haven't done that since the Army Air Corps."

"Well, like I say," Sam gave a shrug, then laughed, "I need to know you could handle the job."

With that, Love peeled off his coat. "Well, all right, since you leave me no choice –" Love did the push-ups, but Sam still did not commit himself to Love's offer.[37]

Minding the store, Sam Jr. implemented important new programs in 1979 to reflect his own theory of a banker's responsibility. To improve officer/employee relations, he formed an Employee Advisory Council.[38] To help staff members find the positions best suited to them, he encouraged "employee preference feedback."[39] Specifically, to help them advance in their careers, he hired a Director of Training.[40]

Apropos now of Sam Jr.'s own career progress, the Texas Bankers Association chose him president-elect in May 1979. The "great honor," as he had already explained to his staff, sent him traveling around over the state for weeks at a time. But now, more clearly than ever, as CEO he demonstrated the worth of his personal managerial style. With a responsible officer in charge at each level, the show went on quite well without him. It was a matter of pride to Sam too that an El Paso banker had achieved such wide recognition. Only once before in the TBA's seventy-five years had an El Paso banker achieved that distinction and that was one of his bank's own officers. Tom Patterson had served as TBA president in 1960.[41]

That fall, almost to Sam's disbelief, the time had come to celebrate another big event in the Bank's history. To mark that occasion, Sam hosted a large party at The El Paso Club, where after the dinner, he read from a letter he had mailed a few days before. "Dear Sammy, it is hard to realize that this quarter of a century has gone so swiftly. I vividly recall your first days in the Bank as an eager but inexperienced banker. How you have matured and gained the respect and love of this community and the banking fraternity! Sammy, I am proud of you and I salute you on this occasion."[42]

If the occasion was partly a chance for Sam to explain his often rough surveillance of Sam Jr. as the Bank's CEO, it was Sam Jr.'s chance now to thank all and sundry for their great help, especially his parents.

Thoughout the year, rumors of an impending sale of the Bank kept crossing Sam Jr.'s desk. There had indeed been overtures, he told his board. Along with Ben Love's, impressive offers had come from Republic, Interfirst and MBank in Dallas and the Bank of the Southwest in Houston. There had even been innuendos of interest from the Frost Bank in San Antonio.[43] "But," Sam Jr. flatly informed his people, "we know what we're worth, and we aren't after any buyers at all."[44]

Yet there was a growing awareness in the board, in the officers, and in Sam Jr. himself that changes in the Texas economy and in the money scene in El Paso – mushrooming now with the ever-expanding twin-plant companies – were foretelling big changes for El Paso National. Could the Bank, no matter how impressive its size, continue to meet, independently, the financial needs of a snowballing industrial economy?

With Sam himself back in harness after more travels, Ben Love tried again to talk "merger." But Sam stood his ground. "Your price is too low. This bank is worth twice its book value."

Talking specifics, Sam was fully aware of Love's background. His Texas Commerce Bancshares holding company was the up-to-date Houston product of that city's long-time financial shrewdness in action. Of the many names that had steered it to its present eminence, Jesse Jones's name stood highest. An original stockholder of the National Bank of Commerce when it was chartered in 1912, he had become a director in 1914. By 1919 he was its major stockholder. Its president from 1922 to 1929 and again in 1934, he was its CB from 1929 till the time of his death in 1956.[45] In the huge enterprise that Jones's little bank had become, his legacy lived on in Texas Commerce Bancshares' view of its role in Texas, in the United States, and the world.

To recognize two big names in El Paso National's own heritage, the January 8, 1980, board meeting raised Sam Jr.'s salary to $120,000. Sam's rose to $55,000, plus bonus. Still in line with that heritage, in July Ernie Roberts circulated throughout the Bank a document dating from Sam's first year as president.[46]

"Friendliness – that is the cornerstone of our policy and it is largely responsible for our success." The thirty-six years since Sam first laid down that policy had proved the worth of that friendly advice. One additional point in that 1944 Bulletin had become a fact as much about Sam as about the people still helping him run many aspects of the Bank. "Never 'talk back' or show your temper. Let me do that for us all."

In the Bank that "temper" had long been legendary. One morning a secretary down in the lobby was slow in answering the phone; it had rung several times when she grabbed it up. "El Paso National Bank," she said. "Hello? El Paso National – " She was repeating the words when a voice bellowed down from the mezzanine. "Damn it, somebody answer that phone!"

The secretary looked up; Sam was glaring down at her.

"I did answer this phone, Mr. Young, but there's nobody on it."

"I know it, dammit. It's me!"[47]

There were still times when too many customers were kept waiting in too many lines and Sam yelled down from the mezzanine. "Put in another teller! Open another window!"[48] But there were still times when that temper apologized: once when his lady tax consultant, Rogene H. Brant, questioned his judgment. "You can't do that, Mr. Young. It wouldn't work."

Sam blushed beet red. "Well, damn you to hell."

"Why – why, Mr. Young, how dare –"

In a moment, Sam leaned forward and patted her hand. "I meant that affectionately."[49]

Though that temper could explode in a flash, it could cool just as quickly. "Grit your teeth," ran the legend backstairs. "He'll be asking you out to lunch in five minutes."

Explosive temper or no, Sam's business connections had matured so effectively by May 1980 that *Texas Business* magazine spotlighted Sam in its story, "Texas' 20 Top Titans." Linking his solid footing in his El Paso National Bank (the state's eighteenth largest, with assets now of $582 million) to his Trans Texas Bancorporation (assets $694 million), to the Republic Bank of Dallas, and to the El Paso Natural Gas Company, *Texas Business* ranked Sam with other bright Texas lights like Perry Bass, George R. Brown, Edward Clark, James Elkins, Jr., Paul Haas, Ben Love, William D. Noel, Arthur Temple, Belton K. Johnson, Jess Hay, Robert R. Stewart III, and Harvey Bright.

"At a vigorous eighty-three, Sam Young is still acknowledged by many as El Paso's No. 1 power. The Horatio Alger-like banker – who spent his early years plowing behind a burr-tail mule and helping out in his father's general store in the southeast Texas hamlet of Woodville – would modestly prefer to regard himself as a banker who's been a builder." And a builder, he has been, *Texas Business* continued, "one of the state's most prodigious builder/financiers," with influence felt throughout the United States, Mexico, and almost "worldwide."

Asked if his father was still active in the Bank, Sam Jr. answered wryly, "You bet. He still calls many of the shots."[50]

Though that statement said more about the Bank's administration than an outsider could have perceived, Sam Jr. called his own shots in November, a new general loan policy expressing both his own financial logic and his personal "feel" for fair play.[51] The Bank, he declared, would treat all parties "in the manner in which we ourselves desire to be treated."

Furthermore, Sam Jr. concluded, no credit-worthy customer should ever be turned away on a loan request without a clear indication of some "viable alternative." No bank ever profited from just saying "No."[52]

Newlyweds Mary Lou and Sam at their wedding luncheon with their families. (Seated from left to right) Mary Lou's son Michael Daves, Mary Lou, Sam. (Standing from left to right) Donna Daves and friend, Deborah Daves Richards and husband Bill, Little Betty and husband Martin Bauman, Marilyn and Sam Young, Jr.

There were powers-that-be, however, in a megalopolis eight hundred miles across Texas that were growing ever more strongly convinced that El Paso National ought to stop playing coy. For its own best interests, reasoned the Texas Commerce people in Houston, the El Paso man ought to say "Yes" to a merger.

In April at a dinner for the El Paso Natural Gas Company board in Hawaii, Mary Lou Daves was sitting next to Ben Love when Love leaned toward her. "You know, I want to be sure you get the right vibes from me. So you can pass them on to Sam Young."

Love leaned closer. "We want to make a merger, but all that Sam says to me is 'Sharpen your pencil.' You have influence with him. After all, Mary Lou, you're going to marry him next month."

To that, Mary Lou smiled. "It's true we're going to marry. But about any merger, Ben Love, you're wooing the wrong person. You should be wooing Sam Jr. If you get *him* on your side, that's the best strategy for you to follow."[53]

There was no time just now for any more thoughts of a merger, not by Mary Lou, not by Sam, amidst the plans for the forthcoming wedding.

On May 11, 1980, the La Jolla Presbyterian Church welcomed the large congregation of family and friends from El Paso, Beverly Hills, Los Angeles, Hollywood and Europe who had come to express their good wishes. With Robert M. Young, Sam's own minister, officiating, Mary Lou's son Michael gave his mother in marriage. Sam Jr. served as best man. Whether or not the La Jolla newspaper reporter had a true ear for accents, he did observe, he wrote the next day, the groom's "unmistakable" Texas heritage when Sam boomed his response to the minister's big question. "Oh, ah will," he declared, smiling at Mary Lou.

A dinner dance at La Valencia Hotel followed the ceremony. Next stop: another celebration party in the presidential suite at the Waldorf-Astoria, then Europe for a long honeymoon.[54]

17

SHOOTOUT AT FORT SAM

Though Ben Love kept "sharpening his pencil," Sam and Sam Jr. felt no rush to say "Yes." The Supreme Court's ruling on their Trans Texas case had made Trans Texas the legitimate, fifteenth largest bank holding company in Texas (assets: $727 million).[1] Though far away in West Texas, Trans Texas – now renamed for clarity's sake, El Paso National Corporation – was clearly no easy pickings.

Consequently, each time Ben came to town with a new hand of cards or cornered Sam in Houston after a Gas Company board meeting, Sam and Sam Jr. played a cool game. El Paso was now the fourth largest city in Texas; its international metropolitan area numbered a million people. Interestingly, it was the state's fifth hottest and fifth largest banking market.

With Interfirst (Dallas) and MCorp (Dallas) and First City (Houston) all fiercely engaged in a neck-and-neck race to dominate the state banking market, Texas Commerce Bancshares had solid reasons to wish to beat them all to the finish. To TCB, El Paso was glowingly attractive: its growth steady, its economic position in its trade area thoroughly sound. In addition, El Paso National itself was impeccable: in its fifty-five years it had never wavered from its always liquid status. Its current capital structure of $50,300,000 was highly impressive. All in all, in Texas the El Paso National Corporation was among TCB's top ten priorities.[2]

Given that picture, Sam knew his worth. His was the biggest bank system in town not yet owned by outsiders. In no way in El Paso could Texas Commerce start up *de novo* and beat Sam's stated price. Besides, TCB was in a position to offer him plenty. It had 39 member banks and 10 overseas offices; its assets had mushroomed to over $9 billion. In size, it ranked third in Texas and 24th in the nation.[3] On TCB's map of Texas, its red-white-and-blue logo flags colored the state east of Odessa. But west of that line, the map was snow white. The El Paso National Corporation, the state's coolest holdout, was the one banking system Ben Love most hotly wanted to own.

It was no small fact, as well, that the Monetary Control and Deregulation Act of 1980 was forcing banks, however august and conservative, to assume drastic new roles. Before now, banks had operated under clear mandates from Congress: interest rates on passbook accounts were set; savings institutions could pay only one-quarter percent more per annum interest than commercial banks; and nobody could pay interest on checking accounts.

In the good old days, one banker joked, he could operate very well on a 3-3-3 rule of thumb: his cost of funds were 3 percent, he added 3 percent for his profit, and by 3 P.M. he was out on the golf course.[4] "Twelve years ago we had two instruments," complained Ira Nathanson, marketing chief for Chicago's Affiliated Bank Group, "one passbook and one certificate." Now, his operation had eighteen instruments, a system that was "depersonalizing cashing a check, making deposits, and even changing a $10 bill." Bankers were no longer the poised, "see-us-when-you-need-us" type people. They were becoming carnival barkers. "Step right up, folks." Let their "incredible Super NOW account" earn depositors "stupendous interest and no-cost checks with a minimum of $1,000."[5]

With aggressive new players now, banking itself was a new game. Sears, American Express, and Prudential Insurance were all pushing competitive products. And every bank, no matter how strong its traditions, was adding a "marketing" department to publicize itself in splashy ads on TV. About Sears especially, Sam had his opinions. "They ought to stick to their knitting. I don't think Sears Roebuck would appreciate it a bit if the banks were to buy up chain stores and go into competition with them."[6]

As president now of the Texas Bankers Association, Sam Jr. faced up to the speechmaking, a task he relished, and official calls around the state. It was a nice coincidence that a second generation William P. Hobby and a second generation Sam D. Young found themselves now in a position to pool their good influence. As lieutenant governor of Texas, Bill Hobby Jr. petitioned TBA President Sam Jr. to assist the Texas school teachers when their paychecks were delayed several days. In a mailing to bankers over the state, Sam Jr. hoped they would please be lenient with all those good folks out there who had time payments to make but couldn't quite meet them on time.[7]

About young Hobby's eminence in Texas politics, Sam himself remembered the summer vacation when Bill learned how to drive, "using my car, out here and in La Jolla. It's great now to see him distinguishing himself as lieutenant governor and" – Sam paused a moment to savor that recollection – "and Sam Jr. distinguishing himself as a banker."[8]

At the first board meeting after Mary Lou and Sam were home from their wedding trip, Sam described the change in his status. "Gentlemen," he chuckled, "I'm under new management."[9] But the next time Ben Love came calling, Sam sang his same banker song. "Houston man, I've already told you. Tune up that pencil."

Now, for Sam and Mary Lou, there were opportunities again to enjoy the sociability each had missed without a companion. At home in La Jolla, "with the ocean as our front yard," they spent quiet evenings out on the deck, gazing seaward into the dark. Or in the late afternoons, watching the whales rise and plunge in the blue rollers as they migrated north. At Del Mar, Sam could laugh when Mary Lou pretended to know "not very much" about playing the ponies.

To their houseguest, Mary Lou's sister Barbara, Mary Lou explained her theory of winning the daily double. "In the first race, pick a long shot. In the second, pick the name you like best. It only costs $2." Like any good teacher, Mary Lou then demonstrated. At the window, she chose her first horse and proudly watched it win. Picking County Kildare for her second, she told Barbara her reason. "I've just had a letter from Desmond Guinness in Ireland; his address is partly County Kildare. So – " Mary Lou placed her $2 bet.

When it came to pass that County Kildare led the pack, Mary Lou joyfully raked in her $3,480, the second biggest $2 payoff in Del Mar's history. Hearing her shriek, Sam told the rest of the party, "The most I ever won was about $1,100."[10]

With Sam, Mary Lou in the fall of 1980 recalled some happy old days when Ronald Reagan brought his presidential campaign to El Paso. After hearing Reagan make his big speech, they were in the crowd at the airport to wave the Reagans goodbye when Nancy cried toward her, "Mary Lou! What are you doing *here?*"

"I live here," Mary Lou laughed. "I married Mr. El Paso himself, Sam Young."[11]

After attending the Reagan inaugural parties in Washington in January 1981, Mary Lou and Sam took to the high seas and the Mediterranean, again.[12] A bonus cruise from the Bank, the trip included a visit with Princess Grace and Prince Rainier in Monaco, a safari through Kenya, and a swing around the Cape of Good Hope.[13] Regarding all the mileage he had covered in the fifty years since his wish "for the chance to travel someday," Sam reaffirmed his zest for it still. Rounding the world on its seas, flying over its continents had only whetted his appetite. "I still want to see the world," he confessed now to a fellow passenger, "what it looks like, how its people live. To see how the Chinese live, to see how the Russians live. In Odessa, I did see a little, I guess."

"Did the Russians talk to you?" asked his new friend.

"They were all pretty closemouthed. Most of them just looked sullen. I wish they had opened up, but their system, I suppose, wouldn't let them. Too bad."[14]

On March 28 while Sam and Mary Lou were still abroad, Dorrance Roderick died at age eighty. Though the Bank's minutes reflected their gratitude for "one of the great citizens of El Paso, Texas, who literally became a legend in his own time in the 20th century history of El Paso,"[15] in Sam's personal case, the loss was profound. Very simply, Sam mentioned his grief to a close confidant. "My friendship with Dorrance Roderick, you couldn't have shaken that with a pecan tree shaker."[16]

In March 1981 soon after its formal opening, the new West El Paso National Bank Building (number five in the holding company's affiliate family) won its architect, Bart Fischer, top prize from the El Paso Chapter of the American Institute of Architects. At the award banquet, President Haskell Monroe of the University of Texas at El Paso praised the building's Hispanic architecture. Having recently moved to

El Paso, his view of the town paralleled Sam's first reactions. "El Paso isn't typically Texas or typically Mexico. It's a frontier; a unique city with a special breed of folks. First of all, El Pasoans were not born in El Paso. This city has been an importer of talent," and its door was wide open still. As twin cities numbering over a million people, El Paso and Ciudad Juarez "already have a head start on showing the rest of the continent what it means to be good neighbors."[17]

Hearing that speech, Sam nodded his full agreement. As it stood now, the community was a realized vision that he himself, for the past fifty-six years, had labored hard to make real.

But ending his year as Texas Bankers Association president at the association's El Paso convention in May, Sam Jr. noted the changes in the banking industry that were making a banker's life increasingly frustrating. In his farewell speech, he urged the bankers to take a firm lead in the fight against inflation and especially against excessive government intervention. "Banking is one of the greatest industries in the world. Having spent nearly all of my adult life in it, it is a very big part of my life, and means a great deal to me. Having been your president is among the highlights of my career."[18]

When Sam Jr. sat down, Mary Lou turned to Sam. "I didn't know that man could talk like that. That was a powerful speech."[19]

Agreeing, Sam smiled, especially when leaving the Civic Center auditorium he overheard an out-of-town banker concur. "Boy, that Mr. Young is a tough act to follow. Tall, handsome, charming, brilliant, and that beautiful silver hair."[20]

Another career man on the Bank team was in for top praise in May 1981. "When a man has put in eighteen hours a day to learn every aspect of his business and to take care of that business for his customers, he's a Banker." Retiring now as vice chairman of the board, Jim Onick could look back on a forty-seven-year achievement that had begun in the mail room. The newsletter echoed Sam Jr.'s own praise. "His genuine concern for people and his warm, friendly manner, exceeded only by his modesty, made him a source of pride for the Bank."[21]

Soon after East El Paso National Bank opened in November 1981 (as number six satellite), Sam was still playing his cat-and-mouse game with Ben Love when Robert T. Sakowitz, the department store magnate, called him from Houston. "I want to buy your bank."

"Why is that, Mr. Sakowitz?"

"Because it's the best managed bank in Texas."[22]

That reputation was based on Sam's still solid conviction that the Bank must remain conservative. In doing his homework before board meetings, he often made it a point to seek out Fred Schneider, knowing that Fred would counsel him just as frankly and as much to the point as Homer Jacobs had done during his many years as Sam's special sounding board. Fred proved particularly valuable now as other younger men on the board insisted that El Paso was ready and open for "creative, aggressive new views" from its money men. Indeed, with the proliferation of many new banks in town, most of them members of out-of-town conglomerates, the El Paso National must open its eyes.[23] At times now, board discussions became vigorous debates between Sam and Sam Jr. about how high a percentage of its lendable funds the Bank ought to commit to new loans.

Sam's traditional wisdom counseled, "Go slow. Don't overextend." Old hands on the Bank team understood Sam's reluctance to bend with more current views, given his worries during the Great Depression. Nevertheless, banking decisions now had to accommodate the creative imagination of younger men highly trained. To meet the ever expanding money needs in the El Paso market, the Bank needed new resources, more "product development capabilities."[24]

The right choice was a matter of judgment and indeed some skill in reading tea leaves. The logical step in the opinion of some, however, might better address a third alternative. If the matter could not be resolved to the satisfaction of the board and Sam and Sam Jr., it was time to address Ben Love's best offer.[25] Specifically, to address what Sam as a negotiator could get for the El Paso National Corp., plus all the perks that Sam could tack on.

Still, Sam insisted, to sell the El Paso National Corporation was not a one-party decision, not his, not the board's. Until major shareholder families like the Harveys, the Prices, the Rodericks, and the Morgans agreed, no sale would occur. So soon after Sam Jr.'s three years of on-the-road service for the Texas Bankers Association, Sam and Sam Jr. confronted a protocol question. "In the negotiations with Love, which of us should represent the Bank?"

"Both of us," Sam said firmly.

"O.K.," Sam Jr. replied, "but it's been your 'baby' from birth; you know the value it has accumulated better than anyone else. You take the lead, and I'll back you up." To Sam Jr. there was an added consideration. In those three years he had had too little opportunity "just to be with Marilyn and my little kids. Now that I'm free, I want to take them to Hawaii for a month. I want to catch up with my family on what all of us, for too long, have been missing. I'll phone you every day. You can phone me whenever you want to."

Talking specifics now with Ben Love, Sam was confronting a financial wizard. "Tall, lean, austere, and intense," *Fortune* magazine had described him in 1979. Love had created that impression throughout the brief years it had taken him to rise from his position as head of a Houston specialty paper manufacturing concern to chief executive of TCB. "I really don't work in a feet-on-the-desk relaxed way," he told *Fortune*.[26]

Nor did he work now, in that manner, with Sam.

At the start of the negotiations in Sam's conference room, Love wanted to trade on the basis of a $40 worth for one of TCB's shares and a $60 worth for one of the Bank's: a share and a half of his stock, that is, for one share of Sam's. Ben also wanted the transaction to be a strictly stock for stock deal.

"But my share," Sam insisted, "is worth much more than $60."

Ben came back with a reaction. "All right, but if your price gets above $67, we cut the number of shares in our offer."

As Sam Jr. had suggested, the telephone consultations between Hawaii and El Paso occurred at least once a day. Each conference lasted close to an hour. Ben's threat to cut down his shares got quick reaction from Sam Jr. "Wait a minute, Dad, suppose it goes the other way."

Sam paused. "So far, it hasn't."

"But if it does go the other way, like below $57, why don't we ask for cash at $62.50? To offset their 'up-side'?"

Sam mulled over that notion. "Cash call him? Will he go for that?"

Sam Jr. answered quickly. "You're a hell of a negotiator. Give it a shot."[27]

Sam Jr. was in town for the final negotiations. Alongside him and Sam, were directors Paul Harvey, Fred Schneider, and attorney Bill Mounce. Love and Tom McDade represented Texas Commerce Bancshares. During that meeting, Faye Hartman was outside at her desk, ready with pencil and pad and typewriter. Every few minutes Tom McDade came out with a legal pad scribbled black with details for Faye to type up. Quickly, she rushed the results back into the meeting. Again and again more drafts came out for her "to make order of the chaos."[28]

With the dickering concluded at last, Ben Love knew he had met in Sam Young a master at defending the interests of those whom he represented. For more than five years, Love had been Sam's pursuer. "It had been an interesting situation for us. In our experience with other Texas bankers, we had often been the pursued." But Love had seen, he reported when he returned to Houston, a master negotiator at work. "He was charming, he was gracious, but, paradoxically, he was right to the point when he insisted on getting the very best terms for his stockholders."[29]

Both parties had come away winners — as Sam had always insisted must be the case in any "good" deal. Love had got the bank holding complex he most wanted. Sam and Sam Jr. and their team of experts had got what they considered the "best deal ever" for their shareholders, $62.50 per share.[30] The battle of wits and "sharp pencils" had left both forces alive and content.

To the directors meeting on July 14, 1981, Sam carried word of the favorable outcome,[31] and two weeks later on July 29, the board approved a motion by Paul and Phil Harvey, finding it apropos that the two sons of the Bank's co-founder had led the decision to sell. Now, the matter must go to the necessary federal regulatory agencies for approval. At the shareholders annual meeting the following April, the El Paso National Corporation's real owners got the last say. They approved the grand total Sam had won for them: $98 million in cash.

On June 29, 1982, Sam did not miss the import of the figures involved in that sale. In the fifty-seven years during which he had presided over the Bank's steady growth (it now had 578 employees and assets of $846,704,000), its worth had increased at an annualized rate of 11.79 percent.

It was time now for the Bank's ads in the El Paso papers to explain the big shift in its status. "With the statewide, national, and international resources of Texas Commerce to draw from, El Paso National Corporation banks can now serve El Paso better than ever before. For example, our lending strength has increased twenty-fold to more than $100 million per customer. That means more capital to fuel the continued growth of our city. For us and our customers, that means progress. We are El Paso. And now we're as strong as Texas." Signed Sam D. Young, Jr.[32]

When the last Federal hurdle — the Justice Department — was successfully leaped in August, the merger was a neat win for Sam and his

Sam with Merriman Morton at the Texas Commerce Bank-El Paso service awards ceremony, June 26, 1985.

Texas Commerce officials Marc Shapiro, Merriman Morton, and Ben Love at an El Paso press conference regarding the merger, September, 1982.

people, a victory plus some honest relief for Ben Love. "The most difficult man to court I ever met," he commented later.[33] But, Marc Shapiro, TCB's chief financial officer, added, "The best negotiator I've ever seen, bar none."[34] Also, Marc added, "We find Sam Jr.'s theory of banking – horizontal administration, that is, not pyramidal – completely compatible with ours."

In addition to the profits Sam realized from the sale of his and his family's 70,095 shares,[35] he came away with a lifetime guarantee of an office suite in the Bank building, a secretary, an automobile, a chauffeur, and an annual consultantship at $125,000. All things considered, a most satisfactory rise from his stipend "in the beginning," $7,500, plus no perks at all.

With those major changes now in his personal status, Sam looked with Little Betty and Sam Jr. at the best use of their newly acquired funds. Sam mused a moment, he looked through the window, then spoke what he had on his mind. "I never did set out just to get rich, and it still doesn't interest me much. I want this money to do some real good, not just be a nest egg for more. I want it to encourage good things in all kinds of good people, support good causes however it can."

On December 1, 1982, when their discussions resulted in the "Sam D. Young Family Foundation," its terms reflected that wish. Monies generated by the Foundation's investments would support worthy "civic, charitable, religious, and educational endeavors."[36]

Merger accomplished, the new institution was in many ways still its own boss with Sam Jr. as CEO and CB. Its new president, Merriman Morton, a dynamic import from a highly successful six-year presidency of TCB's member bank in Corpus Christi, was thoroughly familiar with TCB's headquarters: Houston's new $140 million Texas Commerce Tower. Its seventy-five stories of shining glass, gray granite, and stainless steel made it the tallest building in America outside of New York and Chicago, and, incidentally the tallest bank building in the world.[37] The assets controlled by the Texans inside that behemoth, $16.5 billion, made it Texas' largest bank holding company.

18

A MIGHTY OAK

MUCH AS THE MERGER WITH TEXAS COMMERCE had interested Sam and Sam Jr., another merger of a quite different sort had interested Sam fully as much on July 30, 1982. For months, he had known that his grandson David Hoover was becoming increasingly fond of a young lady named Nancy Jackson. David's friendships were strictly his own business, but when Sam learned the name of Nancy's maternal grandfather – George Matkin – his reaction was loud and quite clear.

Since the angry morning years before when Sam had charged out of Matkin's office at the State National Bank, – "and the hell with you too!" – the door had stayed closed between them. Now, with some amusement, Sam shot David a heavy question. "For heaven sakes, David, out of all the pretty girls in El Paso, why pick a Matkin?"

"Why not, Pappy?" David smiled, accepting the joke. But throughout the spring of 1982 Sam playfully needled him. "Are you still going out with that Matkin girl?" he grinned.

Like David, Nancy played along with Sam's joke. "Though," she recalled later, "I suppose there was some reason for Pappy's apparent concern. After all, I was working as a credit analyst at the State National, fully accessible to highly confidential material. And maybe,

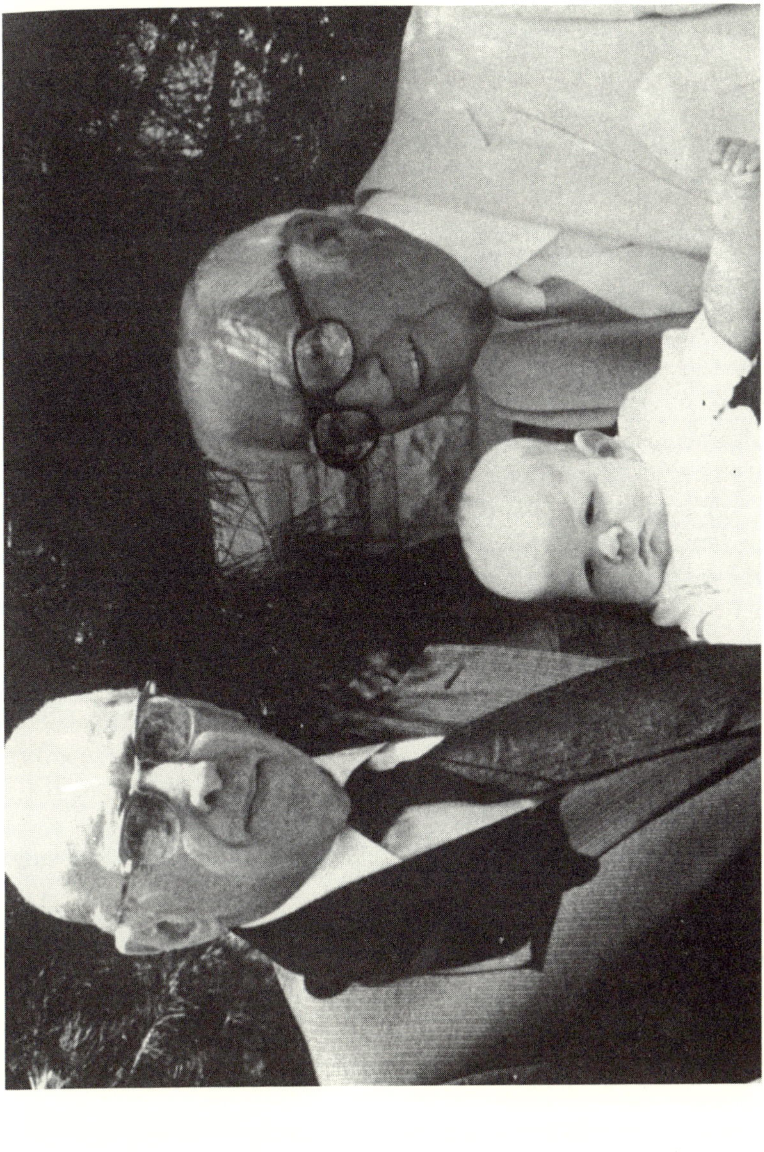

George C. Matkin and Sam with their great-grandson Steven Chadwick Hoover, 1983.

even in spite of the feud or whatever between Granddaddy Matkin and Pappy, I may well have looked like a member of the enemy army."

Again in a few weeks, Sam was grinning and needling David again. "Are you still going out with that Matkin girl?"

"Not just going out with her, I'm marrying her on July 30. And you're invited to come. And so is Mr. Matkin. Can you make it?"[1]

At the wedding in St. Clements Episcopal Church, the old rivals behaved themselves silently, Sam and his family on the groom's side of the aisle, Matkin and his family on the bride's. After the ceremony, no words passed between them, nor was there any exchange almost a year later when a christening featured their bloodlines forever entwined. Afterwards, posing together, they stood for a picture with their mutual great-grandson Steven Chadwick Hoover, Nancy and David's first child. Sam was all smiles for the baby; Matkin stared straight at the camera.

Meanwhile, down at the Bank, evidence was more and more prominent that the merger with Texas Commerce was bringing big changes. In short order the Bank's old logo, its sunburst swirl symbolizing its trade territory, came down. Replacing it now, TCB's red-white-and-blue Texas flag symbol suggested the shift in the Bank's new range: "All over Texas." In short order too the new board of directors set Sam Jr.'s salary at $200,000 (including his pay from the still existent EPNC). Asked about Sam's own value to the Bank, Merriman Morton waxed explicit. "We value his long experience here, his knowledge of the local economy, his incredible ability to sway and influence people in a way that may seem irritating at first, but the next minute he has them charmed off their feet."[2]

Nice words aside, Merriman heard an explosion soon after when in a cost-cutting move throughout the bank, he cancelled one of Sam's favorite daily newspapers. "Morton, how do you folks expect my advice to be worth a damn if I don't keep up with what's happening? Somebody cut off my *American Banker*, and I want it back!"[3]

Typical of the many other employees who were now a part of the new TCB team, young Maria Montes's grace under pressure one afternoon saved the Bank big money. Near quitting time a team of lawyers panicked when they found a substantial mistake in a legal document related to their client's big business plans. Urgent to close the deal *now*, the lawyers were nonplussed about getting the long technical paper retyped. Despite their constant interruptions and the phones jangling around her, Maria perfectly retyped those thirty-five pages. When the sale of that local business to a national conglomerate brought the Bank a $35 million deposit, Polly McFadden praised Maria's cool work. "That's the kind of customer service the El Paso National Bank is proud to give."[4]

For Sam, Mary Lou's own good work was cause for celebration soon after. When her new art anthology, *Lovers* by Mary Lawrence (New York: A and W Press, 1982), was published, he gave a Los Angeles party for the friends who had contributed essays on the one hundred works of art her book featured. Mary Lou's foreword explained her choosing those particular pieces. "A number of the lovers portrayed here are famous lovers from mythology or history; but most are created in the artist's imagination. The varieties of love are as endless as the range of the imagination. Active and passive, creative and receptive, light and darkness, man and woman, yin and yang, forever opposed, forever united, struggling for harmony, striving for love."

The preface by Sophia Loren spoke from the standpoint of all the artists. "It is said that all the world loves a lover. Certainly, works of art which deal with lovers attract the world widely: the actress who portrays romantic roles commands an audience; the writer who describes love sensitively is almost sure to be read; the artist who captures lovers intimately on canvas or in stone is likely to have his work viewed with intense interest. Why are we so drawn to images and tales of love? Perhaps because when we love, we forget our painful sense of being alone."

The book's success was assured when the Literary Guild listed it as one of its fall selections.

Like Mary Lou's interest in art, Sam's concerns for Providence Hospital rode high in 1983 when a hospital holding company approached him. Various people had tried to buy the hospital itself or some of its nine city blocks that had cost the original board $30,000. Of late, Sam had turned away a group of doctors who had offered him $200,000 for a half of one of those blocks. "You can't make any more land and we may need it," Sam had objected. Now, the out-of-town holding company wanted the hospital itself and all its land for $50 million.

"You could use that money in your various charitable works," suggested the buyer.

"Your $50 million," Sam scoffed, "couldn't touch the charity work the hospital already does. We're not selling."[5]

Nor was Sam overlooking another success he had watched with satisfaction for years. In August 1983 when Jack Young, Sam's youngest brother, died, he had been president and chairman of the board of Northgate Bank. Now, his son Randolph succeeded him. Countering the loss of this youngest brother, Sam found Jack's career a testimony to the will-to-succeed that Fanny had early instilled in her flock.

On the same vein, El Paso Natural Gas Company had been bringing good to its town for so long now that concern spread far and wide when rumors reported a pending takeover by outsiders. About that possibility, Sam bristled loudly. And when the sale to Burlington Northern went through in 1983, Henry Crown, Burlington's largest stockholder, heard immediately from his old Hilton colleague. On his call to Chicago Sam came straight to the point. "Henry? I don't know what you folks are planning down here. But I sure as hell hope you bear in mind that our Gas Company is about the best friend this city has got. Are you folks planning some major upset for us?"

Crown spoke equally straight. "Relax, my friend. No major upset, no changes at all. But just to be sure that you hear from us officially, I'm recommending that one of our people pay you a visit quite soon."

That official showed up at Sam's office door the next week. "Mr. Young, I'm Richard Bressler, chairman of Burlington, and I'm here—"

Grinning broadly, Bressler turned one cheek, then the other. "Come on now, give me the beating you have in mind. Henry Crown says you aren't so happy with us."

At Bressler's hearty good cheer and disarming manner, Sam quickly calmed down. "Well, you did do us a dirty trick. But I guess I'm ready to make peace. But only on one condition. You be good to El Paso."

Bressler grinned again, then took his seat. "You don't need to be concerned about anything, Mr. Young," he said, opening his brief case. "We know very well how much this city always meant to Paul Kayser. We aren't planning any change in the vision he felt for this town. El Paso will continue to be headquarters for El Paso Natural Gas. We don't intend to create any disturbance whatever. In fact, under a solid good man like Travis Petty as CB and CEO, we want to help your city as much as we can. That's my personal promise to you."

With that, Sam stood up and shook hands with Bressler. "Well then, I'm taking your word. And I'm holding you to it," he smiled.[6]

Soon after that, Sam was party to a success story related to MacIntosh Muchison. When Jonathan Rogers took charge of Mac's Mortgage Investment Company in 1963, there had been some uncertainty that young Rogers was the right man for the job. Now, in 1984, when El Paso's Mayor Jonathan Rogers and the Murchison family sold their company for $76 million, Sam claimed none of the credit for Jon's impressive achievement. He did take some pride, however, in having been right once again in trusting his confidence in a new "comer."[7]

Again in 1984, Sam entertained thoughts of the past when the view from his office underwent a big alteration. The State National Bank, a member now of MCorp in Dallas, was changing its name to "MBank." For fifty-nine years the State National had been his lusty adversary, but watching "State National Bank" coming down from its skyscraper, Sam was observing the end of an era in his own life. He could not imagine how his bank's statements of condition might have read, had there been no George Matkin at the State National to keep him alert, on his toes.

A ceremony in Dallas in May 1984 indirectly referred to that very point when the Texas Business Hall of Fame added Sam to its pantheon. For Sam's influence upon the money scene far beyond Texas, Robert Dedham, banquet chairman, and Robert S. Strauss, master-of-ceremonies, welcomed the name Samuel Doak Young to the list of those honored thus far. The seventy El Pasoans who attended the banquet had known most of the facts about Sam, but they rose applauding when told that the award placed him among such financial lights as Herman and George Brown, Jesse Jones, Erik Jonsson, Robert Kleberg Jr., L. F. McCollum, William D. Noel, Charles Tandy, Arthur Temple, M. D. Anderson, William Clayton, Oveta Culp Hobby, Stanley Marcus, Clint Murchison, Jr., and Joe C. Thompson. "Sam Young is the only El Pasoan in the list."

Seeing Oveta Culp Hobby's name on that list, Sam smiled as his long thoughts took him back to that dinner meeting in San Antonio when Governor had sought his approval of "this young lady I'm planning to marry." Since 1931 that lady had been at Governor's side as their *Houston Post* waxed ever stronger. In 1983, when Oveta and her two children sold the *Post*, the *New York Times* (October 18, 1983) gave the full story. The sale price: $100 million.

As the ceremony made clear, each honoree was the featured player in a drama that had begun, in more cases than not, in humble circumstances. Joseph Haggar, the Dallas pants man, had left his Lebanon home at age thirteen, penniless, en route to America. "My success here," he declared in his acceptance remarks, "is only partly personal; it is more a proof of the opportunity this great nation of ours afforded us all." Sam's own story affirmed the same point.

"In winning his prize," the Bank's newsletter reported soon after, "he added distinction to the entire El Paso community."

In that same community, Mary Lou had distinguished herself with the local art scene soon after becoming an "adopted El Pasoan" in 1980. Through her friendships with artists, through her service to widely scattered museums that needed "good friends and benefactors," Mary Lou was eager now to encourage the arts in El Paso. As a board member of the El Paso Museum of Art, she joined an ambitious campaign to fund a new building for the Museum's already impressive holdings. Without a larger physical plant, the El Paso Museum of Art could never be a true force in El Paso, she told the board, for encouraging the young and the talented, for acquainting all ages with the world's greatest artistic sensibilities.

That fall, Sam and Mary Lou were en route home from Rome when he suffered another setback with his luggage. There was no angry scuffle this time, merely helpless dismay in New York when, receiving his suitcase at the baggage counter, Sam found a jagged slit in its side. Ruffling through it, he discovered nothing missing until he reexamined his bag at the Waldorf-Astoria. Gone again was his St. Christopher medal, gone were his favorite gold cuff links, and most sadly of all, his beloved old silver dollar that for seventy-seven years he had always held close in case he ever "got in a tight."

Merriman Morton's April 15, 1985, letter to the stockholders announced that on June 30, the name of the Bank would officially change. "For sixty years El Paso National Bank has been recognized by the people of this city, the southwest region of the nation, and northern Mexico as a leading financial institution. Today, its reputation and performance are stronger than ever."

Since the merger, Morton continued, the Bank had used TCB's logo "as a display of our affiliation and our increased capacities," but to achieve full identification with the state-wide organization, "we will now change our name to 'Texas Commerce Bank-El Paso.'" The name would be different, but "our commitment to you and to the city of El Paso remains one of service and dedication with professional excellence."

Sam read that announcement with a twinge of nostalgia, but early in the week of June 30, nostalgia could wait while he hosted a luncheon that a bit of high jinks at UTEP had committed him to. As a city-wide fund raising stunt, the UTEP Women's Auxiliary had billed its 1985 campaign a "slave auction." The "slave" receiving the highest number of bids (at $500 per bid) would host his "buyers" at lunch. When Sam Young "sold" for $4,500, he dutifully sent out his invitations.

Both for its jokes and its gourmet menu that lunch at the Bank helped him acknowledge each guest's investment. Paul Harvey was ill at Providence; Barron Hilton was tied up in a Chicago meeting. But Fred Hervey, Mayor Jonathan Rogers, Pat Haggerty, William Poteet, Tom Thigpin, William Mounce, and Steve DeGroat came hungry and ready with "roasts" about Citizen Sam in the El Paso community.

The wit of the mayor and of "Circle K" Hervey drowned out the retorts Sam attempted, especially when Rogers mentioned his tie-cutting raid around town two weeks before. His Honor had decreed that for the summer all city officials and dignitaries would go without ties or those ties would suffer the whack of his gold-plated shears. "But," the mayor confessed, "the minute I took after Sam, I knew I was risking big trouble: Mayor Cuts Off Banker's Tie, Banker Cuts Off Mayor's Credit." It was that notion that *Time* magazine played up on July 1 with full quotes and a color picture of Sam and the mayor.

Hervey waxed a little more solemn when he testified that it was Sam's faith in Fred Hervey that had funded the expansion of his Circle K stores into Phoenix. "At the time when Sam was willing to stake you with that million-buck loan," somebody asked, "how many stores did you have?"

Hervey grinned. "Thirteen."

"How many stores have you got now?"

Hervey figured a moment. "Three thousand, and more on the way."

Mayor Rogers, a businessman able to sympathize with any other man's losses, chuckled. "A minute ago, Sam here said that for sixty years he has known all of El Paso's mayors and that you and I are two of the best. Fred, how much personal income do you figure your years as mayor cost you?"

Hervey frowned a sad smile. "At least twenty-three million dollars."

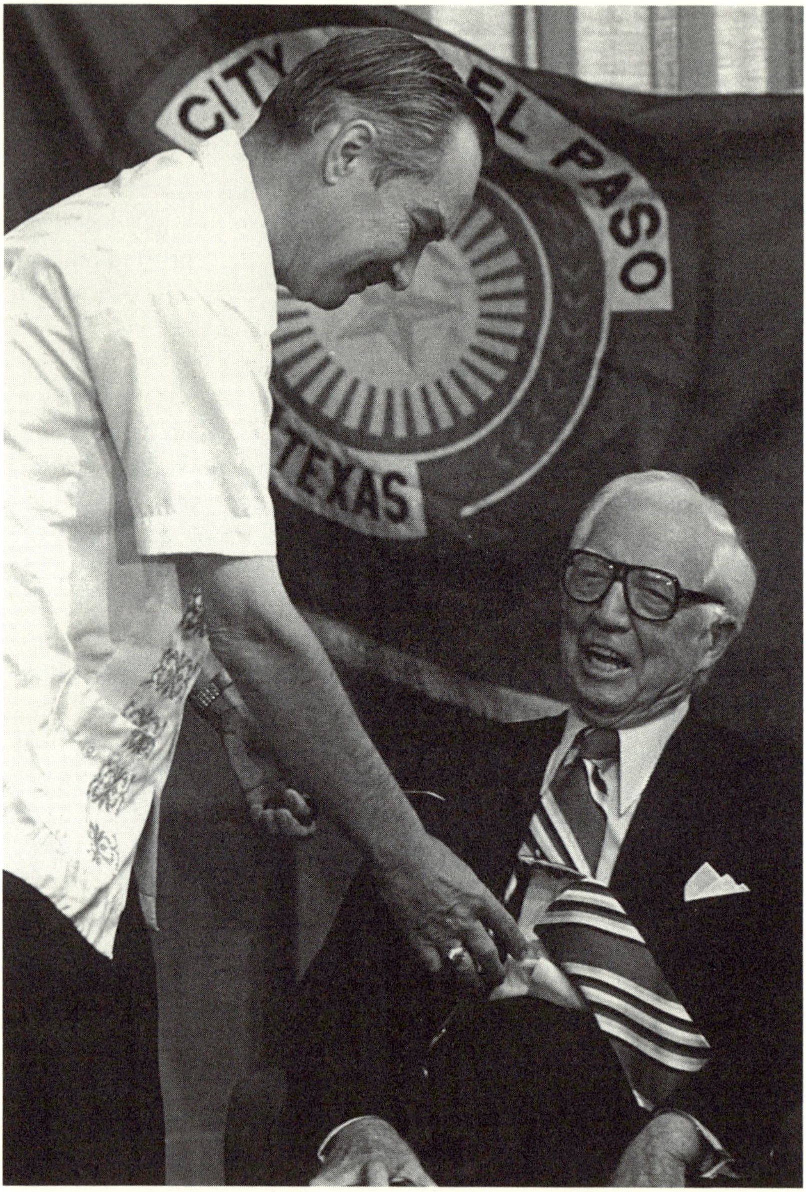

El Paso Mayor Jonathan Rogers decreed that during summer months all city officials and dignitaries would go without ties or those ties would suffer the whack of his gold-plated shears, June, 1985. After cutting off Sam's tie, the mayor confessed that a headline might well read, "Mayor Cuts Off Banker's Tie; Banker Cuts Off Mayor's Credit."

Paling, Rogers surrendered the floor when somebody asked, "Sam, how good a golfer was Hilton?"

Sam gave a big laugh. "Most days Connie shot in the 80s – but he could be hell to play with. Always muttering, 'Hurry up, Sam, dammit, *putt!*' and sometimes I lost my three dollars when he did get me rattled. Still –"

Sam sobered a moment, "He made lots of folks around here plenty rich. Even old Dossie Wiggins who used to be president out at the college. For that $25,000 I made him invest in good Hilton stock, Dossie came away with $350,000."

And about that gold Hilton card Sam carried, had he used it all up?

Sam shook his head. "We checked not long ago with Barron's office about the number of rooms he has now. It came to 97,797. Sleeping one night in each room would take me 267 years. I'm running a little behind."

The next morning, Sam's thoughts were occupied with more talk of Hilton and Hilton Hotels when officials from the Conrad Hilton School of Hotel and Restaurant Management at the University of Houston interviewed him. "As Hilton's earliest major support," archivist Karl Conrad wanted to know, "what did you see in Conrad Hilton that so early impressed you?"

Sam's answer came quick. "His ambition, his zest for life, his excitement in recognizing opportunities that almost nobody in hotels had ever suspected."

"Was yours and Connie's a friendly relationship?"

"Sure. But he was all business when the time came to be and so was I. And he knew it."

On June 26, the Bank spoke its own sense of the week's big significance, when ninety-three of its officers gathered in the Bank's auditorium to receive their new pins sporting "Texas Commerce Bank-El Paso" in place of the old service pins that many had worn for decades. But along with the new pins sporting a diamond for every ten years of service came some laughter and tears. Greeting the group, especially Sam and Mary Lou as they took their seats on the front row, Merriman gestured toward the long banner facing the audience. "Texas Commerce Bank-El Paso National Bank," he read. "New Name – Same Strength."

Morton hoped, he explained, that the staff would think of the week, not as the close of an era, but as the start of a bright, new chapter in the Bank's story. Noting their loyal stability, he recognized each member according to his or her length of service. Sixty-six people had served more than 5 years; 41 more than 10, 14 more than 20, and 8 more than 30. Distributing the appropriate pins, Morton paused, smiling. Since everyone here looked "forward to many good things ahead, I think we can all give each other a good round of applause."

Nodding toward Sam, Merriman pointed out the ceremony's special chance to express "our respect and affection for Mr. Sam D. Young, the founder 60 years ago of this bank."

From his seat, Sam called out, "All right, folks, but don't I get a new service pin like the rest of you?"

"Later," Merriman laughed, "in a minute."

As Merriman ushered forward the officers with the longest records, each spoke his thoughts about his time with the Bank. Sandy Caviness's happy memories spanned 31 years. Ruth Knott's covered 33 years. Les Walker (38 years) remembered how short the Bank's personnel roster had been when he started. Maria Castruita (39 years) received special applause for having served longest. Cecilia Solem (39 years) choked up a little when she gave Sam a smile. "Mr. Young, you raised us."

As Mary Lou and Merriman escorted Sam to the podium, the audience rose, applauding, as he turned to them. "I do believe I see some pretty girls I haven't seen before," Sam winked, when Merriman presented him his 60-year pin.

Under the glare of TV cameras, Sam smiled at the crowd. "The name El Paso National Bank," he said slowly, "has been like a family name to me. And I do regret a little the name change"—his voice cracked—"but the new name will mean many good things ahead. Our employees have worked hard for us, and we have all profited. The good Lord has guided me at every step of the way, and I know the Lord has prospered us all in the Bank."

Leaning forward, Sam's hands gripped the head of his cane. "I do hope the Bank will continue to lead and participate in community improvements. The business community always supporting the arts and community developments—that's the main thing we need."

With that, his glance swept the crowd. "You'll always be in my heart and in my mind."

Head down, Sam accepted their applause.

That occasion expressed the Bank's thanks to those members present but if a similar ceremony could have honored those hundreds who had given similarly valuable service over the years, the list chosen by consensus of the Bank's long memories would have included at least the following: Harold Browning, Kenneth Dean, Emil Jay Dittmer, Frank Harriss, George Hogan, Helen Kitt, Walter Marquis, Harry Moore, Jr., Tom C. Patterson, and Don Ridgway. From there, the list could have extended indefinitely.

Since the merger, Sam had known the Bank would eventually change its name. But he was not quite ready when that day arrived. He had never regretted the deal he had made with Ben Love: "My policy was to put service ahead of profits, but we didn't make as much money as they are making now," he told a *Times* reporter in 1984.[8]

Case in point was an irate lady who protested to lobby official Walt Klinikowski a new service charge on her checking account. "I've had an account here for thirty years and never had a service charge. Why are they charging me now?"

"It's bank policy, ma'am," Walt explained.

"Well, if Mr. Young were still here, I wouldn't question it. With him still in charge, there'd be a good reason."[9]

June 30, 1985, the Bank's sixtieth birthday plus one day, saw proof that a new era had replaced the "old Young years," as a pun throughout the building expressed it. For several days now flesh-and-blood workers had been riding up and down on the tower, dismantling the El Paso National Bank sign, letter by letter. "It makes me kind of sad when I think of what's going on up there, right above this office," Sam explained to a friend when his voice choked.

A *New Yorker* cartoon of four sour-faced men in a club lounge caught his mood exactly. "It's all gone to hell," read the caption. "Sandy's been acquired, Herb disappeared in a hostile takeover, Ted went to Chapter 11 to duck lawsuits, and now Eddie's operation is changing its name."[10]

A better statement of the day's meaning for the old personnel was a bit of poetry, "Old 88-15" read to them by their own "Oliver Wendell William Woodyard." Recognizing the title as a reference to the Bank's routing number for its customers' checks, they gave Will Woodyard, investment officer, full marks.

Aye, tear her battered logo down!
Long has it hung on high,
And many an eye has danced to see
That emblem in the sky;
Beneath it rang old Big Sam's shout,
And burst his temper's roar;
The beacon of the desert air
Shall grace the smog no more.

As the Bank's name was changing, so were the names in its inner sanctum. From the earliest days of the merger, Sam Jr. had sensed that Texas Commerce was "much more intent on reshaping El Paso National Corporation into its own image than in establishing a partnership on more individualistic operating styles." Sensitized by his experiences with Sam, Sam Jr. concluded that none of the people involved "could benefit from having two chairmen of the board," himself and somebody else. Though he had helped to effect a smooth transition to the merger, he told his friends that he did not wish to remain in El Paso, either with TCB or with "some other institution now competing with an institution to which he had given the best part of his life."[11]

At its board meeting on August 31, 1985, Sam Jr. announced his retirement. His point was succinct: he and his family were moving to La Jolla. The board sat silent, but in a moment Sam himself spoke up, emotion choking his voice. "Well, California's a mighty fine place, but El Paso is very special. In five years, you'll miss it and want to move back."[12] Sam Jr. nodded, but he had already spoken his piece.

At that meeting the board had made no official response, but at its October 8 session the directors adopted a tribute to Sam Jr.'s twenty-eight years of leadership. In his rise to president, CEO, and CB, his contributions "have been numerous and significant;" he had installed modern management practices vital to the Bank's development. Yet "among his many contributions none will be longer nor more favorably remembered than the emphasis he placed upon people," bank employees and bank customers alike. "Sam Young Jr. will be remembered as a sensitive, caring, friendly person with an extremely high regard for his fellow man." That relationship had helped him create "a management style that put people first in his priority system. This," concluded the tribute, "is his legacy as a manager."[13]

The following week Texas Commerce hosted Sam Jr. and Marilyn to a farewell dinner at the El Paso Club for 150 executives of its eight El Paso banks. After the ceremony, CEO Merriman Morton introduced Sam Jr.'s successor, President Richard Hickson and his wife Janet.[14] With a B.S. degree from the University of Georgia, Richard had been executive vice president of TCB-Houston's banking group handling national corporations. He had been chairman of the Texas Commerce International Bank.

"Now," Morton continued, "you'll all be happy to know that this is not the total goodbye to our good friends the Youngs. Sam Jr. will be returning each month to attend the El Paso National Corporation's board meeting and the board meeting of TCB-El Paso itself."

19

FAITH IN THE MAN

SAM JR.'S OWN TIME AT THE BANK was complete. Ceremonially, his dedication and hard work had been recognized and applauded. Free now to make his own commitments to new enterprises in La Jolla and elsewhere, he shook hands all around in farewell.

As for Sam Sr., he would remain with the team. Far more than a "dignitary" retained merely out of respect, he would advise, he would forewarn, he would share the fruit of his long experience. "Soon after that farewell dinner," Richard Hickson said later, "Mr. Young showed me some of his cancelled checks. Several had been deposited at a competitor bank. 'How come?' he wanted to know. 'Those people used to bank here. Why did we lose them? How can we get them back?' That kind of question from him," Richard declared, "is good for us."

"More than that," Richard continued, "almost daily he increases my insight about matters we need to examine long range. The influence of military spending here. El Paso's real estate growth. Every day he examines our loan agenda. Still the hands-on banker, he is always concerned for our customers: the big ones, of course, like the Hiltons, Fred Hervey, the Tony Lamas, the Zachrys who have been with us for years. But also the little accounts like the ones he himself built with a friendly smile and handshake.[1] And he still wants us to lead El Paso's best efforts to improve the quality of life here. Merriman led the United Way's latest campaign. Right now, I'm leading the drive to re-establish the old Plaza Theatre as a cultural asset."

"But true to his policy," Richard concluded his salute to Sam's era, "we also want to make a profit." Shortly before he came to El Paso, Ben Love had told him, "TCB-El Paso is one of our battleships, not merely a PT boat in the flotilla."

"And our total profits last year certainly proved that," Richard smiled. "Of Texas Commerce Bancshares' total profit of $50 million, TCB-El Paso's $8 million was a very respectable 16 percent."[2]

Capping the climax of the merger, on November 5, 1985, Ben Love hosted a large party at the El Paso Marriott Hotel. His tribute to Sam was broadly detailed and colorful: "Sam grew up knowing the sweat of hard work, whether driving a wagon and team, serving as stock boy in his father's small country store, or serving at the ripe old age of twelve as the Woodville agent for a laundry in Beaumont. One wonders how he feels now, amidst all his friends, home safe with his honors. It is for those reasons we have congregated tonight, to celebrate – with him – his good works and his achievements."

Ben lifted his glass. "Sam Young, remarkable El Pasoan. Sam Young, big Texan among Texans, in that grand old Texas tradition."[3]

After delivering his own tribute to Sam, Merriman gestured around to the guests. "You've been wondering why I asked you not to open that big envelope in the center of each of your tables. Now you can open it."

Inside it, they found printed copies of a letter dated October 30, 1985.[4] "We had it sized to insert in the programme leaflet," Merriman explained, "in case you'd like to take it home as a souvenir."

Sam delivered a graceful response not only to Love for the party, but in particular, to his "right hand men," Homer Jacobs, Sheley Warnock, Gus Bianche, and Joe Moreno. He thanked Sam Jr. "And," he concluded, "I am especially thankful to the Grand Architect of the universe, who was my guide throughout my career. I had already found that you couldn't go it alone and that the Lord's guidance, with the help of loyal and devoted friends, was necessary to success."[5]

Appropriately, Mayor Jonathan Rogers had already declared November 5, 1985, "Sam Young Day."[6]

A little note from Margaret Jacoway Stocker rounded out a long bit of history. The daughter of the young bridegroom who had given Sam

THE WHITE HOUSE

WASHINGTON

October 30, 1985

Dear Mr. Young:

I understand El Paso will be celebrating Sam Young Day on November 5, while that night a group of your friends and admirers are giving you a testimonial dinner. Naturally a biography is under way. And at mid-month you'll be marking -- and many will be celebrating -- the 50th anniversary of your 39th birthday. I could congratulate you on any of these, and I want to congratulate you on all of them. America, not just Texas, is proud of you.

It will take that biography to list all your achievements, and all your contributions to the State of Texas. I want to single out the wise counsel you have given the Federal government, and the constructive role you have played helping us to maintain good relations with our neighbor to the South. For all this, I salute you, and on behalf of all the American people, I thank you.

Nancy joins me in sending warmest regards to you and Mary Lou. God bless you.

Sincerely,

Ronald Reagan

Mr. Sam D. Young, Sr.

El Paso, Texas

This letter from President Ronald Reagan was inserted in the printed program at a large dinner honoring Sam in 1985. Ben Love, chairman of Texas Commerce Bancshares, hosted the party which capped the climax of the El Paso National Bank-Texas Commerce merger.

the silver dollar was delighted now to hear of Sam's honor. "My parents would be so proud, but not surprised!"[7]

After that, there remained the special birthday festivities at Sam's beloved Paso del Norte Hotel (now the Westin Paso del Norte) on the evening of November 15, 1986.

Word had circulated that the dinner for three hundred guests would be an ideal opportunity for testimonies to Sam. As the evening drew near, however, hostesses Mary Lou, Little Betty, and Marilyn stood firmly opposed: Sam had heard plenty of presentations. Tonight, his friends and his family wanted merely to shake his hand and wish him "Happy Ninetieth Birthday!"

Throughout the evening, the crowd, young and old, danced to the tunes that Sam most enjoyed. Seated with Mary Lou, Little Betty and her husband Wally Taber, and Sam Jr. and Marilyn at a table beside the dance floor, Sam was easy to reach for congratulations. After the dinner, the orchestra leader called for "The grandchildren, please, the grandchildren." Little Betty's seven children: Robert T. Hoover III, Doak Hoover, David Hoover, Elizabeth Hoover Sergent, Ruth Hoover Sprout, Erin Bauman and Kristin Bauman; and Sam Jr.'s five: Sam D. Young III, Blair Young, Lisa Roesler, Emily Williams and Allison McGuire, ushered forward their own children and spouses and formed a circle in front of the orchestra. The music struck up, the twenty-one young people glanced at each other, then laughed and burst into song.

To the tune of "Give My Regards to Broadway" they chorused, "Let's give our regards to Pappy. Tell him just how much we care. Tell all the world how much we love him. Where he is, we'll all be there."

They took deep breaths, then sang to the tune of "Happy Days Are Here Again": "All together, shout it now / With our love and then a great big Wow! / Happy birthday, Sam, it's here, it's now / Pappy's day is here again!" Then joining hands to the beat of the music, they gave a grand finale to the tune of "Hello Dolly": "So hello, Pappy, well hello, Pappy / It's so nice to be with you where we belong. / You're looking swell, Pappy / We can tell, Pappy / You're still glowing, you're still crowing, you're still going strong. / We feel the room swaying' and the band's playin' / one of your old favorite songs from way back when. / Now here's your cake, Pappy. / Ninety wishes make, Pappy / Lots of love from all of us to you!" Waving at Sam, his whole clutch of family shouted, "Happy birthday, Pappy!"

Sam had been told, "No speeches," but he did not resist the urge to tell the crowd how he felt. Using his cane, slowly making his way to the bandstand, Sam turned, swallowed, then thanked everybody for the love and friendship he had enjoyed with everyone there – he smiled around at the crowd – for most of their lives: Phebe from Woodville and Margaret from Houston (his only siblings left now), Betty's sisters Jo Lipscomb and Martha and her husband Dean Herman, Olga Roderick and Winnie Schuster and other special friends from his earliest days in El Paso. From England, Switzerland, France, Italy, La Jolla, Los Angeles, and Mexico he recognized Eloy Vallina, Jr. and his wife and his mother Maria; Elizabeth Lambert; Marion Pike; and Eleanor (Mrs. Brian) Aherne.

Musing a moment next day, Sam said of that big occasion, "It was *the* party of my career."[8]

The birthday party had been a delight, but it had reminded Sam once again, as he told the crowd that evening, "I don't have many contemporaries left." He made no mention of his own life expectancy, but such thoughts had lain heavy on his mind long before the big party: pain in the bladder had plagued him for weeks.

The medical exam discovered the worst. Sam's jaws clinched when he heard the word "cancer." But each morning as he dressed for his office, he told Mary Lou, "I've got too many projects unfinished to give in to whatever my fate holds in store." But as major surgery took place, and then in a few weeks further surgery, he spent more and more days – this time as a patient himself – at Providence.

When he felt able, he insisted on attending "his" hospital board meetings. Later, banker Tom Hussman commented on that kind of dedication. "From my experience on the board of another local hospital, I know that hospital management is much more complicated than bank management. Hospitals must pay their bills even though their customers may or not pay them. Mr. Young is a banker professionally so he's supposed to be good at that. But running a hospital – at no salary – well, that comes right out of his high standards for himself. That's a fantastic contribution."

Between bouts with his malady, Sam still appeared at the Bank board meetings; he and Mary Lou kept up their busy routine in El Paso and La Jolla. But as Christmas 1986 approached, they knew that the cruise they had booked on the *Royal Viking Sky* was beyond possibility. Whenever Sam felt well enough, he asked his chauffeur, Ted Toliver, to drive him down to the farm where he could ride slowly along, watching Jay Martin, his farm manager, directing the pecan harvest crew. Then, parked in the yard of the house he had remodeled when Little Betty and Sammy were growing up, he and Jay plotted the chances for better farm prices next season or a more ample water supply from Elephant Butte.

Driving back into town, it upset him to see the valley land that almost overnight was being paved over for new shopping centers and tract housing. "I hate it," he said. "Developers ought to expand into the sand hills and leave our good farm lands alone."[9]

To brighten his spirits, Mary Lou assembled the family down at the farm several times to tumble around and watch fireworks, or sit immersed in the cool silence after sundown, together.

Back at his office, he kept up his correspondence. Almost daily he went over his books with Faye Hartman and Dolores Najera, his bookkeeper, shuffling investments. Many times Sam summoned Bill Mounce, his personal attorney, to consider again the terms of his will. Some days those terms reflected exactly what he had always intended, but some days he found them glaringly vague. One afternoon, the discussion with Mounce centered on Little Betty and Sam Jr. "I want to change some of these details along here," he indicated to Mounce, "both should get more than this says. Make it —" He specified a sizable increase for Little Betty; he specified the same "raise" for Sam Jr. The hour was late, the session had been knotty and time consuming. Suddenly, Sam looked at Mounce. "Now, Bill, what can I do for you?"

"Whatever you say, Mr. Young." Bill thought a minute, then grinned. "Adopt me?"[10]

When Sam was content with such weighty matters, he was especially glad when friends dropped by "just to chat." One afternoon, he mentioned the year 1919, and his biographer responded, "You came out here to El Paso in, well, a rather unpromising time, didn't you?"

Sam shook his head. "It wasn't that way for me. I can't imagine a more interesting time to have lived than the time I was given. I'd have picked it intentionally if I'd had the choice."

Because it turned out to be a good time to make money?

"Because it was a good time to do what you could with what the Lord gave you, a good time to watch what you did bear some fruit."

Any regrets that he had had to start out without that proverbial silver spoon in his mouth?

"None at all. Making the money – in your own honest way – is a good part of the worth of that money. Money, just money, isn't much good. Don't let it fool you."

Any thoughts on the money he had spread around to help other folks working hard to make theirs?

"Sure, a banker is maybe all things to all people, but to me, a *good* banker is the man who likes money the way that, down at the farm, I like seeds. I like to plant seeds. I like to see the crop that comes up. I like to know that in some way I've helped some good things to grow."

Did he make many good loans, good in that sense?

"Thousands. Some of those loans made a lot of folks rich."

Where?

"Look out the window."

Did it take wealth to be happy?

"Of course not."

But it helps?

"It can, but it's no guarantee. Everybody's got a right to work hard and discover that fact for himself."

But if sweat doesn't always pay off, is there no room for charity?

"Plenty of room, for the sick and the cripples. But no room at all, when charity *makes* cripples."

In 1919 if his boss hadn't sent him out west to examine banks along the Mexican border, how might his story have shaped up?

"It's hard to think about that, and I'm glad I don't have to. I can't imagine a better place."

To grow up in?

"There was no better place. Not for me."

So, what's next? Back to that other good place – La Jolla?

"I kind of like to sit out there on my porch after the ponies have run at Del Mar. I like to gaze out to sea. It's a good feeling, watching those whales."

"You told me once," commented the writer, "that back there in Woodville, your mother said again and again that what you don't understand in the Scriptures, try not to worry about. Have faith and the Good Lord will listen. He'll see you through." Any thoughts about that?

"Lots of thoughts," Sam nodded slowly, "oh, lots of thoughts. I learned from her, and from every day since, that the Lord is ready to guide you. But He can't guide if you don't ask Him to help. I regard all the good fortune that my life has brought me to the Lord's promise, 'And He shall direct thy path,' and I think He has done so constantly until this very hour."

"Sometime ago," the writer remarked, "Merriman Morton commented that, in light of the state of Texas as a whole, he found you unique. The special fact about you, money-wise, he said, was your ability to read El Paso's financial potential. In an area in far West Texas that had no oil and gas (when for the last fifty years the foundation of the Texas economy had been oil and gas) you built a billion dollar organization without energy dollars.[11] Any thoughts about that?"

"Sure. But we did have the military, the cotton and the cattle, the copper, and the mining and manufacturing. Most of all, we had good people willing to work. Lots of people have the same feel I do about this part of the world. People with vision and the will to roll up their sleeves. That's the real backbone of any area's potential."

And back in Woodville, remembered the writer, a teacher named Brown cried out in frustration when you quit school without a diploma saying, "You're ruining your life!" Any thoughts about that?

Sam glanced through the window. High in his tower overlooking the vibrant, international city below, he cleared his throat. "Whatever my life has become," he said, as if picking his words one by one, "I had a lot of good help from others."

About 2 A.M. on April 14, 1987, Mary Lou came awake, hearing the nurse in Sam's room saying gently, "Rouse up now, Mr. Young. So I can give you some water. Fine. Now take a good sip."

Overhearing that little exchange from her own room, Mary Lou realized that Sam could indeed hear, though for the past three days he had made no response to anything said. After the nurse had straightened Sam's pillows and gone back to her chair, Mary Lou leaned close to Sam's ear.

"Sam, can you hear me?" Sam opened his eyes a little. "I do want to tell you I do thank you, Sam, for all the good times we've had together, the good trips, the cruises, the talks we have shared, looking out over the ocean. Sam, can you hear me?"

There was no response.

"Sam, if you can hear, please squeeze my hand." After a moment, Sam squeezed her hand, then closed his eyes.

Early next morning, Little Betty tried to get through to him. When Sam made a feeble effort to speak, she asked, "Are you waiting for Sammy?"

Sam nodded.

At noon, when Sam Jr. arrived from La Jolla, he asked, "Do you need anything, Dad?" Sam's eyes came alert; he shook his head.

On April 15, at 9:15 in the evening, Mary Lou and Little Betty and Sam Jr. and many other members of the family were at home with Sam when he died.

Robert M. Young, Sam's pastor at First Presbyterian Church, conducted the funeral on Saturday morning, April 18. His text: Matthew 25:14-29. To one servant the master gave five talents, to another two talents, and to another only one talent. When the master returned, he was pleased with the servant who had invested his five talents; he was pleased with the servant who had invested his two. But for the man who had merely buried his one, the master had only scorn. "You ought to have invested my money with the bankers, and at my coming I should have received what was my own with interest. So, take the one talent from him and give it to him who has the ten talents. For to everyone who has, will more be given, and he will have abundance; but for him who has not, even what he has, will be taken away."

Closing his Bible, the minister spoke of Sam's worship "here in this sanctuary. He loved this place and he cared for it. It was he who placed the Holy Bible in the pew pockets and funded many other improvements. But he did not reserve his faith merely for stated occasions of worship and praise. His faith was expressed where it really counts, out on the main streets of life. He used his own mind and his own abilities – his talents – in the very best ways, and he helped others to become successful in their chosen professions. How many persons sought his wisdom and guidance and counsel! And from whence came those talents?"

The minister looked at the casket, then at the congregation. "From whence came those talents?" he asked again. "Sam Young knew!"

As pallbearers, Sam's grandsons Rob Hoover, Doak Hoover, David Hoover, Sam D. Young III, and his grandsons-in-law Tim Williams and W. R. Sprout escorted the casket up the aisle of the church and then to Restlawn Cemetery.

In a day or so, other voices spoke of Sam's influence. From Beverly Hills Barron Hilton declared, "Whenever my father wanted unvarnished advice, he turned to Sam Young, his banker in El Paso. Without Young, Hilton Hotels Corporation, under my father's leadership, would never have flourished as it did. He was a pivotal force in our company."[12]

Richard Feuille, one of Sam's many dedicated board members over the years, remembered him now "as a smart, tough businessman," who would help people when they were down. "It was always good to pray with him in hospitals, to see that side of a businessman like him."[13]

Members of the Bank family, Rachel Garcia of the credit department among them, expressed their own sober thoughts. "Back in the seventies, I was pretty new at the bank, but my children Ralph and Beki were in college and my husband Rafael, who also worked for the Bank, and I wanted them to finish their degrees. Since their doing that would require me to work, I needed to know if I could expect my job to last quite a while at the Bank. I went to Mr. Young and told him what I had on my mind. He understood immediately. 'Nothing is more important than giving those children a good education. We'll do everything we can to see that they get it. Go ahead, you and Rafael are doing fine work with us. Make your plans.'"

Recalling that little conversation now, Rachel smiled proudly. "Ralph and Beki came out with college diplomas and our youngest child Robert will soon receive his degree. We all owe some of that achievement to Mr. Young's confidence in Rafael and me."[14]

Another member of the team, Isabel Champion had her own insights into Sam's nature. "When it came to helping oldtimers out of a tight spot, many folks around here knew Mr. Young's tender side. If he heard of a family crisis, a serious illness, or some other heartbreak, he sought those people out. And any money he lent them was strictly between them and him."[15]

Faye Hartman, Sam's executive secretary for twenty-three years, had "the greatest admiration for his abilities as a businessman as well as a philanthropist,"[16] particularly through the Sam D. Young Family Foundation.

In a large display in the *Times*, Providence Hospital spoke of the unpaid volunteer who for thirty-seven years had chaired its full operations: "His life, a legend. His legacy, a hospital. His model of excellence endures."[17]

For the Bank team, Richard Hickson, Ernie Roberts, and Barbara Austin deliberated at length for the right words to speak of their Bank's co-founder. The morning of the funeral itself, their decision appeared in a full newspaper page with a portrait captioned, "Sam D. Young, 1896-1987. Chairman Emeritus."

"Financier. Humanitarian. Innovator. Friend. We mourn his death. We celebrate his life."[18]

REFERENCE MATTER

APPENDIX

DIRECTORS OF TCB-EL PASO TO DATE

(Alphabetical Listing)

	Years of Service
J. D Abrams	3/78-2/85
Edward Azar	3/83-Present
W. Martin Banner	1/29-6/49
Martin F. Bauman, Jr.	2/72-1/80
Warren T. Burns	4/82-Present
Henry A. Cline, Jr.	1/29-3/30
G. Lee Conner	4/81-6/83
Douglas C. Crowell	1/29-7/40
Robert H. Cutler	4/76-Present
James Farah	1/62-1/64
William F. Farah	1/64-3/77
Richard H. Feuille	1/64-Present
George W. Finger	8/87-Present
Frank B. Fletcher	1/30-3/69
Henry G. "Tif" Frost	11/33-3/42
Herbert W. Gehring, Jr.	4/77-10/79
A. H. Goldstein	6/25-12/33
Thornton Hardie	1/34-1/69
William B. Hardie, Sr.	1/64-2/83
Charles M. Harvey	6/25-2/52
Chas. M. Harvey, Jr.	1/29-1/30
Eldon P. Harvey	1/53-Present
Paul Harvey	1/26-4/88
John C. Hayes	6/25-1/55
Richard G. Hickson	9/85-Present
Conrad N. Hilton	1/51-4/79
Conrad N. Hilton, Jr.	1/60-2/69
Robert T. Hoover, Jr.	1/62-Present
Woody L. Hunt	3/83-Present
Homer A. Jacobs	1/27-7/57
Travis C. Johnson	9/84-Present
Carroll S. Jones	4/80-Present
William J. Kastrin	2/72-Present

James A. Keller	9/84-Present
Will E. Keller	1/32-2/35
E. M. Kelley	1/59-4/82
John T. Kelley	3/83-Present
Joe N. Kidd	4/86-Present
Martin N. Lettunich	1/64-1/65
Wm. P. B. McSain	6/14-1/20
W. B. Miller	1/28-5/37
J. Francis Morgan	1/47-8/80
W. Merriman Morton	8/82-Present
William J. Mounce	11/83-Present
Guillermo Ochoa	6/86-Present
James E. Onick	1/68-2/81
Thomas C. Patterson	11/63-1/77
Travis H. Petty	5/73-Present
J. Hart Ponder	1/64-4/85
Max R. Prestridge	1/60-12/63
Max Prestridge, Jr.	1/64-10/77
Robert B. Price	1/45-9/74
G. P. Putnam	6/25-1/29
Dr. R. L. Ramey	7/25-11/33
George A. Rancich	1/64-Present
Dorrance D. Roderick	1/54-3/81
Fred D. Schneider	2/72-Present
Leo R. Schuster, Jr.	3/88-Present
A. Schwartz	1/27-1/30 and 1/34-1/38
Edward F. Schwartz	1/62-Present
Manuel Schwartz	1/29-1/30
Marc J. Shapiro	9/82-3/87
Carlos Trouyet	1/65-3/72
Eloy S. Vallina, Jr.	1/71-3/86
W. S. Warnock	1/43-1/77
I. Weiss	6/25-1/27
Sam D. Young	6/25-4/87
Sam D. Young, Jr.	1/58-Present

NOTES

In these notes several symbols mean as follows: SDY = typescript of taped interview between Leach and the person named on the tape. YFA = Young family archives. Als = autograph letter signed. Bk min = Minutes, El Paso National Bank Board of Directors meeting.

CHAPTER 1

A Little Acorn

1 SDY 37A, 4
2 Lewis W. Newton and Herbert P. Gambrell, *Texas: Yesterday and Today* (Dallas: Turner, 1949), 103
3 Phebe Young Armstrong, "Memoir," 7, unpublished manuscript, YFA
4 Armstrong, "Memoir," 16
5 Samuel Doak Young, "Memoirs," 2, unpublished manuscript, YFA
6 Armstrong, "Memoir," 8
7 Young to author, in conversation
8 Young to author, in conversation
9 Armstrong, "Memoir," 9
10 Young to author, in conversation
11 SDY 1 B, 1. Young to author, in conversation. YFA
12 SDY 37 A, 2 and 3. Young to author. YFA
13 Young to author, in conversation
14 Young to author, in conversation
15 SDY 17 A, 1. Young to author. YFA
16 Young to author, in conversation
17 Young to author, in conversation

CHAPTER 2

He's in the Army Now

1 SDY 16 B, 5. Young to author. YFA
2 Young to author, in conversation
3 SDY 16 B, 7. Young to author. YFA
4 SDY 16 A, 1. Young to author. YFA
5 El Paso Times, December 18, 1978
6 Young to author, in conversation
7 SDY 31 A, 1. Young to author. YFA
8 SDY 43 A, 1. Young to author. YFA
9 SDY 16 B, 5. Young to author. YFA
10 SDY 16 B, 5. Young to author. YFA
11 SDY 16 B, 5. Young to author. YFA
12 SDY 43 A, 2. Young to author. YFA
13 Frank Mangan, *The Pipeliners* (El Paso: Guynes, 1977), 16
14 Quoted in T. Harry Gatton, *The First Century: the Texas Bankers Association 1885-1985* (Austin: no publisher, 1984), 91
15 William B. Hamby quoted in Gatton, *First*, 105
16 Samuel Eliot Morison, *The Growth of the American Republic* (New York: Oxford, 1969), II, 344
17 Young to author, in conversation
18 SDY 16 B, 5. Young to author. YFA
19 Young to author, in conversation
20 *El Paso Times*, June 8, 1964
21 SDY 34 A, 6. Margaret Young Parker to author. YFA
22 SDY 16 B, 5. Young to author. YFA
23 SDY 16 B, 5. Young to author. YFA
24 SDY 37 A, 3. Young to author. YFA
25 Newton, *Texas*, 281
26 Young to author, in conversation
27 SDY 16 B, 5. Young to author. YFA
28 SDY 16 B, 5. Young to author. YFA
29 SDY 31 A, 8. Young to author. YFA
30 Phebe Young Armstrong to author, May 27, 1985, in conversation
31 Newton, *Texas*, 281
32 *El Paso Times*, June 8, 1964
33 SDY 16 B, 5. Young to author. YFA
34 Young, "Memoirs," 5
35 Young, "Memoirs," 5
36 SDY 30 A, 2. Young to author. YFA
37 Young to author, in conversation
38 SDY 30 A, 3. Young to author. YFA

CHAPTER 3

Young Man Going Places

1 SDY 28 A, 2. Young to author. YFA
2 SDY 28 A, 2. Young to author. YFA
3 SDY 31 B, 9. Young to author. YFA
4 SDY 31 B, 9. Young to author. YFA

5 Young, "Memoirs," 6
6 SDY 32 A, 4. Young to author. YFA
7 SDY 32 A, 4. Young to author. YFA
8 SDY 32 A, 5. Young to author. YFA
9 SDY 32 B, 1. Young to author. YFA
10 Quoted in Conrad Hilton, *Be My Guest* (Englewood Cliffs, N.J.: Prentice-Hall, 1957), 189
11 Young to author, in conversation
12 SDY 33 A, 1. Young to author. YFA
13 SDY 32 B, 6. Young to author. YFA
14 SDY 32 B, 7. Young to author. YFA
15 *El Paso Herald-Post*, February 1, 1932
16 Hilton, *Be*, 148
17 Young to author, in conversation
18 Walter L. Buenger and Joseph A. Pratt, *But Also Good Business: Texas Commerce Banks and the Financing of Houston and Texas, 1886-1986* (College Station: Texas A and M Press, 1986), 76
19 SDY 32 A, 1-2. Young to author. YFA
20 Armstrong, "Memoir," 10
21 SDY 33 A, 2. Young to author. YFA
22 SDY 32 B, 6. Young to author. YFA
23 SDY 5 A, 3. Young to author. YFA
24 Young, "Memoirs," 8
25 Young, "Memoirs," 8
26 SDY 33 A, 2. Young to author. YFA
27 SDY 28 A, 4. Young to author. YFA
28 Jose Fuentes Mares, *Don Eloy S. Vallina* (Mexico City: Editorial Jus., 1968), 39
29 SDY 16 B, 6. Young to author. YFA
30 SDY 16 B, 6. Young to author. YFA

CHAPTER 4

Home Base at Last

1 SDY 34 A, 10. Margaret Young Parker to author. YFA
2 SDY 33 A, 3. Young to author. YFA
3 Young, "Memoirs," 55
4 Young, "Memoirs," 55
5 Armstrong, "Memoir," 11
6 SDY 33 A, 4. Young to author. YFA
7 SDY 35 A, 4. Young to author. YFA
8 SDY 34 A, 10. Young to author. YFA
9 SDY 32 A, 2. Young to author. YFA
10 SDY 32 A, 3. Young to author. YFA
11 SDY 33 A, 2. Young to author. YFA
12 SDY 28 A, 4-5. Young to author. YFA
13 Young, "Memoirs," 124
14 Young, "Memoirs," 185
15 SDY 33 A, 3. Young to author. YFA
16 SDY 33 A, 4. Young to author. YFA
17 Young, "Memoirs," 56
18 SDY 35 A, 1. Young to author. YFA
19 Young to author, in conversation.
20 Actually, "ex-Governor" since January 18, when Pat Neff succeeded him into office.
21 Young, "Memoirs," 10
22 Young, "Memoirs," 10 and SDY 35 A, 4. Young to author. YFA
23 Young, "Memoirs," 11
24 Young, "Memoirs," 13
25 SDY 35 A, 5. Young to author. YFA
26 SDY 35 A, 6. Young to author. YFA
27 Young, "Memoirs," 13
28 SDY 35 A, 5. Young to author. YFA
29 Young, "Memoirs," 126
30 Young, "Memoirs," 13
31 Young, "Memoirs," 14
32 Young, "Memoirs," 129

CHAPTER 5

Go West, Young Man

1 SDY 14 A, 2. Young to author. YFA
2 SDY 36 A, 1. Young to author. YFA
3 SDY 36 A, 1. Young to author. YFA
4 Young to author, in conversation
5 Hilliard Bryan, "Memoirs," unpublished ms, 44
6 SDY 36 A, 2-3. Young to author. YFA
7 SDY 8 B, 2. Hilliard Bryan to author. YFA
8 SDY 35 A, 7. Young to author. YFA
9 SDY 28 A, 7. Young to author. YFA
10 Young, "Memoirs," 129
11 SDY 31 A, 7. Young to author. YFA
12 SDY 31 A, 7. Young to author. YFA
13 Bk min, March 4, 1941, 549
14 SDY 31 A, 4. Young to author. YFA
15 SDY 31 A, 4. Young to author. YFA
16 SDY 17 A, 1. Young to author. YFA
17 Floyd Fierman, *The Schwartz Family of El Paso: The Story of a Pioneer Jewish Family in the Southwest* (El Paso: Texas Western Press, 1980), 10ff
18 SDY 24 A, 2. Phil Harvey to author. YFA
19 Phil Harvey to author, in conversation
20 Young, "Memoirs," 1721 Bk min, June 6, 1925
22 Young, "Memoirs," 18
23 SDY 35 A, 1. Young to author. YFA
24 Young, "Memoirs," 19
25 Young, "Memoirs," 19

26 Young, "Memoirs," 187
27 Bk min, June 22, 1925, 2
28 SDY 31 A, 6. Young to author. YFA
29 Young to author, in conversation
30 SDY 33 B, 6. Young to author. YFA
31 Quoted in *Fiftieth Anniversary, 1925-1975* (a special bulletin printed by the Bank celebrating its golden anniversary), 1
32 Young to author, in conversation
33 Bertha Bull Knight to author, in conversation
34 SDY 22 A, 2. Bertha Bull Knight to author, May 27, 1986
35 *Fiftieth Anniversary*, 1
36 SDY 31 A, 6. Young to author. YFA. Also Young to author, in conversation.
37 Young to author, in conversation
38 Young to author, in conversation

CHAPTER 6

The Founding Father

1 Young, "Memoirs," 19
2 Young to author, in conversation
3 SDY 21 A, 2. Young to author. YFA
4 Walter Feinberg to author, in conversation
5 John Garrett to author, in conversation
6 Young to author, in conversation
7 Faye Hartman to author, in conversation
8 SDY 17 A, 1. Young to author. YFA
9 SDY 37 A, 10. Young to author. YFA
10 Mares, *Don*, 41
11 Young to author, in conversation.
12 SDY 22 A, 1. Bertha Bull Knight to author. YFA
13 Quoted in *El Paso Times*, June 27, 1976
14 Young, "Memoirs," 44
15 SDY 35 A, 1. Young to author. YFA
16 SDY 20 A, 3. John Garrett to author. YFA
17 SDY 20 B, 2. John Garrett to author. YFA
18 Joe Moreno. Statement of Condition report ms. YFA
19 SDY 43 A, 2. Young to author. YFA
20 SDY 43 A, 1. Young to author. YFA
21 Quoted in SDY 38 A, 2. Young to author. YFA
22 Young to author, in conversation.
23 Young to author, in conversation
24 SDY 22 A, 2. Bertha Bull Knight to author. YFA
25 Letterhead typed statement. YFA
26 Untitled El Paso newspaper clipping, December 31, 1926. YFA
27 Bk min, December 31, 1927
28 SDY 34 B, 5. Margaret Young Parker to author. YFA
29 SDY 34 A, 8. Margaret Young Parker to author. YFA
30 SDY 37 A, 6. Young to author. YFA
31 SDY 36 A, 4. Young to author. YFA
32 SDY 39 A, 4. Young to author. YFA
33 Joe Moreno. Statement of Condition report. December 31, 1927. ms in YFA
34 SDY 38 A, 1. Young to author. YFA
35 El Paso National Bank bulletin, November 23, 1927. YFA
36 El Paso National Bank bulletin, December 8, 1927. YFA
37 SDY 37 A, 9. Young to author. YFA
38 El Paso National Bank bulletin, August 7, 1928
39 SDY 22 A, 2. Bertha Bull Knight to author. YFA
40 SDY 22 B, 1. Bertha Bull Knight to author. YFA
41 SDY 16 A, 3. Young to author. YFA
42 SDY 39 A, 1. Young to author. YFA
43 *El Paso Times*, September 11, 1953
44 Richard Hancock, *Chihuahua: A Guide to the Wonderful Country*, (Norman: University of Oklahoma, 1978), 37
45 SDY 39 A, 2. Young to author. YFA
46 Bk min, February 27, 1973, 2454, and April 12, 1977, 2768
47 For background, see William J. Hooten, *Fifty-two Years a Newsman* (El Paso: Texas Western Press, 1974), 3
48 SDY 31 B, 11-12. Young to author. YFA
49 SDY 10 A, 2. Young to Karl Conrad and author. YFA
50 Young typed recollection ms in Conrad Hilton biographical file, 1963. YFA
51 SDY 10 A, 2. Young to Karl Conrad and author. YFA
52 Telegram in Box 5, folder 4. YFA
53 SDY 38 A, 1. Young to author. YFA
54 *El Paso Herald-Post*, October 15, 1979
55 SDY 39 A, 1. Young to author. YFA
56 SDY A, 1. Young to author. YFA
57 Quoted in *El Paso Herald-Post*, October 15, 1979
58 Young, "Memoirs," 22-23
59 Young, "Memoirs," 23

CHAPTER 7

Rough Times on the Border

1 Mangan, *Pipeliners,* 53
2 Joseph Leach, "Farewell to Horse-back, Mule-back, Foot-back and Prairie-Schooner: The Railroad Comes to Town," *Password,* (May, 1956), passim
3 SDY 10 A, 2. Young to Karl Conrad and author. YFA
4 Hilton, *Be,* 150
5 *El Paso Times,* October 29, 1929
6 Hilton, *Be,* 148
7 *El Paso Herald-Post,* October 15, 1979
8 Quoted in *El Paso Herald-Post,* October 15, 1979
9 Young to author, in conversation
10 SDY 9 B, 3. Hilliard Bryan to author. YFA
11 Bryan, "Memoirs," 49
12 Quoted in *El Paso Herald-Post,* October 15, 1979
13 *El Paso Herald-Post,* October 15, 1979
14 Young, "Memoirs," 222
15 Quoted by Tim Williams to author, February 17, 1987
16 Quoted in *El Paso Herald-Post,* October 15, 1979
17 Young, "Memoirs," 24
18 Rickie Feuille to author, in conversation, April 17, 1987
19 Hilton, *Be,* 151
20 Hilton, *Be,* 151
21 *El Paso Times,* February 13, 1930
22 *El Paso Times,* February 13, 1930
23 Young to author, in conversation
24 SDY 1 B, 2. Young to author. YFA
25 SDY 37 A, 8. Young to author. YFA
26 SDY 37 A, 7. Young to author. YFA
27 SDY 40 A, 5. Leslie Levy to author. YFA
28 SDY 2 B, 4. Young to author. YFA
29 SDY 61 A, 3. Young to author. YFA
30 SDY 16 A, 3. Young to author. YFA
31 Young to author, in conversation
32 Young, "Memoirs," 52
33 Bk min, January 14, 1930, p. 152
34 SDY 5 A, 1. Young to author. YFA
35 Young to author, in conversation
36 Young, "Memoirs," 39-40

CHAPTER 8

A Time of Deep Depression

1 Bryan, "Memoirs," 46
2 Young, "Memoirs," 24
3 Young, "Memoirs," 89
4 Young, "Memoirs," 25
5 Young, "Memoirs," 41
6 Young, "Memoirs," 42-43
7 Young, "Memoirs," 72 and 61a
8 Typescript of Karl Conrad interview with Young and author, June 28, 1985, p. 15. YFA. Also Young, "Memoirs," 79
9 SDY 1 A, 2. Young to author. YFA
10 SDY 37 A, 5 and SDY 1 A, 2. Young to author. YFA
11 SDY 37 A, 6. Young to author. YFA
12 Young, "Memoirs," 46
13 Young to author, in conversation
14 Olga Roderick to author, interview, April 1, 1986
15 SDY 45 A, 3. Sam D. Young, Jr. to author. YFA
16 SDY 2 B, 5. Young to author. YFA
17 SDY 14 A, 1. Betty Young Taber to author. YFA
18 SDY 14 A, 2. Betty Young Taber to author. YFA
19 Moreno, Statement of Condition report. YFA
20 Young to author, in conversation
21 James Graham McNary, *This Is My Life* (Albuquerque: University of New Mexico Press, 1956), 264
22 Young to author, in conversation
23 Quoted in Morison, *Growth,* II, 484
24 Quoted in Gatton, *First,* 145
25 Young, "Memoirs," 84

CHAPTER 9

Playing the Double Sixes

1 Quoted in Gatton, *First,* 146
2 Young, "Memoirs," 84
3 Young, "Memoirs," 84
4 Bryan, "Memoirs," 48
5 Young, quoted in *El Paso Times,* June 27, 1976
6 SDY 14 A, 1. Betty Young Taber to author. YFA
7 Young to author, in conversation
8 Als H. A. Jacobs to Banco Mercantil, May 6, 1933 in Hilton file. YFA
9 Hilton, *Be,* 168
10 SDY 11 B, 2. Young to Karl Conrad and author, YFA
11 Hilton, *Be,* 169

12 SDY 2 B, 4. Young to author. YFA
13 SDY 17 A, 5. Young to author. YFA
14 Young to author, in conversation
15 Young to author, in conversation
16 SDY 28 A, 7. Young to author. YFA
17 SDY 28 A, 7. Young to author. YFA
18 SDY 2 A, 5. Young to author. YFA
19 SDY 28 A, 7. Young to author. YFA
20 SDY 43 A, 4. Young to author. YFA
21 Bk min, January 8, 1935
22 SDY 13 A, 4. James Onick to author. YFA
23 Young, "Memoirs," 118
24 SDY 31 A, 3. Young to author. YFA
25 Moreno, Statement of Condition report. YFA
26 Young to author, in conversation
27 SDY 39 A, 3. Young to author. YFA
28 SDY 45 A, 4. Sam Young, Jr. to author. YFA
29 SDY 45 A, 4. Sam Young, Jr. to author. YFA
30 SDY 2 B, 6. Young to author. YFA
31 SDY 14 A, 2. Betty Young Taber to author. YFA
32 Bk min, January 14, 1936
33 *El Paso Times*, May 30, 1936
34 SDY 45 A, 5. Sam Young, Jr. to author. YFA
35 *El Paso Times*, December 24, 1978 and SDY 14 A, 5. Betty Young Taber to author. YFA
36 Hilton, *Be*, 177
37 Hilton, *Be*, 178
38 Thomas Ewing Dabney, *The Man Who Bought the Waldorf* (New York; Duell, Sloan and Pearce, 1950), 123
39 SDY 10 A, 2. Young to Karl Conrad and author. YFA
40 Young, "Memoirs," 63
41 Young, "Memoirs," 61b
42 Sam Young, Jr. to author, interview, October 10, 1985
43 Young, "Memoirs," 82
44 Dabney, *Man*, 63
45 Young, "Memoirs," 63
46 SDY 10 B, 2. Young to Karl Conrad and author. YFA
47 SDY 6 A, 1. Paul Poling to author. YFA
48 SDY 45 A, 4. Sam Young Jr. to author. YFA

CHAPTER 10

Warfare and Business

1 Bryan, "Memoirs, Supplement," 7
2 Bryan, "Memoirs," 5
3 Als Sam to Mama and Papa, May 2, 1941. YFA
4 SDY 14 A, 5. Betty Young Taber to author. YFA
5 Bryan, "Memoirs," 51
6 Bryan, "Memoirs," 51
7 Jeanette Dority to author, September 19, 1985, in conversation
8 Als Hilton to Young, April 26, 1941, Hilton file. YFA
9 John Middagh, *Frontier Newspaper: The El Paso Times* (El Paso; Texas Western Press, 1958), 299
10 *El Paso Times*, December 8, 1941
11 *El Paso Times*, December 9, 1941, 4
12 Als Sam to Mama and Papa, February 2, 1942. YFA
13 SDY 32 A, 3. Young to author. YFA
14 "Texas Classics," printed programme Texas Business Hall of Fame Banquet 1984, 8. YFA
15 Young, "Memoirs," 37
16 Als Sam to Mama and Papa, March 5, 1942. YFA
17 Bk min, May 12, 1942
18 SDY 11 B, 3. Young to Karl Conrad and author. YFA
19 Als Sam to Hilton, March 27, 1942. Hilton file. YFA
20 SDY 13 A, 4. James Onick to author. YFA
21 Als Sam to Hilton, November 20, 1942. Hilton file. YFA
22 Als Hilton to Young, December 12, 1942. YFA
23 Bk min, March 24, 1942, 617
24 Als Sam to Mama, November 16, 1942. YFA
25 Als Sam to Mama, March 4, 1943. YFA
26 Als Sam to Mama, March 4, 1943. YFA
27 SDY 2 B, 5. Young to author. YFA
28 Als Young to Sister, February 27, 1943. YFA
29 Als Sam to Margaret, September 13, 1943. YFA
30 SDY 37 A, 5. Young to author. YFA
31 Als Sam to Roderick, December 7, 1943. YFA
32 Young, "Memoirs," 65
33 Hilton, *Be*, 199
34 SDY 36 A, 4. Young to author. YFA
35 SDY 36 A, 4. Young to author. YFA
36 C. M. Harvey quoted in Young, "Memoirs," 27-28
37 Bk min, January 12, 1944, 656

38 Moreno, Statement of Condition report. YFA
39 Als Young to Sister, January 15, 1944. YFA
40 Als Roderick to Young, Roderick file. YFA

CHAPTER 11

The Men Who Bought the Waldorf

1 Young, "To Our Bank Family," Bulletin No. 82, September 11, 1944. YFA
2 Hartrick to author, May 1, 1987, interview
3 Als Young to Sister, February 7, 1944. YFA
4 Als Young to Roderick, August 24, 1944. YFA
5 Als Young to Bob Hoover, November 21, 1944. YFA
6 Als Sam to Mama, December 1, 1944. YFA
7 Als Young to Roderick, April 24, 1945. YFA
8 "Analysis," Stock file. YFA
9 Bk min, June 29, 1945, 712-713
10 Bk min, May 1, 1945, 698
11 SDY 25 B, 4. Phil Harvey to author. YFA
12 SDY 3 A, 1. Fred Hervey to author. YFA
13 SDY 2 A, 2. Young to author. YFA
14 SDY 10 B, 4. Young to Karl Conrad and author. YFA
15 SDY 10 B, 4. Young to Karl Conrad and author. YFA
16 Hilton, *Be*, 213
17 Whitney Bolton, *The Silver Spade* (New York: Farrar, Straus and Young, 1954), 146
18 *El Paso Times*, August 15, 1945, 1
19 Young to author, in conversation
20 Sam Young, Jr. to author, October 10, 1985, interview
21 SDY 46 A, 3. Sam Young, Jr. to author. YFA
22 Young, "Memoirs," 78
23 Hilton, *Be*, 206
24 SDY 13 B, 5. James Onick to author. YFA
25 Sheley Warnock, Jr. to author, April 15, 1987, interview
26 Als Sam to Mama, February 3, 1947. YFA
27 Young, "Memoirs," 28a
28 Young to author, in conversation.
29 Als Sam to Mama, May 26, 1947. YFA
30 "To All Officers," Bank bulletin, September 19, 1947. YFA
31 Sam Young, Jr. to author, in conversation
32 Joe Moreno, autobiographical sketch. YFA
33 Kastrin to author, interview
34 Young, "Memoirs," 142
35 Young, "Memoirs," 106, 136 and 158
36 SDY 11 A, 1 and SDY 10 B, 5. Young to Karl Conrad and author. YFA
37 Young, "Memoirs," 67
38 Typescript Karl Conrad interview with Young, 30. YFA
39 Als Young to Herndon, June 1, 1948, Hilton file. YFA
40 Als Herndon to Young, June 5, 1948, Hilton file. YFA
41 Als Herndon to Young, November 4, 1948. YFA
42 Als Young to Herndon, February 3, 1949, Hilton Corp. file 1949. YFA
43 Als Young to Connie, February 15, 1949, Hilton Corp. file, 1949. YFA
44 Crown quoted in SDY 10 B, 5. Young to Karl Conrad and author. YFA
45 Young to author, in conversation
46 Young to author, in conversation
47 SDY 28 A, 6. Young to author. YFA
48 Young, "Memoirs," 178
49 *Southwestern Medicine*, May 1949, 87
50 SDY 2 A, 3. Young to author. YFA
51 SDY 17 A, 1. Young to author. YFA
52 Young, "Memoirs," 159
53 SDY 2 A, 3. Young to author. YFA
54 Young, "Memoirs," 170
55 Young, "Memoirs," 171
56 Young, "Memoirs," 178
57 Young, "Memoirs," 178

CHAPTER 12

Be My Guest

1 Young, "Memoirs," 84
2 Als Young to Briggs, March 23, 1950. YFA
3 Als Sam to Mama, March 1, 1950. YFA
4 SDY 25 A, 1. Phil Harvey to author. YFA
5 Als Sam to Mama, March 1, 1950. YFA
6 SDY 25 A, 1. Phil Harvey to author. YFA

7 Typescript Karl Conrad interview with Young, 51. YFA
8 SDY 14 A, 4. Betty Young Taber to author. YFA
9 SDY 46 A, 2. Sam Young, Jr. to author. YFA
10 Bk min, January 9, 1951, 904
11 Als Moss to Young, July 7, 1950. YFA
12 Als Wallace to Young, July 17, 1950. YFA
13 Als Wightman to Young, August 18, 1950. YFA
14 Als Young to Hilton, July 5, 1950. YFA
15 SDY 15 A, 2. Foreman to author. YFA
16 Nelan quoted in SDY 15 A, 2. Foreman to author. YFA
17 John Garrett to author, May 22, 1986, interview
18 Hilton quoted in Young, "Memoirs," 28
19 Hilton quoted in SDY 11 A, 1. Young to author. YFA
20 Als Sam to Connie, January 17, 1951. YFA
21 SDY 11 B, 4. Young to author. YFA
22 Young in Karl Conrad interview, 61. YFA
23 Hervey memo to Sam, November 19, 1985. YFA
24 SDY 46 B, 5. Sam Young, Jr. to author. YFA
25 SDY 45 A, 4. Sam Young, Jr. to author. YFA
26 Als Sam to Mama, July 2, 1951. YFA
27 Als Sam to Mama, September 1, 1951. YFA
28 Untitled El Paso newspaper clipping, January 12, 1952. YFA
29 Young to author, February 4, 1986, in conversation
30 Bk min, March 27, 1952, 973
31 Als Sam to Mama, March 18, 1952. YFA
32 Als Sam to Connie, December 31, 1952. YFA
33 Als Connie to Sam, January 5, 1953. YFA
34 *El Paso Times*, September 9, 1952
35 Young, "Memoirs," 40
36 Young, "Memoirs," 40
37 SDY 46 B, 5. Sam Young, Jr. to author. YFA
38 Als Sam to Phebe, April 9, 1954. YFA
39 Bk min, April 23, 1954, 1084
40 Young, "Memoirs," 80a
41 Quoted in Hilton, *Be*, 251
42 Hilton, *Be*, 251
43 SDY 15 A, 1. Foreman to author. YFA
44 *American Banker*, January 31, 1955
45 Sandy Caviness to author, February 19, 1986, in conversation
46 SDY 2 B, 5. Young to author. YFA. Also Young, "Memoirs," 210
47 Quoted by Lloyd Shearer in *Parade Magazine, El Paso Times*, July 21, 1963
48 Precis of the case in its file. YFA
49 Als Sam to Mama, November 1, 1956. YFA
50 Young to author, in conversation
51 Sister Ramona to author, June 14, 1986, interview
52 Als Young to Sister Francetta, May 8, 1957. YFA
53 Young, "Memoirs," 218-219
54 Young to author, in conversation

CHAPTER 13

A Dream in Concrete and Steel

1 *El Paso Times*, December 24, 1978
2 SDY 46 B, 3. Sam Young, Jr. to author. YFA
3 SDY A, 2. Fred Hervey to author. YFA
4 SDY 39 A, 2. Young to author. YFA. Also SDY 34 A, 2. Young to author. YFA
5 SDY 39 A, 4. Young to author. YFA
6 Als Young to Jackson, July 30, 1957. YFA
7 Bk min, August 13, 1957, 1320
8 Bk min, August 13, 1957, 1321
9 Bk min, August 13, 1957, 1323
10 *Saturday Evening Post*, June 20, 1976
11 Bk min, January 14, 1958, 1356
12 Bk min, December 6, 1957, 1337
13 Als Sam to Cullee Mann, May 5, 1958. YFA
14 Young to author, in conversation
15 Als Sam to Martha and Dean, July 15, 1958. YFA
16 SDY 2 B, 5. Young to author. YFA
17 Young, "Memoirs," 33
18 Young, "Memoirs," 104-105
19 *El Paso Times*, February 26, 1960
20 Young to author, in conversation
21 Young to author, in conversation
22 SDY 18 A, 2. Strickland to author, YFA
23 *American Banker*, June 10, 1959
24 *American Banker*, June 10, 1959
25 Young, "Memoirs," 213
26 SDY 2 B, 7-8. Young to author. YFA

27 Young, "Memoirs," 210
28 SDY 18 A, 2. Strickland to author. YFA
29 Young, "Memoirs," 73
30 Alan Riding, *Distant Neighbors: A Portrait of the Mexicans* (New York: Vintage, 1986), 202
31 Als Young to Maria, May 31, 1960. YFA
32 Sam D. Young, Jr., *A Comparison Between the High Lights of Mexican and American Commercial Bank Law*, an unpublished thesis presented to the Faculty of the Southwestern Graduate School of Banking (Dallas, Texas: June, 1960), iii
33 SDY 45 A, 2. Sam Young, Jr. to author. YFA
34 Young to Shareholders, quoted in Bk min, January 10, 1961, 1540
35 SDY 2 B, 5. Young to author. YFA
36 Bk min, January 9, 1962, 1614
37 SDY 15 A, 1. Foreman to author, YFA
38 Bk min, December 1, 1961, 1591
39 Bk min, January 9, 1962, 1622
40 SDY 2 A, 1-2. Young to author. YFA
41 Als Young to Friedkin, Chamizal file. YFA
42 SDY 5 A, 2. Young to author. YFA
43 SDY 5 A, 2. Young to author. YFA
44 SDY 5 A, 2. Young to author. YFA
45 Young, "Memoirs," 217
46 Als Sam to Paul Kayser, January 11, 1963. YFA
47 Young to author, in conversation
48 *El Paso Times*, February 26, 1963
49 Bk min, April 12, 1963, 1700
50 Young, "Memoirs," 68-69
51 Young, "Memoirs," 38
52 Als Hilton to Sam, March 16, 1963. YFA
53 Als Sam to Connie, March 19, 1963. YFA
54 SDY 22 B, 2. Bertha Bull Knight to author. YFA

CHAPTER 14

Hands Across the Border

1 Als di Tullio to Young, June 26, 1963. YFA
2 Young, "Memoirs," 42
3 The framed scroll. YFA
4 SDY 47 A, 5. Sam Young Jr. to author. YFA
5 *El Paso Times*, January 15, 1964
6 SDY 34 A, 5. Young to author. YFA
7 Phebe Armstrong to author, interviews, March 24, 1988
8 "Resolution Adopted October 8, 1985 by the Board of Directors of Texas Commerce Bank-El Paso in Appreciation of Sam D. Young, Jr.". YFA
9 Bk min, January 12, 1965, 1812 and 1816
10 Bk min, January 12, 1965, 1812
11 Faye Hartman to author, in conversation
12 *El Paso Times*, April 1, 1964
13 Quoted in *El Paso Times*, June 8, 1964
14 SDY 43 A, 7. Young to author. YFA
15 Als Young to Mr. President, May 5, 1965. YFA
16 Als Lyndon B. Johnson to Sam, May 14, 1965, LBJ file. YFA
17 Als Young to Tamillo, June 29, 1965. YFA
18 Bk min, September 14, 1965, 1849
19 Bianche quoted in *El Paso Times*, December 18, 1978
20 Als Young to Rob, October 11, 1965. YFA
21 *New York Daily News*, December 10, 1965
22 "El Paso National Bank News," 5. YFA
23 James Turnage to author, September 22, 1986, interview
24 Quoted by Young to author, in conversation
25 *El Paso Times*, March 26, 1967
26 *Trans Texas Quarterly Dividend* magazine, Spring, 1979, 4
27 Quoted in Young, "Memoirs," 98
28 The bronze plaque. YFA
29 Typescript Young's speech, Aztec Eagle scrapbook. YFA
31 *El Paso Times*, June 23, 1968
32 S.C.R., No. 16, June 25, 1968. YFA
33 Als Tom to Young, Washington, D. C., August 6, 1968. YFA
34 Als Rob to Pappy, Bauman family file. YFA
35 Faye Hartman to author, in conversation

CHAPTER 15

Have a Good Day and Pass It On

1 Board Minutes, Providence Memorial Hospital, June 14, 1968
2 SDY 42 A, 2. Jack Curlin to author, December 19, 1986. YFA

3 Young to author, in conversation
4 June Fore to author, September 30, 1987, in conversation
5 June Fore to author, September 30, 1987, in conversation
6 Sam Young, Jr. to author, in conversation
7 SDY 47 A, 1-2. Sam Young, Jr. to author. YFA
8 Bk min, January 13, 1970, 2187
9 Als Oveta to Sam, October 6, 1969. YFA
10 Als Young to Doak, December 11, 1970, Bauman file. YFA
11 Als Doak to Dear Pappy, December 14, 1970, Bauman file. YFA
12 SDY 5 A, 3. Young to author. YFA
13 *El Paso Times*, July 27, 1971
14 Deposition, Young misc. file 1975-76. YFA
15 SDY 47 A, 2. Sam Young,, Jr. to author. YFA
16 *El Paso Times*, October 27, 1971
17 Bk min, December 14, 1971, 2326
18 SDY 5 A, 4. Young to author. YFA
19 Young to author, in conversation
20 Bill Deffebach in Young, "Memoirs," 190
21 Young, "Memoirs," 190
22 Young, "Memoirs," 190
23 Deffebach in Young, "Memoirs," 192
24 "El Paso National Bank Note," April, 1972
25 "El Paso National Bank Note," May, 1972
26 Gunning to author, in conversation
27 *El Paso Times*, December 28, 1978
28 SDY 39 A, 5. Young to author. YFA
29 SDY 21 A, 1. Garrett to author. YFA
30 Bill Stevens to author, November 14, 1985, in conversation
31 *El Paso Herald-Post*, September 25-27, 1972
32 Bk min, February 27, 1973, 2429
33 Bk min, February 27, 1973, 2453
34 Quoted in *El Paso Herald-Post*, May 7, 1973
35 Young, "Memoirs," 197
36 *El Paso Times*, June 19, 1973
37 SDY 11 B, 5. Young to author. YFA
38 Young, "Memoirs," 82
39 Als Rob to Munna and Pappy, July 13, 1974. YFA
40 Als Young to Rob, April 17, 1974. YFA
41 Als Young to Rob, April 17, 1974. YFA
42 Young to author, in conversation
43 SDY 14 A, 5. Betty Young Taber to author. YFA
44 SDY 43 A, 7. Young to author. YFA
45 *Financial Trends*, June 7, 1976. Also Malcolm Harris to author, interview
46 Bill Deffebach to author, February 10, 1987, interview
47 *El Paso Times*, May 15, 1975
48 *El Paso Times*, May 15, 1975
49 The plaque. YFA
50 *El Paso Times*, July 1, 1975
51 "50th Anniversary," 6. YFA
52 Als Young to Board of Directors, August 12, 1975. YFA

CHAPTER 16

Old Heads and Young

1 Banquet speech script. YFA
2 SDY 44 B, 4. Ernie Roberts to author. YFA
3 SDY 28 A, 7. Young to author. YFA
4 Als Oveta to Sam, June 28, 1976. YFA
5 SDY 11 A, 2
6 SDY 37 A, 8. Young to author. YFA
7 SDY 42 A, 1. Jack Curlin to author. YFA
8 *El Paso Herald-Post*, November 17, 1977
9 *Trans Texas Quarterly Dividend* magazine, Spring, 1979, 4
10 "El Paso National Corporation Bank Note," April-May, 1978
11 SDY 15 A, 2. Foreman to author. YFA
12 "El Paso National Bank Newsletter," December 13, 1978
13 *El Paso Times*, May 29, 1978
14 Travis Johnson to author, September 24, 1985, interview
15 Travis Johnson to author, September 24, 1985, interview
16 Memo Young to President Jimmie Carter. YFA
17 Quoted in *El Paso Herald-Post*, April 16, 1987
18 SDY 12 A, 1. Mary Lou Young to author. YFA
19 SDY 12 A, 3. Mary Lou Young to author. YFA
20 SDY 12 A, 3. Mary Lou Young to author. YFA
21 Mary Lawrence, *Mother and Child* (New York: Crowell, 1975), 80
22 SDY 13 A, 1. Mary Lou Young to author. YFA
23 Young, "Memoirs," 79-80
24 *New York Times*, January 5, 1979, B 5

25 *New York Times*, January 17, 1979, A 11
26 Young to author, in conversation
27 *El Paso Times*, December 17, 1978
28 *El Paso Times*, December 18, 1978
29 Young quoted in *El Paso Times*, December 20, 1978
30 Young quoted in *El Paso Times, December 22, 1978*
31 *El Paso Times*, December 28, 1978
32 *El Paso Times*, December 24, 1978
33 SDY 12 A, 5. Mary Lou Young to author. YFA
34 Quoted in *El Paso Times*, December 28, 1978
35 Bk min, January 9, 1979, 2905
36 Bk min, January 9, 1979, 2908
37 Ben Love to author, April 18, 1987, interview
38 "The Sunshiner, El Paso National Bank Newsletter," November 30, 1979, 2
39 "Sunshiner," December 14, 1979, 1
40 "Sunshiner," November 30, 1979, 1
41 Bk min, May 19, 1960, 1506
42 Als Young to Sammy, October 1, 1979. YFA
43 SDY 47 A, 4. Sam Young, Jr. to author. YFA
44 Ernie Roberts to author, October 3, 1985, interview
45 Buenger, *But*, 76
46 El Paso National Bank Bulletin, No. 82, September 11, 1944. YFA
47 SDY 20 B, 3. John Garrett to author. YFA
48 Paul Mueller to author, in conversation
49 Rogene Brant to author, in conversation.
50 Quoted in "Power: Texas' 20 Top Titans," *Texas Business*, May, 1980, 46
51 Bk min, November 24, 1980, 3083
52 Bk min, November 24, 1980, 3083
53 SDY 12 A, 5. Mary Lou Young to author. YFA
54 SDY 12 A, 6. Mary Lou Young to author. YFA

CHAPTER 17

Shootout at Fort Sam

1 Buenger, *But*, 294
2 Marc Shapiro to author, May 29, 1985, interview
3 "Banker's Hours," Newsletter Texas Commerce Bancshares, XVIII, No. 1, 1980
4 Don German and Karen Petitte, "Step Right up to Your New Bank," *Consumer Digest*, September/October, 1984, 53
5 German, "Step," 53
6 *El Paso Times*, April 15, 1984
7 William P. Hobby, Jr. to author, September 26, 1985, interview
8 SDY 43 A, 7. Young to author. YFA
9 Bill Mounce to author, November 26, 1985, interview
10 SDY 12 A, 4. Mary Lou Young to author. YFA
11 Mary Lou Young to author, interview
12 SDY 12 B, 6 and SDY 13 A, 2. Mary Lou Young to author. YFA
13 Bk min, January 13, 1981, 3204
14 SDY 5 B, 3. Young to author. YFA
15 Bk min, October 31, 1981, 3182
16 SDY 43 A, 7. Young to author. YFA
17 "El Paso National Corp. Bank Note," March-April, 1981, 6
18 Sam Young, Jr. speech outline, 1981 note file. YFA
19 SDY 16 B, 7. Young to author. YFA
20 "El Paso National Corp. Bank Note," May-June 1981, 3
21 "El Paso National Corp. Bank Note," May-June 1981, 6
22 Young to author, in conversation
23 Ernie Roberts to author, February 4, 1986, interview
24 *El Paso Herald-Post*, September 9, 1981
25 Sam Young, Jr. to author, May 14, 1986, interview
26 Alexander Stuart, "Ben Love Conquers Houston," *Fortune*, November 15, 1979, 125
27 SDY 47 A, 5. Sam Young, Jr. to author. YFA
28 Faye Hartman to author, in conversation
29 Love to author, April 8, 1987, interview
30 Sam Young, Jr. to author, May 26, 1987, interview
31 Bk min, July 14, 1981, 3158
32 Newspaper ads *El Paso Times* and *El Paso Herald-Post*. YFA
33 Ben Love to author, April 8, 1987, interview
34 Marc Shapiro to author, May 29, 1985, interview
35 1982 stockholder poster. YFA
36 Faye Hartman to author, March 24, 1988
37 Buenger, *But*, 325

CHAPTER 18

A Mighty Oak

1 Nancy and David Hoover to author, interview, July 19, 1988
2 SDY 19 A, 3. Morton to author. YFA
3 Ernie Roberts to author, interview
4 Quoted in "Sunshiner," April, 1983, 2
5 SDY 7 A, 3. Paul Poling to author. YFA
6 Young, "Memoirs," 118-119
7 Young to author, in conversation
8 *El Paso Times*, April 15, 1984
9 Klinikowski to author, July 17, 1986, in conversation
10 May 19, 1986, 20
11 Sam Young, Jr. to author, May 26, 1987, interview
12 Travis Johnson to author, September 24, 1985
13 Bank Board resolution, October 8, 1985
14 *El Paso Herald-Post*, October 15, 1985

CHAPTER 19

Faith in the Man

1 Hickson to author, April 8, 1988, interview
2 Hickson to author, March 19, 1986, interview
3 Ben Love's speech script. YFA
4 Als Ronald Reagan to Young. YFA
5 Young's speech script. YFA
6 The framed certificate. YFA
7 Als Margaret Jacoway Stocker to Faye Hartman, February 21, 1986. YFA
8 SDY 37 A, 1. Young to author. YFA
9 SDY 28 B, 3. Young to author. YFA
10 Mounce to author, in conversation
11 SDY 29 A, 4. Morton to author. YFA
12 Barron Hilton quoted in *El Paso Herald-Post*, April 16, 1987
13 Rickie Feuille, quoted in *El Paso Times*, April 17, 1987
14 Rachel Garcia to author, in conversation
15 Isabel Champion to author, in conversation
16 Faye Hartman quoted in *Times*, April 17, 1987
17 *El Paso Times*, May 3, 1987
18 *El Paso Times*, April 18, 1987

INDEX

The Paper

on which this book was printed is 60-pound Glatfelter. It is acid free and has an effective life of at least three hundred years. Typeface for the text is 11 point Paladium, set by Camille in El Paso, Texas. Headings are set in Romic. This book was printed by Thomson-Shore, Dexter, Michigan; binding by John H. Decker & Sons, Grand Rapids, Michigan.

Those involved in the publication of this work gratefully acknowledge funding support from Fred Schneider, from Travis Petty and El Paso Natural Gas Company, and from Providence Memorial Hospital.